HUMAN FAMILY SYSTEMS

HUMAN FAMILY SYSTEMS
An Evolutionary View

Pierre L. van den Berghe

WAVELAND

PRESS, INC.

Prospect Heights, Illinois

For information about this book, write or call:
Waveland Press, Inc.
P.O. Box 400
Prospect Heights, Illinois 60070
(708) 634-0081

CONTENTS

ACKNOWLEDGMENTS

This book grew out of an increasing interest over the last decade in bridging the chasm which has long separated the social sciences from biology. In an earlier book (van den Berghe, 1973a), I explored the biological and cultural bases of age and sex distinctions in human societies. The rapid growth of sociobiology in the last few years prompted me to reexamine anthropological and sociological thinking in the field of kinship and marriage. This was another long-standing interest of mine stretching back to my graduate student days with Claude Lévi-Strauss and George C. Homans in the 1950s. The ideas that follow therefore owe a considerable debt to both the anthropological tradition of kinship theory and to the emerging paradigm of sociobiology. Students and colleagues, both in and out of the sociobiological persuasion, have contributed to the development of my thinking through discussions and critical reading of portions of this manuscript, but, of course, I must take full responsibility for the flack I am about to receive in response thereto. I am especially grateful to Richard D. Alexander, David P. Barash, Napoleon Chagnon, Daniel Chirot, Richard Dawkins, Jean Paul Dumont, Stephen T. Emlen, Bernard Farber, Penelope Greene, Edward Gross, Thomas Hall, William D. Hamilton, John Hartung, Judith Heerwagen, Charles F. Keyes, Hilda Kuper, Joan S. Lockard, Robert D. Lockard, Gordon H. Orians, Simon Ottenberg, Pepper J. Schwartz,

Joseph Shepher, David Spain, Robert L. Trivers, James Watson and Edward O. Wilson. In addition, Penelope Greene and Judith Heerwagen helped me with the computer programming of the HRAF data.

As is always the case in an exploding field of knowledge, new ideas "float around" and spread so fast that their parenthood is often in doubt. I did my best to acknowledge their source where I was conscious of it, and such ideas as I seem to claim as my own are mostly derived from sociobiological theory and applied to anthropological kinship theory. No doubt, my thinking independently converged with that of others concerned with the same issues, because the power of the sociobiological paradigm is sufficient to make many inferences, deductions, and hypotheses plausible and logical. At the same time, human applications are still quite tentative and I must therefore apologize to my readers if I sometimes sound more definitive than I ought to do.

To my wife Irmgard and my sons Eric, Oliver and Marc I owe not only the joys of kin selection and reciprocal altruism, but an appreciable amount of new data for the day-to-day experiential testing of sociobiological hypotheses. It is to their credit that they put up with my disagreeable self during the difficult gestation period.

Beulah Reddaway, Mary Whiting, Karen Wayenberg, Alice Fowler and Barbara Davis converted my unsightly scribblings into a publishable typescript, a task requiring considerable patience and graphological skills.

Finally (in chronological order), William Gum, friend and veteran editor of four previous books of mine, not only gave me the gentle prods necessary to keep me productive and honest, but he personally copy-edited my prose. He eliminated about 25 percent of my commas and 80 percent of my hyphens; he was right 95 percent of the time. The residual 5 percent of error or unclarity is entirely attributable to my pigheadedness.

Pierre L. van den Berghe
Seattle

According to the materialist conception, the determining factor in history is, in the final instance, the production and reproduction of immediate life. This again, is of a twofold character: on the one side, the production of the means of existence, of food, clothing and shelter and the tools necessary for that production; on the other side, the production of human beings themselves, the propagation of the species. The social organization under which the people of a particular historical epoch and a particular country live is determined by both kinds of production.

Frederick Engels
Preface to the First Edition of
The Origin of the Family, Private Property and the State (1884)

We can no more stop within the limits of our own species, when trying to find the root of our psychical and social life, than we can understand the physical condition of the human race without taking into consideration that of the lower animals.

Edward A. Westermarck, *The History of Human Marriage* (1891)

HUMAN FAMILY SYSTEMS

1

INTRODUCTION

By now, it should be clear that the innumerable "schools of thought" in social science have not led us much of anywhere in understanding human behavior, at either the individual or the collective level. Aside from a great mass of ethnographic data, rich in descriptive detail but difficult to compare and frequently of unverifiable validity, we really know little more about human societies than we did a century ago, or indeed 2500 years ago, in the days of Confucius, Plato and Aristotle. The social sciences, in short, are still largely at a proto-scientific, minimally cumulative stage of development.

Yet, during the century of self-conscious existence of the social sciences, biology has developed a powerful theoretical paradigm to account for the diversity of life forms on our planet: Darwinian evolutionary theory. While the social sciences stagnated, biology made spectacular advances. Now that evolutionary theory in biology is being systematically and successfully applied to the behavior and social organization of thousands of animal species, it seems extraordinarily foolish to resist *a priori* its application to our own species.[1] Such an application seems most urgent and promising in the most basic and universal aspects of human social organization, kinship and marriage, or what biologists call the mating and reproductive system. We seem to be at the stage where the social scientist should belatedly join T. H. Huxley who, on first exposure to

Darwin's theory of evolution, exclaimed, "How stupid of me not to have thought of that!" Hence, this book.

THE CONTRIBUTIONS OF ANTHROPOLOGY, PSYCHOLOGY AND SOCIOLOGY

Kinship and marriage have been at the very core of anthropological theory for a century, if only because most of the "simpler" societies of concern to anthropologists have been largely organized on the basis of blood and matrimonial relations. Much of the anthropological literature on the subject, however, is highly technical, sometimes pedantic, often intellectually dazzling but generally inaccessible to the uninitiated (Lévi-Strauss, 1969; Murdock, 1949; Radcliffe-Brown and Forde, 1950). Until Robin Fox (1967) published his elegant little introductory book a decade ago, the beginning student had to be satisfied with brief treatments in the standard kinship chapter of introductory anthropology textbooks. [Bohannan (1963) is among the best.]

The sociological literature on the family rivals in size the anthropological one, and it is much more readable, but, alas, with a few notable exceptions (W. Goode, 1963; Coser, 1964; N. Bell and Vogel, 1960), it is scarcely worth reading. It lacks for the most part the intellectual sparkle of the anthropological works and much of it consists of textbooks geared to how-to courses on "Marriage and the Family." The shortcomings of much of that literature are many. It is provincial, dealing overwhelmingly with Western or even American society, with only an occasional illustration from non-Western societies thrown in to inject an exotic note. It is frequently full of moralistic or ideological cant, peddling the currently fashionable brand of professorial liberalism. In recent years, family textbooks have followed the mass media in kow-towing to feminism and including an obligatory chapter or two on "alternate lifestyles," but there is also a long-standing tradition of treating "deviant" forms of family (such as the "matrifocal" black lower-class family) as "social problems" and symptoms and sources of "social pathology."

Luckily, the anthropological literature on the family is of much superior quality to the sociological one. Anthropologists are more knowledgeable on the average about non-Western societies and, hence, have a better grasp of the range of variability in human behavior. Furthermore, through extensive field work, anthropologists have accumulated a vast amount of empirical data in the last half-century or so. For all its theoretical sophistication, however, the anthropological treatment of the family suffers from three interrelated limitations. First, it tends to assume that the structure of the human family is, first and foremost, the product of a set of culturally codified rules of behavior, terms of address, and so on. Second, as a corollary of this view, anthropologists have stressed the variety of human systems at the expense of the species-wide uniformities: cultural rules have been regarded as largely arbitrary. Finally, the emphasis on cultural rules has steered anthropologists away from attributing much importance to actual behavior, and toward assuming that people actually behave as they say they do or should. Many anthropologists, when they describe a kinship system, do not so much relate what they have observed people doing. Instead, they give an ideal and schematic account of rules of conduct. Often, these rules are not even explicit in the culture in question but are inferred by anthropologists from verbal reports, kin terminology and, with luck, nonverbal behavior.

To some extent the tradition of psychology known as behaviorism has corrected some of these biases by insisting that what people do is more important than what they say they do (Bandura, 1969; Burgess and Bushell, 1969; Skinner, 1971). However, behaviorism, too, has its stringent limitations. Three main ones are its extreme environmentalism; its nearly complete absence of an evolutionary perspective; and its almost exclusive reliance on the experimental method. Behaviorists, by and large, have had far too flexible a model of learning processes. They have tended to see the mind, whether of a man, a rat or a pigeon, as a *tabula rasa* that could learn and be made to behave in practically any way the experimenter chose in response to "schedules of reinforcement." Experimental manipulation of rewards and punishments could lead, they demonstrated, to considerable behavioral modifications, but not indefinitely or at random. In biological terms, behaviorists have been almost exclusively interested in the ontogeny (individual development) of learning and have shown only minimal concern for its phylogeny (evolution). In their eagerness to demonstrate flexibility of behavior, they have been far more concerned with modifying behavior under the neatly controlled and artificial conditions of the laboratory, rather than observing behavior under natural conditions. Consequently, the insights and findings of behaviorism, while sound as far as they go, do not go very far.

Behaviorism has made some contribution to the study of the human family, especially in the area of applied pedagogy. But then, most parents did not need behaviorists to tell them that a good spanking or a lollipop, judiciously administered or withheld, can be an effective means of modifying their children's behavior in a desired direction. Most parents also know that "schedules of reinforcement" do not always work. In defense of behaviorism, however, it must be said that other traditions in psychology have contributed even less. Psychoanalysis makes a great many pronouncements about the nature of family bonds, based on the hunches of that early 20th-century Viennese shaman, Sigmund Freud, but the efforts of thousands of practioners of the sect for over half a century have singularly failed to produce the kind of empirical support for psychoanalytic theories that conforms to the canons of scientific evidence. Other currently fashionable brands of psychology and social psychology, like "symbolic interactionism," "ethnomethodology" and others, boil down either to pretentious and recondite ways of stating the obvious (e.g., that humans communicate through symbolic language), or to techniques of recording observations—or both.

The three central behavioral sciences, anthropology, sociology and psychology, all give us fragmentary and incomplete views of human behavior in general and of the human family in particular. Of the three, anthropology has made the largest contribution by far, because it has greatly increased our recorded knowledge of a wide range of human societies. Behaviorist psychology has helped us to specify under what environmental conditions behavior can be modified in accordance with the subject's pursuit of his interests. Sociology, in my perhaps overly jaundiced view of my own discipline, has taught us very little.

THE SOCIOBIOLOGICAL APPROACH

Obviously, an important part of the puzzle is missing—one which this book intends to supply. I am referring to the rapidly growing contribution of biology, and especially of sociobiology, ecology, behavior genetics and ethology, to our understanding of animal behavior (Barash, 1977; Dawkins, 1976; Wilson, 1975, 1978). In a trivial sense, every anthropology and sociology textbook mentions sex and reproduction as "biological functions of the family." However, after a few perfunctory paragraphs wherein the biological imperatives of a long period of gestation, lactation and infant dependency are duly mentioned, and in which the sex drive is conceded to have a partly physiological basis, sociologists and anthropologists typically proceed as if virtually every other aspect of human family structure and behavior were the product of learning, cultural norms and social scripts, subject to an almost infinite range of variability from society to society, from individual to individual and from epoch to epoch (Erich Goode, 1978; Laws and Schwartz, 1977; Schneider, 1965; Witherspoon, 1975).

Here, I shall take issue with this view of human social behavior, and I shall attempt to show that

1. like other species, we share a phylogenetic history of adaptation to complex environmental conditions;
2. this common history gives us a gene pool that predisposes us to behave in certain ways and that *channels* our responses to our environment;

3. our behavior is best understood in evolutionary perspective, by systematic comparison and contrast with that of other species, and as the product of an extraordinarily complex process of interaction between genotype and environment.

Applied specifically to the family, this means that the human family reflects our species' mating and reproductive system. Some features of it we share in varying degrees with varying numbers of other species. Other aspects of the human family are both universally found in our species *and,* as far as we know, unique to it. Others yet vary from one human society to another, or indeed even from family to family within a given society. Therefore, to understand what kind of an animal we are, *we must compare humans to other species as well as compare human societies to one another.* Furthermore, we must look at our social arrangements as the product of a long process of evolutionary adaptation to environmental changes. This evolutionary process began long before the appearance of hominids on the planet and continues today. Our social and cultural evolution is in important respects part and parcel of our biological evolution, and in other respects an emergent outgrowth from it, but it cannot be divorced from it.

Such an outlook is still anathema to the great majority of social scientists [e.g., Harris (1975, 1977) and Sahlins (1976)] who perceive the recent development of sociobiology as a threat to their professional position, a challenge to their self-proclaimed expertise, and even a devious political plot of fascists, racists and reactionaries. Little purpose would be served by engaging in polemics, but, because the approach suggested here has been misrepresented and stigmatized as one of "biological reductionism," I must clarify what I *am* and what I *am not* saying.

I am definitely *not* saying that everything or even most things about human behavior are most parsimoniously reducible to biology. Some aspects of our behavior are reducible, beyond biology, to biochemistry and ultimately to biophysics. Others are now best understood as genetically channeled predispositions to act in certain ways in response to certain environmental conditions. This, be it noted, is no return to simple, mechanistic instinct theory, because we now know that genetic programs can be and often are extremely complex and quite flexible and facultative. What I am, however, suggesting is that behavior be studied comparatively in terms of levels of generality:

1. There are behaviors that we share with many other species, such as nepotism, or preference for kin. Such behaviors, though subject to environmental variation, are most likely to have a genetic basis in humans as well as in other animals. The argument is often advanced by social scientists who seek to reject sociobiology that animal comparisons constitute "mere analogies" to human behavior. It is true that

different species frequently converge through different evolutionary paths on amazingly similar solutions to similar sets of environmental constraints. This is true, for instance, of what biologists call "territorial behavior," a broad category of behavior that was probably independently evolved thousands of times by different species. The more distantly related species are, the more likely it becomes that an outwardly similar behavior phenotype is analogous rather than homologous (i.e., the product of convergence, rather than evolution from a common origin). However, to say that a human phenotype is "merely analogous" to similar behavior in another animal is *not* to say that it has no genetic basis in humans.

2. Some human behaviors are shared with some but not most species, and, there too, a genetic basis cannot be lightly discounted especially if one or both of the following are found. If the behavior syndrome is found in most of a group of closely related species, then the probability of a homology is high. If on the other hand, the behavior is found in less closely related species that have adapted to similar environmental constraints, then it is probably the product of convergent evolution and an analogy rather than a homology. Even then, there is a high probability of a genetic evolution in man. An example is food-sharing, a trait we do not significantly share with any primate, but which is conspicuous in many social carnivores (lions, hyenas, wolves, African hunting dogs). It obviously pays for members of species that make irregular and chancy kills of large game to share the bounty. There is no *a priori* reason to suppose that if hyenas and lions have been genetically selected to share food, humans have arrived at the same solution through a purely cultural invention.

3. Some forms of behavior seem uniquely or almost uniquely human, but are universal or nearly universal in our species. Anything pan-human can also be presumed to have a genetic basis. An example is our ability to communicate through symbolic language. It is true that human societies often transmit cultural inventions to one another, and, therefore, it is theoretically conceivable that the cultural invention of speech could have spread from one society to the whole of humanity. It is also conceivable that all human societies should have independently hit on the idea of symbolic speech. Both of these possibilities are, however, far-fetched and fit poorly with what we know of the ontogeny of speech in human infants: it is virtually impossible for a human in contact with another human *not* to evolve a mutually understandable system of symbols to communicate complex, abstract meanings—barring such gross physical defects as mental retardation, or auditory and visual impairment.

4. Finally, human societies differ substantially from one another in cer-

tain forms of their behavior. The French, for example, do a lot of hand-shaking when they meet; the British much less. When one tries to explain these intraspecific differences, the presumption clearly leans toward a cultural hypothesis. *Some* intraspecific differences in human behavior may have a genetic basis, but, so far, this has only been firmly established in cases of severe deficiencies attributable to gross chromosomal abnormalities like Trisomy 21 or "mongolism." There is also some evidence of a biochemical basis of some forms of mental illness, but, so far, no differences in human behavior between large populations have been clearly attributable to differences in the frequencies of alleles in their gene pools. Differences in the distribution of some genes (e.g., the ABO blood types) have been found between large human groups, but no significant linkages with behavior have yet been established.

At present, then, most intergroup behavioral differences in humans are most readily explainable in cultural terms. Even that statement, however, must be expanded in two ways. Culture itself is the product of a process of natural selection specific to our species. It is our species' way of adding to natural selection a new and faster mechanism of adaptation to our environment. Culture is therefore itself an outgrowth of biological evolution, not the antithesis to it that so many social scientists seem to make it. Ultimately, the ability to be a cultural animal has a genetic basis.

Secondly, a cultural adaptation is often not the kind of random, arbitrary creation subject to infinite variability that some extreme cultural determinists seem to assume. Even when it is not subject to any specific genetic program, it is still often constrained by the conditions of the nonhuman environment—physical and biotic.

HEREDITY AND ENVIRONMENT

I am most assuredly *not* saying that heredity is more important than the environment. Such a general statement is quite meaningless. Geneticists have great difficulty building models complex enough to account for polygenic traits, and most human social behaviors are probably under the influence of multiple genes. Feldman and Lewontin (1975, p. 1168) conclude that, at present, no statistically reliable techniques of assessing heritability of polygenic traits in humans exist. They write:

At present, no statistical methodology exists that will enable us to predict the range of phenotypic possibilities that are inherent in any genotype, nor can any technique of statistical estimation provide a convincing argument for a genetic mechanism more complicated than one to two Mendelian loci with low and constant penetrance. Certainly the simple estimate of heritability, either in the broad or narrow sense, . . . is nearly equivalent to no information at all for any serious problem of human genetics (p. 1168).

Besides, any statement concerning the causes of behavior in terms of heredity versus environment is, in principle, wrong. A phenotype, behavioral or somatic, is the product of a complex *interaction* of genes and a multiplicity of environmental factors. Both heredity and environment are, in principle, equally important. In some traits, the heretability factor is high; in others it is low. For extraordinarily complex aspects of behavior, such as, for instance, "intelligence," which are probably under the influence of an unknown but large number of genes, it is at present impossible to determine heretability.

People like Arthur Jensen (1969), who make silly statements such as that 80 percent of the variance in intelligence is inherited, are not competent geneticists; they are biologically naive psychologists. Such statements not only go much beyond the present state of knowledge in behavior genetics, but implicitly assume that such culture-bound instruments as IQ tests are valid measurements of genotypes.

Biologists, then, are in nearly unanimous agreement about a complex interaction model of behavior as the product of *both* heredity and environment. Most social scientists, however, still adhere to an overwhelmingly environmentalist view of human behavior. It is with the one-sided dogmatism of extreme environmentalism that this book will take issue.

Many social scientists are not only environmentalists; they are also cultural determinists; that is, they regard learned, man-made culture as virtually the only aspect of the environment that matters in explaining human behavior. A good exemplar of this viewpoint is David Schneider who, in his book, *American Kinship* (1968), explicitly defines his topic as "the culture of American kinship," and excludes "the patterns of behavior as formulated from systematic observations of each of its actual occurrences" (1968, p. 6). "This book," he states, "is intended to be an account of the American kinship system *as a cultural system, as a system of symbols, and not as a 'description' of any other level*" (p. 18, italics are Schneider's). Schneider further sees the cultural and the behavioral elements of kinship as *"independent* of each other" (p. 6, italics are Schneider's). My book, on the other hand, takes the position that the cultural institutions of kinship, far from being independent of behavior (and its biological underpinnings), are derivations and codifications of behavioral patterns.

To cultural determinists à la Schneider, a society's system of kinship and marriage *is* the system of cultural symbols used to charter relationships between kinsmen and in-laws. It just so happens, they would argue, that in American or Western society, these symbols are *culturally* defined in *biological* terms. The following quotations from Schneider (1968) make this clear:

> ... sexual intercourse is the symbol in terms of which members of the family as relatives and the family as a cultural unit are defined and differentiated in American kinship (p. 31).

> Women bear children, nurse them, and care for them. This, according to the definition of American culture, is part of woman's nature (p. 35).

> The American cultural premise is that the newborn child is quite helpless and requires a great deal of care and protection for its survival (p. 35).

> The biological elements in the definition of kinship have the quality of symbols (p. 52).

> What is out there in nature, say the definition of American culture, is what kinship is. Kinship is the blood relationship, the fact of shared biogenetic substance (p. 107).

According to this view of kinship and marriage, the present work is but a cultural product of Western society. It merely reflects the particular cultural view that blood and affinal ties have something to do with biology. Sahlins (1976) in his polemical rejection of sociobiology extends this line of argument even further. Sociobiology, he claims, is merely the pseudoscientific expression of Western capitalist ideology. By further extension of the argument, then, all modern science is a cultural product of a particular type of society at a particular moment in history.

As a low-level descriptive statement, the above arguments are not so much wrong as limiting and question-begging. Of course, science develops within a specific cultural and temporal context; sociobiology is no exception. Of course, kin and marriage relationships are culturally codified according to a symbolic system expressed in human language. Nor is it wrong to assert that these cultural symbols determine behavior. In an immediate, proximate, descriptive sense, they do indeed. But as an explanation of behavior, the simple cultural determinist approach is extremely limiting. It completely begs the question of *why* there is a systematic relationship between cultural models of human behavior and biological facts. This relationship exists, not only in Western societies since Darwin and Mendel, but in all known societies, present and past. All cultural models of kinship and marriage bear a demonstrable relationship to the real world, although not all societies have equally accurate models of the biology of reproduction and heredity. In Chapter 5 we will see the tortured absurdity to which the Schneider approach leads when used by one of his disciples (Witherspoon, 1975) in the attempt to show that the Navajo, being matrilineal, regard patrilateral relatives as in-laws rather than kinsmen.

All known, self-perpetuating cultures, in short, have taken the biology of human mating and reproduction into systematic account. They have operated on a set of cultural premises broadly congruent with sociobiology. All cultures have a brand of science in general (biology in particular) that bears a demonstrable relationship to the external, objective realities of their physical and biotic habitat. A number of experimental groups, as we will see in Chapter 3, have attempted, more or less consciously, to ignore important features of human biology, but they have either met with failure, or they have reverted to more conventional views and practices. Some groups, like celibate religious orders, have long endured, but only as a small subgroup of larger societies, not as sexually reproducing, self-perpetuating societies in their own right.

In conclusion, the extreme cultural determinist view of human behavior is, at its best, a proximate description of verbal behavior. It reiterates verbal rationalizations for behavior given by native informants. It assumes not only that the native is always right, by definition, but also that his conscious, verbalized behavior is, to all significant intents and purposes, the only one with which the social scientist needs to concern himself. One of the main objectives of this book is to show the stringent limitations of this perspective as a theory of human behavior.

Some anthropologists have given attention to ecology as an influence on culture, especially on technology, but even they have largely neglected the direct effect of the physical and biotic environment on human behavior (Harris, 1974, 1975, 1977; Sahlins and Service, 1960; Service, 1966, 1971; Steward, 1955, 1977; White, 1959). As for sociologists, they have, with a few exceptions (Hawley, 1950; Lenski, 1978), virtually reduced their conception of human ecology to spatial distribution of human populations. This book subscribes to the view that, for man, the environment is an extraordinarily complex thing where culture is but one major component among several. The physical environment (climate, topography, hydrography, latitude, altitude, mineral resources, etc.) and the biotic environment (i.e., the thousands of plant and animal species with which we interact on the basis of symbiosis, parasitism or predation, including, of course, the endoparasites that have periodically decimated our species) both exert considerable determinism over our behavior, culture and social organization.

When we look at a human population, therefore, we must not tear it out of its physical and biotic environment. We must, instead, see it as occupying certain niches in a habitat shared with many other forms of life. Indeed, our environment does not even stop at our skin, as we all carry millions of organisms inside our skin, and, at a deeper level yet, we each carry an intraorganic environment in which the genes themselves are an environment to each other. The effect of a gene is often affected by that of other genes, and different gene combinations produce different effects.

Having said all this, culture clearly *is* important for humans, but *not* all-important. Whether culture is unique to man is a matter of definition. If by culture we mean "socially transmitted, learned behavior," then we share it with a number of higher vertebrates (birds and mammals), and certainly with many primates. Animal ethologists generally use the word "tradition" to refer to such phenomena as bird populations of the same species learning different songs in different areas, or different monkey troops of the same species learning the use of different foods. As in human cultures, some of these forms of behavior are clearly learned, not inherited; and they are socially passed on from individual to individual through observation and imitation. A classic instance is the spread of a tradition of food washing in a troop of Japanese macaques (monkeys) on Koshima island, Japan. Five years after the new behavior was invented by a young female, it had spread to nearly 80 percent of the younger monkeys in the troop (Kawai, 1965; Kummer, 1971). Human culture does have an additional element, however, which, so far as we know, does not exist naturally in any other species. That is, of course, symbolic language. Many other animals have sophisticated signaling systems, which are sometimes called "languages," but human language is made up of signals (largely verbal ones, but also visual ones) that are meaningful only through learned social conventions. Chimpanzees have the intellectual ability to learn a rudimentary type of symbolic language with a simple syntax, but they only do so when laboriously taught by humans. As far as we know, only man uses symbolic language "in the wild," and all humans learn to do so by age two, unless they are mentally retarded or have been deprived of all human contact.

Presumably, the reader now has a clear picture of the author's view of human behavior, thanks to the few thousand meaningful little black symbols arranged so as to conform to English syntax on this and prior pages. So culture is indeed important. Neither of us inherited our ability to communicate in English. I only developed that ability at age 17. However, our ability to communicate is entirely contingent on the fact that we are both members of the same biological species. The specific language we use is culturally learned; the ability to use it is biologically evolved. All human languages share features that make them unmistakably human because we all share the genes that make us humans, rather than chimpanzees or ostriches. To a limited extent, we can communicate meanings to chimpanzees or even to dogs, but we assuredly cannot discuss baseball or Hindu philosophy with them. When it comes to goldfish, crocodiles or ants, our ability to share meanings with them drops to zero or near zero. The point of this trivial illustration is that culture itself must be seen within the wide biological framework of our evolutionary history as one life form among many.

SOCIETIES AND POPULATIONS

A society, whether of humans or of other animals, consists of *interacting conspecifics.** The degree of sociality shown by different species varies enormously: some, like ants, termites and bees are highly social; others, like tapeworms and orangutans, only minimally so. There are also many species that congregate in great numbers, but whose interaction is largely limited to moving and feeding in concert, and who therefore do not constitute genuine societies. Schools of fish, for instance, are more conglomerations of animals than societies, in the sense of systems of *structured* interaction, involving dominance hierarchies, division of labor, specialization of function and other standard features of social organization. In practice, of course, social behavior is on a continuum and there is no exact point at which a conglomeration turns into a society.

The social boundaries of an animal society or subsociety are sometimes unclear, but, typically, it is fairly easy to identify clusters of ties that link groups of individuals much more closely to each other than to any organism of their species outside the group. Individuals may interact with others outside their group, or may migrate back and forth between groups; groups may interact with other groups as collectivities; and larger groups may be subdivided in a hierarchy of subgroups. Nonetheless, it is usually not difficult to determine the boundaries of animal societies, and, indeed, the size of these groups is often fairly uniform within a species.

In the nature of the case, physical propinquity is a basic property of groups. Animals have to be in physical, visual, auditory or olfactory contact with each other to interact. Therefore, spatial distribution, access to space and the use of space as a resource are important features of all animal societies. Abstractly put, animals of necessity interact in a space—time continuum. Animals necessarily share a habitat with other members of their species and with many other species, and their use of space is inevitably *structured,* not haphazard.

In the last analysis, animals interact to survive and to reproduce. This is, of course, not to say that they consciously do so. Man may possibly be the only self-conscious animal with a sense of destiny and even he does not always act consciously. Nor does this statement imply that there is a

*Technical terms are defined in the Glossary (pp. 222—227).

mysterious ultimate purpose to society—or indeed to evolution itself. What is meant is that behavior, like anatomy, is the product of a long process of biological evolution. Forms of behavior will be selected for to the extent that they contribute to the fitness (i.e., the reproductive success) of those animals that exhibit it. Naturally, different environments will select for different behaviors, so that the process of behavioral evolution never stops since no environment remains static. *Social* behavior, then, will be selected for if it contributes to the fitness of interacting animals. Conspecifics are selected to cooperate if by doing so, they help each other pass on their individual genes (again, with no conscious purpose implied).

An animal society, therefore, must be seen, among other things, as a reproductive system. A group of interbreeding conspecifics is what biologists term a population; the sum total of genes represented in such a population is that population's *gene pool*. Different species have different reproductive systems: some are monogamous, some polygynous, some promiscuous. Some have pair-bonds between reproductive males and females; some do not. Some species invest more in raising their young than others and different species differ widely in the contribution of males and females to raising the offspring. Some species have stable family groups, others not. Variety is the name of the reproductive game, but, as we shall see, that variety is not capricious or random.

It might be thought that the boundaries of a society and of a population, in the sense that we have just defined them, tend to be coterminous, but this is not necessarily so. Many essentially solitary or nonsocial animals manage to reproduce quite well, often asexually. Even sexually reproducing animals often have but the most fleeting of encounters. A number of highly social species have nonreproducing groups, for instance, segregated male groups waiting for a chance to take over a reproductive group from another male.

As Wilson (1975) suggested, the central problem of sociobiology is that of the relationship between society and population. Throughout the animal world, from social insects to higher vertebrates, there is a relationship between mating and other forms of interaction. By and large, and to the extent that a species is social, animals tend to interact cooperatively with genetically related animals. The reason is simple: helping an organism that is related to ego by common descent is an indirect way of helping oneself, or, more precisely, the genes shared between it and ego. This is true even when the act of helping costs the helper some reduction in fitness. This widespread phenomenon of helping kin has been called "kin selection," "inclusive fitness," or, misleadingly, "altruism" by biologists (Hamilton, 1964; Maynard Smith, 1964).

THE BASES OF SOCIALITY:
KIN SELECTION, RECIPROCITY, COERCION

"Altruism" (defined as behavior that increases the fitness of alter at the cost of reduced fitness to ego, again without any assumption of conscious decision) had long presented a major problem for evolutionary theory, until Hamilton (1964) suggested a very simple solution. How could behavior that reduced the fitness of the individual be selected for? Would not "altruists" be selected against and, hence, in the long run fail to pass on their genetic propensity to do others a good turn? Complex and, on the whole, unconvincing arguments had been presented that even though altruists might suffer, the groups to which they belonged benefited, and therefore altruism was passed on through group selection (Wynne-Edwards, 1962). Hamilton, on the other hand, advanced that "altruism" could be expected if the cost—benefit ratio of the altruistic act was smaller than the coefficient of relatedness (proportion of genes shared by common descent, e.g., 0.5 between full siblings, 0.125 between first cousins, and so on) between altruist and beneficiary of altruism. In concrete terms, I can be expected to help my full sister or my son (both of whom share half of their genes with me through common descent) if they receive more than twice the benefit from my act compared to the cost to me. For a nephew or a grandchild (related by a factor of $\frac{1}{4}$), the benefit—cost ratio would have to be greater than four; for a first cousin ($\frac{1}{8}$ related to me) greater than eight, and so on.

"Altruism," in short, is really ultimate genetic selfishness. By being altruistic to relatives, we pass on our genes by proxy if not directly. We are therefore selected to do so, whether we are conscious of it or not. Indeed, given the universality of nepotism in our species, and its similarity to kin selection in other social animals, there is no reason to seek a nonbiological basis of human nepotism. For humans, then, as for other social animals, kinship is a major cement of sociality. Sociologists and anthropologists have, of course, long proclaimed that the family was the basis of human social organization, but they took it for granted without explaining why. What we call the human family is the social unit resulting from our species-specific system of mating and reproduction, as we will see in detail later. Most of us pair off with members of the opposite sex and together we raise children. That has been the standard human way of reproducing since prehistoric times.

To study the human family, then, is synonymous with studying the most fundamental basis of human social behavior. And because so many other social species behave in ways in some respects so strikingly like ours, it is imperative that we explore the biological bases of our social behavior, and especially of our kinship and marriage systems.

Kin selection does not explain all of man's social behavior, nor even all of his family-related behavior. As we will see in Chapters 4, 5 and 6, there is a considerable range of cultural variability in human family systems. But the variability is far from infinite. Before we turn to a comparative study of mating and reproductive systems in man and in other animals in Chapters 2 and 3, I should like to suggest that there are three bases of sociality in humans:

1. *Kin selection, the propensity to favor kin, which we share with countless other species.* Therefore, it has almost certainly an important genetic basis in humans also, although it is modifiable by culture as we shall see.
2. *Reciprocity [or "reciprocal altruism" as Trivers (1971) terms it], cooperative behavior beneficial to others which is extended without considerations of genetic relatedness, and even at some cost to ego, but in the expectation that the good turn will be paid back at some time in the future.* This rather complex form of social behavior is most highly developed in humans, although it may not be completely absent in other intelligent animals, such as monkeys and apes, as suggested by recent field work. Packer (1977) found that pairs of Savannah baboon males (who were presumably unrelated) solicited each other's help in stealing females in oestrus from other males and that favors were reciprocated on subsequent interactions. In any case, reciprocity presupposes a level of cerebral development sufficiently high for long-term memory and recognition of individual conspecifics (Trivers, 1971). Reciprocity, an exchange of mutually beneficial favors, is in fact the pursuit of calculated self-interest, and clearly plays a large role in human societies. It must have evolved much later than kin selection in hominids, and, once the intellectual threshold for reciprocity was reached, it probably became a powerful basis of further selection for intelligence, and, hence, the development of human culture.

   Indeed, reciprocity invites cheating or freeloading; the temptation is always strong not to return the favor received. Therefore, cheaters must be punished and freeloaders must be eliminated from further transactions if the system is to continue working. This, in turn, invites more and more cunning ways of cheating undetected, which then calls forth better and better ways of detecting cheaters. And so, *ad infinitum.* This game of wits is still with us as computer technology opens enticing new vistas for sophisticated cheating. To work, reciprocity must be based on "trust," that is, on controls reliable enough to make cheating rare and unprofitable.
3. *Collective coercion for purposes of intraspecific parasitism.* Obviously not all human relationships are mutually beneficial; many are one-sidedly

exploitative. Exploitative relationships are typically not gladly entered; people have to be coerced into them by force or the threat of force. The development of collective means of coercion for the purpose of parasitizing unrelated conspecifics is overwhelmingly a *cultural* development of the last few thousand years. It essentially grew with the rise of states—that is, of societies in which one group, typically a minority, attempted to monopolize the means of violence to extract surplus production from the rest of the population. The history of the world for the last five or six thousand years is largely the history of the rise of ever larger and more complex societies held together by ever increasing degrees of coercion and inequality. So far, no complex, large-scale human society has ever existed that was not based on a large measure of inequality and coercion, and, therefore, of exploitation and intraspecific parasitism. To be sure, coercion is not entirely absent in other species. The male hamadryas baboon, for instance, forces the females in his harem to remain close to him by means of threats and neck bites (Kummer, 1968). However, organized coercion exercised over conspecifics who are neither kin nor mates, and for purposes of extracting the product of their labor, has been elaborated in humans to a degree incommensurable with any other animal societies. Some ant species have "slavery," but they generally "enslave" other species—not their own (Wilson, 1971, 1975).

These three fundamental bases of human sociality—kin selection, reciprocity and coercion—evolved sequentially and are now present in all but the remotest nonliterate, stateless societies that still manage to escape control from large state societies. Even in large state-organized societies, however, the family is still a mode of social organization based primarily on kin selection, although elements of reciprocity and coercion are not absent from relations between kinsmen and spouses. Conversely, larger non-kin-based organizations (states, business firms and the like) often create myths of familism to legitimize their coercion. The emperor is a "father" to his subjects; the company is a "big family," and so on. Even the most complex human societies still retain an important genetic element in their sociality, and, therefore, a study of human society, and more particularly of the human family must start with the oldest, biological basis of our sociality. To do so successfully, we must compare ourselves, especially our systems of mating and reproduction, to those of other animals. That is what I propose to do in the next chapter.

NOTES

1. A basic understanding of Darwinian evolutionary theory is taken for granted here. To summarize the theory adequately would lengthen this book by a full chapter, and would only rehash ground well-covered in most introductory biology texts. For a lucid sum-

mary of evolutionary theory applied to animal behavior, the reader should turn to Chapters 2 and 3 of Barash (1977). In van den Berghe (1978c), I attempt to make explicit some of the common misconceptions that social scientists have about evolutionary thinking in biology and to bridge the conceptual gap between the two sets of disciplines. A broader application of sociobiology to human societies can be found in my *Man in Society* (1978a).

SUPPLEMENTARY READINGS

The student interested in sociobiology would do best to start with Barash (1977) as a nontechnical introduction, then graduate to Dawkins (1976) and finally to Wilson (1975). Together, all three of these books give a good general overview of the field, and the last one is, by far, the most extensive reference work in sociobiology. Among the key theoretical articles are Alexander (1971, 1974, 1975), Hamilton (1964), Maynard Smith (1964, 1966, 1971) and Trivers (1971, 1972, 1974), but these should only be tackled after reading Barash, Dawkins and Wilson, as they are both more technical and less general in scope. A number of these articles are conveniently reprinted in the useful collection by Clutton-Brock and Harvey (1978a).

2

MATING AND
REPRODUCTIVE SYSTEMS IN NONHUMANS

The simplest way for organisms to reproduce is by *mitosis* or cell division. While simple, the method has a fundamental limitation: when a cell divides, it makes an exact genetic duplication of itself. This, in turn, makes random mutation the only genetic source of adaptive evolution in asexually reproducing species. Most multicellular organisms, whether plants or animals, developed sexual reproduction as a more versatile way to evolve by recombining their genetic material. Through a complicated process of cell division accompanied by a halving of the numbers of chromosomes *(meiosis)*, two different types of *haploid gametes*, ova and sperm, are produced. The two types of germ cells have to fuse to create a normal *diploid* individual, which has again the full complement of chromosomes for that particular species.

SEXUAL REPRODUCTION

Meiosis and fertilization are each accompanied by a great shuffling of genes and chromosomes that greatly enhances the adaptive capability of organisms. During meiosis, *chiasmata* or chromosome cross-overs take place, in which sets of paired chromosomes switch sections. During fertilization, the half-set of chromosomes of the egg gets paired off with homologous chromosomes on the half-set of sperm chromosomes, thereby reconstituting a normal *diploid* individual.[1]

There are variations on the game of sexual reproduction. Sometimes the two gametes are produced by the same individual *(hermaphrodite)* that is therefore capable of fertilizing itself (although hermaphrodites do not necessarily do so). Some colonial invertebrates, like sponges and corals, are hermaphroditic. Sometimes haploid individuals are produced from unfertilized ova, one of the forms of reproduction known as *parthenogenesis.* Such is the case of thousands of species of social insects of the order of *hymenoptera* (wasps, ants and bees) that produce haploid males and diploid females. Generally, however, separate individuals, males and females, specialize in the production of sperm and eggs, and have to mate to produce offspring. This is almost universally true among vertebrates, to which we belong along with tens of thousands of species of fish, reptiles, amphibians, birds and mammals.

When we speak of mating and reproductive systems, therefore, we will confine ourselves to species that reproduce sexually, since otherwise there can be no mating. Mating, however, does not necessarily involve direct physical contact. Most fish and amphibians, for instance, have external fertilization of the eggs. Mating and reproductive systems are, in the last analysis, interaction systems between reproductive males and females, and between parents and offspring. Relations between mates are largely determined by the conditions necessary for the successful rearing of offspring: reproduction, not sex, is the name of the biological game.

INCLUSIVE FITNESS

Mating and reproductive systems are most parsimoniously seen as interaction systems in which every actor is biologically selected to behave so as to maximize its *individual inclusive fitness.* Individual organisms in such systems are then both *competing* and *collaborating* with each other to maximize their own reproductive success and that of their relatives both in the present and the future. Since resources conducive to fitness are almost always in limited supply, it is inevitable that conflicts continually crop up between relatives and mates. Yet, relatives and mates, because of shared genetic interests, also indirectly enhance their own individual fitness by helping each other. Inclusive fitness theory explains the ubiquity of both facets of social relationships: cooperation and conflict.

In simplest terms, every individual in a diploid species can be said to have a 100 percent genetic interest in itself (and its monozygotic twins), a 50 percent interest in full siblings, parents and offspring, a 25 percent interest in grandparents, grandchildren, half siblings and full nephews, and so on. The interest in an unrelated mate lies in the investment in the common offspring: the nature of the sexual bond between mates is primarily a function of the contribution parental cooperation makes to their common offspring's fitness. Again, we use the terms "game" and "interest" without any implication that the actors *consciously* recognize kin, seek to reproduce or are otherwise *motivated* to behave in the ways for which they are biologically *selected* to behave. Humans are, of course, self-conscious animals that have motives, but consciousness or motivation has no bearing on the theory of natural selection.

A classical instance of this genetic calculus of inclusive fitness is the conflict over weaning between mother and offspring in mammals (Trivers, 1974). So long as mother and neonate (related by a factor of $\frac{1}{2}$) both increase their fitness by continuing lactation, there is no conflict between them. Should the mother stop lactating too early, the infant would die and both would reduce their fitness. The mother would lose her already considerable investment in the infant, and, of course, the infant's fitness would be reduced to zero. When lactation no longer makes a significant contribution to the infant, continuing lactation is also to the detriment of both insofar as it detracts from the mother's investment in other offspring who would be related to both of them. There is a time in between, however, when the mother would "like" to wean the infant earlier than the latter would choose. The weaning conflict occurs when lactation still makes a substantial though no longer essential contribution to the offspring's fitness. The older infant is valuable to the mother, but only half as valuable as the infant is to itself. Therefore, there is a temporary asymmetry in the cost–benefit ratio of weaning for mother and offspring, and the conflict is only resolved when the fitness loss of weaning to the infant becomes smaller than its potential fitness gain from having new siblings.

PARENTAL INVESTMENT

A central concept in mating and reproductive systems is that of *parental investment,* namely, the contribution (often best measured in energetic terms) parents make to the fitness of offspring (Trivers, 1972). Investment in present offspring is frequently at the cost of investment of potential future offspring, and thus affects parental fitness. Since parents and offspring in diploid species share only half their genes, their genetic interests overlap but are not identical. Sexual reproduction and, hence (except for the few hermaphroditic species) reproductive specialization into male and female morphs, entails differential parental investment between males and females. Females make the bigger investment by producing fewer, bigger, less motile and energetically more costly gametes than males. This, known as *anisogamy,* is so basic a difference between females and males as to be the best criterion of sex determination in a species. That morph of a species that produces the bigger gametes is, *by definition,* the female. In short, sperm are plentiful and cheap relative to eggs. This gender asymmetry in the reproductive process has a fundamental consequence: the female is almost invariably the scarce resource for the male, rather than vice versa. Females are seldom in want of males to fertilize them, whereas males seldom have access to all the females they are capable of fertilizing.

Sexual access to females, then, becomes a potentially bargainable resource that can be exchanged for male contributions to the fitness of both the female and her offspring. In some species, e.g., in some spiders, this may take the extreme form of the female cannibalizing the male after copulation, though typically the cost of copulation to the male is much smaller. With few exceptions, however, males compete for females rather than the other way around. The converse of this is that females are choosier than males, as well they should be, because their reproductive mistakes are costlier than those of males.

The extent to which there is *differential parental investment* for males and females varies greatly from species to species. In some species (e.g., many birds), the male's investment is almost as great as that of the female after egg laying. In many of the altricial birds (those whose fledglings have to be fed), the male takes an active part in constructing the nest, hatching the eggs and provisioning the fledglings. On the other hand, the males of many species make virtually no contribution to the fitness of their offspring other than fertilization of the females. Marine mammals like seals, sea lions and sea elephants are cases in point, and so are many species of precocial birds (whose chicks start feeding themselves as soon as they hatch). There are also species in which paternal investment is optional. Under some environmental conditions they contribute a great deal—in others much less. Such is the case of hoary marmots which, depending on circumstances, alternate between being doting fathers and philandering mates (Barash, 1975). In general, paternal investment is more optional to offspring survival than maternal investment.

MATING AND PAIR-BONDING

Closely linked with parental, especially paternal, investment, at least in higher vertebrates (birds and mammals), is the nature of the pair-bond between mates. At one end of the spectrum are those species that mate monogamously for life, like some geese and foxes. At the other extreme are animals that are quite promiscuous and seem to form no stable pair-bonds at all: a female in heat will mate in quick succession with almost any male in sight. Males, in turn, show little if any possessiveness of females. Dogs and chimpanzees, for example, are among the more promiscuous species. The great majority of higher vertebrates, man included, fall somewhere in a broad middle ground that comprises a great deal of variation in mating patterns.

Some species, including many altricial birds, are monogamous during a mating season but change partners from season to season. A great many animals, like a number of precocial birds, ungulates, pinnipeds and some primates, are more or less polygynous, i.e., several females share a single male and form a "harem." Yet others, such as the savannah baboon, form temporary "consort" relationships, preferably with one of the dominant males in the group, but the female may change partners during a single oestrus period. A very small number of animals are polyandrous, i.e., have a single female stably mated to several males. Less than one percent of bird species (e.g., the Tasmanian native hen) are polyandrous (Barash, 1977; Jenni, 1974; Lack, 1968). Among mammals, polyandry is even rarer—the best known case being, occasionally, humans.

The kind of mating system that a species has evolved is closely linked with the requirements of the offspring, and those in turn contribute directly to the fitness of the mates. Mating, then, is but another form of the fitness game. Generally, stable pair-bonds, especially monogamous ones, are found in species where males make a considerable parental investment through such activities as nest-building, provisioning the young, defending a foraging territory against intruders, or protecting the female and brood against predators. Monogamous pair-bonding is the avian strategy par excellence. Some 92 percent of bird species are monogamous (Lack, 1968). Conversely, in highly polygynous or promiscuous species, paternal investment is less crucial and typically much less substantial. Mates stick together, in short, not so much because they "love" each other, but for the fitness of the young, which is also the fitness of their own genes. At the root of both parental and conjugal love is, once again, the ultimate genetic egoism. Mates "fall in love," or, more prosaically, become imprinted on each other, in species where it serves their individual fitness to do so. Sexual love, in the last analysis, is genetic self-love.

SEXUAL SELECTION AND DIMORPHISM

We have seen that, in sexually reproducing species, females are almost invariably a scarce resource for males, rather than vice versa. This means that males compete for females, a process referred to by Darwin as *sexual selection*. There are basically two ways in which males can compete: they can seek to attract females (*epigamic* selection), or they can seek to out-compete other males *(intrasexual* selection). Far from being mutually exclusive, many species practice both, though some stress one or the other. Both types of sexual selection lead to *sexual dimorphism,* i.e., the differences in external appearance between the two sexes of the same species. Since the males, in addition to other selective pressures that they share with females, also compete with each other over access to reproductive females (something which females obviously do not), it stands to reason that males should, in some respects, come to look different from females.

Where the stress is on epigamic selection, the males are often of more striking appearance. This is true of many birds where males attract females through bright plumage. On the other hand, in species where males fight each other rather than woo females, sexual dimorphism, at least in vertebrates, takes the form of greater size, strength, musculature or fighting equipment (antlers, teeth) in males.[2] Generally, the more sexual selection, the more sexual dimorphism there is. Some species are so minimally dimorphic that the sexes cannot be readily distinguished, as, for instance, among hyenas (where females even have a pseudo-penis). In other species, e.g., in a number of insects, sexual dimorphism is so pronounced that zoologists have sometimes erroneously assigned the two sexes of the same species to different species. In some mammals, e.g., in pinnipeds and many terrestrial primates, adult males weigh twice to three times as much as adult females. In some birds, drab and cryptic females have resplendent males—for instance, with peacocks.

Often, where the male is much bigger than the female, it takes him longer to reach his full reproductive age, a phenomenon referred to as *sexual bimaturism.* Both sexual dimorphism and sexual bimaturism are directly related to the extent to which a species is polygynous, and result principally from intrasexual selection, but also from a multiplicity of ecological conditions (Clutton-Brock and Harvey, 1978b). Highly dimorphic males typically have a shorter reproductive lifespan than females. This is not true, however, of the only moderately dimorphic humans where the female lives long past the menopause but where males typically retain some fertility into old age.

With lesser male parental investment and its resulting sexual selection on males, *variation* in reproductive success is greater for males than for females. On the average, reproductive success tends to be equal for males and females. This is so because sex ratios in most species tend to be very close to parity, and, of course, every offspring has a single parent of both sexes. However, to the extent that sexual selection operates, some males are completely or almost completely debarred from reproducing, while others produce greatly disproportionate numbers of offspring. In monogamous species, there is relatively little sexual selection. Conversely, the more polygynous a species is, the more sexually dimorphic it tends to be, and the greater the variability in male reproductive success. In some species, for instance, young maturing males are chased away from the parental harem, and forced to join peripheral all-male groups, or to live as solitary males until such time as they successfully steal a harem from another male. This is the case, for instance, among some antelopes (e.g., the impala) and in some primates (e.g., langurs). In such animal societies, most males never mate, but those that do sire enormous progenies.

We stated earlier that sexual selection and mating systems have much to do with parental investment, especially with *differential* parental investment between males and females. In general, the more polygynous a species is, the smaller the male's parental investment in relation to the female's. In a sense, that statement is a tautology. Since polygynous males have more offspring than any one of their females, their contribution to any one of their young can only be a fraction of that of any female, even if the males devote a substantial amount of energy to their offspring collectively. Beyond that trivial observation, however, many polygynous males do not invest much in their young, even collectively. For one thing, they often spend much of their time and energy denying other males access to their females. In effect, males in highly polygynous species play long shots: they incur considerable risk or at least energetic expense to win a harem, and, once this is achieved, keeping the harem is far more important to their fitness than whatever marginal contribution they might make to an individual offspring.

An extreme example of this is the sea elephant, a pinniped where the male is about three times as heavy as the female and where dominant bulls attempt to monopolize harems of scores of females (LeBoeuf, 1974). They are continuously challenged by bachelor bulls eager to take over. Hence, they have to be constantly on the lookout for intruders and if necessary, they have to fight to repel them while at the same time avoiding injury. Not only are they challenged by fully grown males willing to fight them, but they also have to watch out for younger males who try to sneak into the harem and have surreptitious copulations at an age when they are still small enough to be difficult to distinguish from females. The males make no perceptible direct parental investment. Indeed, they sometimes accidentally kill their own offspring. When maneuvering their mass of blubber to fight off other males, the males occasionally smother to death some of their own young because the females and pups are tightly aggregated on rookeries near the sea. This behavior obviously reduces their fitness but far less than the potential threat of losing the harem. They belong to a species where only a few males get to reproduce at all, but those who succeed do so spectacularly well that the occasional smothering of a pup makes relatively little difference.

FERTILITY: K AND r SELECTION

Another way in which species differ conspicuously is in their fertility. Why should not all animals evolve so as to maximize the number of offspring at birth? Why should we not lay thousands of eggs, like insects or fish, instead of laboriously giving birth to a single baby every couple of years? The answer is obvious: once the environment is saturated, i.e., once a species makes optimum use of the niche for which it has adapted, every reproductive couple can only expect that, on the average, two of their offspring will themselves reach reproductive age. There are two basic evolutionary strategies, respectively called in biological jargon "K" and "r," that a species can take. The K strategy (where K stands for the carrying capacity of the environment) consists of putting a lot of investment in a small number of offspring, while the r strategy (r for reproduction) produces many young but invests less heavily in them. In other words, K strategists go for quality, while r strategists opt for quantity.

The fewer the offspring, the heavier the investment in each and the lower the mortality; what the K strategist loses in fertility, he makes up in survival rates.[3] The reverse is, of course, true of r strategists. The general evolutionary trend has been toward the K strategy. For instance, among vertebrates, fish and amphibians lay many more eggs on the average than reptiles and reptiles lay many more than birds. Birds and mammals are on the whole the least prolific of vertebrates.

Of course, this is all a relative matter, so there is no point at which r strategy may be said to end and K strategy to begin. Furthermore, there have been many evolutionary reversals of this general trend toward K. For instance, most felids and canids, feeding on large prey (such as ungulates), are more prolific than their prey animals, suffering much higher infant mortality rates, in spite of the fact that they are often at or near the apex of their respective food chains and thus are relatively free of predators. They die mostly of hunger.

Despite their high fertility (with litters typically ranging from three to twelve for most canids and felids) relative to their ungulate prey animals (who typically have single or at most twin births), predators are far less numerous than prey animals. Predator biomass is typically less than one tenth of the biomass of their prey. A highly fertile species is not necessarily more abundant than a relative infertile one. Generally, there is some association between fertility and numbers, because smaller species tend to be both more fertile and more numerous in a given environment than big ones. Obviously, an African savannah, for instance, can carry far more termites per square kilometer than elephants or rhinoceroses. However, controlling for size, there is no close association between fertility and abundance of a species in a given environment. What, then, determines whether a species will, within the limitations of its previous phylogeny, evolve toward a K or an r strategy?

The answer must be sought in the stability of its resources, especially food, of course. K strategists exploit relatively stable resources and have relatively stable populations that are at or close to the carrying capacity of their environment. That is, they maximize their reproductive capability and minimize wasteful losses through mortality by restricting their fertility (obviously with no conscious intent) to something not greatly in excess of their resource base, plus an allowance for predation, disease, accidents and so on. The danger of the K strategy is that, should an environmental catastrophe strike, K species take much longer to replenish their numbers; but they usually replenish because every species possesses enough fertility to multiply should the opportunity arise.

The r strategist, by contrast, exploits unstable resources and is characterized by wildly fluctuating populations. His high fertility is adaptive insurance against catastrophe in an environment where catastrophe is highly probable. The frog that lays its eggs in a puddle of stagnant water, for example, is unconsciously betting on highly variable conditions of rain and insolation. Its risks are high, but, should it be successful, it hits the jackpot. Another nice feature of the r strategy, despite its inevitable high losses, is that an r species has the capability of swiftly colonizing and multiplying in new, vacant niches and, therefore, of making the most of sudden opportunities. Anybody, for instance, who has experienced the sudden apparition of a mosquito swarm in the spring will testify to the superiority of mosquitoes over humans as environmental opportunists.

SPACING AND TERRITORIALITY

Mating and reproductive systems of animals are thus clearly and drastically influenced by a wide variety of environmental conditions. Of the resources essential for survival, sheer space is perhaps the most basic, for without its control, most other resources become elusive. This is why the way animals relate to space is such a universally important feature of their social organization—therefore of their mating and reproductive systems. The two main ways in which animals relate to space are *spacing* and *territoriality*. Spacing refers to the distance kept between conspecifics, the invisible bubble of space that moves about with animals. Territoriality is the defense of relatively fixed space against use or occupation by conspecifics. Both spacing and territoriality are closely related to the social organization of animals. For instance, spacing and related "displacement behavior" (where a dominant animal approaches another, and the latter yields ground) reveal an animal group's dominance structure. Within family groups, spacing often corresponds to an age- and sex-based hierarchy, which in turn determines order of access to the group's resources.

Territoriality takes different forms in different species. Some species are by nature much more territorial than others. Territorial behavior is also determined to a large extent by environmental variables, such as the distribution of food (Emlen and Oring, 1977). Where food resources are relatively stable and evenly spread in a species' habitat, a territorial response is common. Available real estate is divided up and monopolistically exploited by individuals or small, mutually exclusive groups that are often reproductive units. But, when food sources are seasonal and/or highly concentrated (e.g., fruiting trees for primates or the carcass of an animal for scavengers), temporary congregations of animals take place and territorial behavior is much less evident.

Not all territories are for purposes of foraging, however. At least two other types of territory are especially important to breeding groups, namely nesting or breeding territories that are defended principally to ensure the safety of the offspring and to secure mating grounds *(leks)*. Many birds, for example, have leks during the mating season: males defend small territories around them, into which they attract receptive females by means of ritualized displays.

Another important feature of mating and reproductive systems is the extent to which they are inbred or outbred. A *population,* in the biological sense, is an inbred group. There may be migration in and out of the population, so inbreeding is often not absolute; but a population is stable enough as to have a *gene pool* that is, in respects to some genes, significantly different from that of neighboring populations. Otherwise, by definition, it is not a population. A population is said to be *panmictic* if all the reproductive adults of one sex have an equal probability of breeding with any member of the opposite sex in the population. Although statistical models of population genetics sometimes assume that populations are panmictic, very few actually are. Such factors as physical propinquity, dominance order and sexual selection typically result in gross departures from random mating. This is, of course, especially true in strongly polygynous species.

In the nature of the case, animal populations are often (though not necessarily) *societies,* as previously defined. That is, their members are in physical proximity, and interact cooperatively with one another. We have also seen that animals are likely to contribute to each other's fitness to the extent that they are genetically related. It follows then that social species tend to consist of kin-related groups since kinship seem to be the main basis of sociality in animals. This is carried to extremes in the *eusocial* insect societies of *hymenoptera* (bees, wasps and ants) where the sterile female workers in a colony are related to each other by a factor of $\frac{3}{4}$, and to their mother the queen by a factor of $\frac{1}{2}$.[4] Indeed, the social insects are unparalleled in the animal kingdom for both the size of their societies (commonly running into the tens of thousands) and their degree of social cohesion. Among higher vertebrates, societies are typically much smaller and much more loosely integrated. The members of avian and mammalian societies are also much less closely related on the average, though kin selection clearly is the principal basis of such sociality as they show.

INBREEDING AND SOCIALITY

If animal societies are held together by kin relatedness, why do not all animal societies maximize inbreeding? The more incestuous a society, the more cohesive it could be expected to be according to kin selection theory. In fact, however, most sexually reproducing animals have mechanisms of "incest avoidance": they are far less than maximally inbred, though also often far short of being panmictic. In many, perhaps most, species, incest avoidance is achieved through sheer spatial dispersal. In species where little or no parental care is needed, e.g., in most fishes, both sexes disperse soon after hatching. Among birds and mammals, the dispersal often takes place shortly before sexual maturation, and it may only affect one sex—often the males. But why do not most sexual species evolve toward highly cohesive, highly incestuous societies?

The answer is twofold. First, sociality is not an absolute "good" toward which all species should tend. For some species, a high level of sociality increases individual fitness under given environmental conditions; other species do quite well with solitary existence. There is no general evolutionary trend toward more sociality. If anything the reverse is true. Sexual reproduction itself is an antisocial force since it produces individual variability: the more unlike individuals in a population are, the less their genetic interests overlap, and, hence, the more diluted the kin selection benefits of cooperation. Most of the more recently developed species, such as birds and mammals, tend to be much less social than many species with a much longer phylogenic history, such as termites, ants or bees. The reason is that, among the eusocial insects, the coefficient of relatedness between colony members is much higher than in any vertebrate population of comparable size.

A species will only develop as much sociality as will contribute to the individual fitness of its members in a given environment. If fitness optimization requires a reduction in societal size and cohesion, that species will evolve in that direction—and vice versa. There is nothing intrinsically good about being social. It all depends on the kind of environment in which one finds oneself.

The second half of the answer has to do with the evolutionary benefits of both sexual reproduction and of heterogeneity in a gene pool. Sexual reproduction is a great evolutionary leap forward because it permits a great shuffling of genetic material at each generation, and therefore greatly enhances the ability of a species to adapt to changing environments. The shuffling, however, is only effective to the extent that substantial numbers of genes in the species' gene pool have more than one allele for each locus on a chromosome. In other words, the more heterozygous individuals a population has for the greater number of genes, the more adaptive potential that population has. Inbreeding has the effect of reducing heterozygosity, and therefore that adaptive potential.[5] Therefore extreme inbreeding cancels out the benefits of sexual reproduction itself. The logical extreme of inbreeding would be to have haploid organisms reproducing parthenogenetically, which, in effect, would make for an all-female species. This prospect might enchant some feminists, but the cost in evolutionary adaptability would be high, since it would revert to mutation as the only source of adaptive change.

BEHAVIOR AND NATURAL SELECTION

In this chapter, we have presented a general way of looking at mating and reproductive systems in which such systems are seen as the product of a process of natural selection. Animal behavior, in general, and their mating, reproductive and parental behavior, in particular, are genetically programmed adaptations to a multiplicity of selective pressures in their environment. The genetic program can be quite flexible and compatible with a wide range of phenotypic responses to different environmental circumstances. Indeed, in the more intelligent animals, such as birds and mammals, genetic programs for behavior are demonstrably modifiable through learning; so, to speak of genetic programs is not to reduce behavior to simple, automatic reflexes. Some behaviors are highly stereotyped and ritualized; others much less so. The more neurologically complex an animal, the more flexible its genetic programs. There is, however, a genetic base, direct or indirect, to the behavior of all animals.

Natural selection, whether of anatomical or behavioral phenotypes, results from differential reproductive rates between individual animals, that is from differential fitness. Ultimately, however, the unit of selection is not the individual organism but the gene. Evolution is a process whereby competing alleles of the same gene change their relative frequencies in the population's gene pool. Sexually reproducing organisms are ephemeral and unique combinations of genes thrown together by mutations, sexual recombination and chromosomal cross-overs during meiosis. They are ultimately little more than gene-shuffling machines resulting in combinations of different fitnesses in different environments. In Dawkins' (1976) vivid imagery, organisms are perishable survival machines for potentially eternal genes.

What matters from the point of view of evolution is thus not simply an individual's own direct reproduction, but the passing on of its genes, either directly or indirectly through the reproduction of individuals that share its genes—in short, its *inclusive* fitness. Individuals have a genetic interest in their kin to the extent they share genes. Preference for kin, or *kin selection,* is thus a fundamental basis of sociality in animal societies. No animal society, therefore, can be understood without reference to its mating and reproductive system and to the groups of cooperating mates and kin to which these systems give rise.

In the next chapter, we will see that humans, too, fit rather well into that biological scheme of things.

NOTES

1. This chapter presents a pedagogical problem: to introduce readers to elementary genetics (including population and behavior genetics), ecology and evolutionary theory—all of which would make a book. Therefore, I take a nodding acquaintance with elementary biology, especially Mendelian genetics, for granted, rather than restate that material here. For introductory background material relevant to this and the following chapters, the reader should turn to the supplementary sources suggested at the end of this chapter.
2. In many invertebrates, such as insects and spiders, the male is often smaller than the female. This may be partly selection of females as prodigious egg-laying machines. Termite queens represent a grotesque extreme of this.
3. The inverse relationship between parental investment on one hand, and fertility and infant mortality on the other, was clearly understood by Westermarck (1891). In Chapter 1 of his great classic, we find a nearly modern version of parental investment theory, including the notions that parental investment is asymmetrical by sex; that the investment of males varies greatly from species to species; and that the pair-bond is a fitness-enhancing mechanism. Unfortunately, later generations of social scientists were so eager to reject everything Westermarck had said, especially his instinctual theory of incest, that they stopped reading him seriously, and thereby further sealed the 20th century divorce between the social sciences and biology. Contemporary sociobiology is merely the rediscovery and more systematic application to animal behavior of a theoretical model developed by Darwin well over a century ago.
4. This is not the place to explain in detail why this is the case, but the high degree of relatedness of members of social hymnenoptera colonies is due to two factors: the single fertilization of the queen and their haplodiploidy, i.e., the fact that, while females are diploid, males are produced from unfertilized eggs and are thus haploid (Wilson, 1971).

Females share *all* the genes of their father and half of the genes of their mother, being thus ¾ related to each other.
5. The effect of inbreeding is to reduce the frequency of recessive alleles of genes in a gene pool. Inbreeding brings forth more homozygous recessive individuals who often have lower fitness and are less likely to pass on these recessive alleles. In a more panmictic population, recessive alleles can be passed on indefinitely by heterozygotes who do not exhibit the fitness-reducing phenotypes as do the homozygous recessives. A recessive allele, however, which under present environmental conditions under lower fitness, may acquire a higher fitness under changed conditions; therefore, individuals who retain such flexibility keep adaptive insurance against future environmental change. There are also cases of recessive alleles that are deleterious, indeed lethal, in the homozygous form but, which, in the heterozygous form, have higher fitness than the homozygous dominants. This conditions, known as *heterosis* or heterozygote superiority, is exemplified by sickle cell anemia in humans. This recessive gene is lethal in its homozygous form, but it affords some immunity to malaria to the heterozygote carriers; the latter are thus fitter in malaria-endemic areas than the homozygous dominants.

SUPPLEMENTARY READINGS

Perhaps the best general treatment of the material summarized in this chapter is Daly and Wilson (1978). An application of sociobiology to humans requires at least minimum knowledge of the social behavior of primates. Rowell (1972), Kummer (1971) and Jane Lancaster (1975) provide a good short introductions to behavioral primatology. Stine (1977) and Bodmer and Cavalli-Sforza (1976) are useful textbooks in human genetics. Hinde (1974), Mazur and Robertson (1972), Tiger and Fox (1971) and van den Berghe (1974, 1978a) all represent attempts to reintroduce behavioral biology into the social sciences. More technical articles include Alexander (1971, 1978), D. T. Campbell (1975), Hartung (1976), Parker (1976), Shepher (1971), Trivers (1971, 1972, 1974), van den Berghe (1974, 1977) and van den Berghe and Barash (1977).

3

THE SOCIOBIOLOGY OF
HUMAN MATING AND REPRODUCTION

Anthropologists delight in stressing the diversity of human systems of marriage and kinship, and, indeed, there are important cultural differences within our species, as we will see in subsequent chapters. However, the illusion of almost infinite flexibility in our mating and reproductive systems, an impression one can easily gain by steeping oneself in the ethnographic literature, can only be sustained by studiously ignoring biology. At a trivial level, sociological and anthropological treatments of the family do, of course, mention biology and deal, if only superficially, with the physiology of gestation and lactation, with sex hormones and menstruation, with infant dependency and child development. There is usually a brief mention that we are mammals and primates, but the dominant social science viewpoint is still that the biological constraints on our mating and reproductive behavior are much less limiting than for any other animal, and indeed are so broad as to be inconsequential, or, at the very least, uninteresting.

Many social scientists are even more dogmatically environmentalist than I have just suggested. Erich Goode (1978, p. 312), for example, writes, "In a nutshell: sexual behavior, sexual custom, and sexual deviance are all dictated not by the body's animal or hormonal makeup, but by the society and the culture in which we live." Amusingly, Goode dedicates his book: "To My Mother, Sangu du me sangu," which translates "blood of my blood." It is interesting that he should have chosen an inaccurate transliteration of Sicilian dialect to hide his closet biological sentiments, while loudly proclaiming his cultural determinist orthodoxy in the King's English. Even authors like Alice Rossi (1977, 1978) who take an eminently sensible position of the importance of human physiology on behavior (especially on sex differences) are skeptical about the validity of cross-species comparisons. Yet, without comparing humans with nonhumans, a full understanding of our behavior in evolutionary perspective is impossible. What possible intellectual ground is there for rejecting any source of evidence?

It is probably in the study of kinship that dogmatic cultural determinism has achieved its most extreme, indeed ethereal, expression. Through the influence of theorists such as David Schneider in the United States and Claude Lévi-Strauss in Europe, an idealist view of human kinship has come to dominate much of contemporary social science. According to that perspective, the ultimate reality of kinship is not individual interaction, but the *model* that a more or less hypothetical native philosopher has of his society's kinship structure. The mental construct is the ultimate reality, irrespective of whether it bears a recognizable resemblance with what people do. Lest I be accused of drawing a caricature of this position, I quote Lévi-Strauss (1953, p. 115), the high priest of "structuralism" in kinship analysis: "In my mind, models are reality and I would even say that they are the only reality."

There are of course, a number of important exceptions to this general neglect of biology in social science—most of them in anthropology. Marxist materialist tradition going back to Engels' 1884 classic, *The Origin of the Family, Private Property and the State,* based on Morgan's *Ancient Society* (1877), paid attention to the relationship between production and reproduction. However, by stressing almost exclusively the former, it failed to see that production was itself ultimately reducible to a means of reproduction. This is still a shortcoming of more recent anthropological works that are, broadly, in the materialist tradition (Harris, 1974, 1975, 1977; Goody, 1976; Goody and Tambiah, 1973; Meillassoux, 1977). They are almost exclusively focused on the social organization of production and the cultural superstructures regulating the production, distribution and inheritance of resources.[1] Malinowski (1929, 1960) believed that biological drives underlaid human behavior and that much social organization derived from biologically based kin ties, but, of the major figures in the British anthropology of the next generation, only Fortes (1953, 1959, 1969) followed his lead.

Here I argue that we must first carefully examine what kind of an animal we are; how we came to evolve the way we have; and how our mating and reproductive system both resembles and differs from that of other animals. The most directly relevant basis of comparison will be the other primates because of their phylogenetic proximity to us; however, sometimes our adaptation will show interesting parallels with other species, such as social carnivores, because of similarity of environmental conditions.

In a number of basic respects we stand at an extreme of mammalian evolution, even among primates. We are clearly on the "K selection" end of the spectrum. Like other primates, we are unprolific, and therefore have, until recently, had relatively stable populations that tended to remain close to the carrying capacity of the environment. In the last few thousand years, dramatic technological changes have produced several human population explosions, but, before the development of agriculture, human populations grew very slowly (Cowgill, 1975). Even during the population growth produced by the development of agriculture in the Middle East some 10,000 years ago, the growth rate was estimated at no more than one per thousand per year (Carneiro and Hilse, 1966).

Not only are single births the rule, but pregnancy and lactation are prolonged and maturation is slow, even by primate standards. Only the three large living species of anthropoid apes—gorillas, chimpanzees and orangutans—approach us in these respects among primates, and, among other mammals, only some very large species like elephants share these demographic characteristics with us. In short, for our size, we reproduce slowly, both because we have few young and because human generations cover about 20 years.

INFANT DEPENDENCY

The most fundamental human bond—the one which is absolutely essential to survival under any but recent industrial conditions—is, of course, the mother–infant bond which we share with all mammals. Recent technology now allows the substitution of surrogates for the mother—often at considerable physical or emotional cost. Safely feeding infants by parasitizing another species for milk requires an advanced industrial technology of food sterilization and processing and is still beyond the economic means of much of the human population, especially in the tropics. As for the cost of providing institutionalized care of infants in the first few years of life, it is high—in economic and in emotional terms. The sustained, continuous, loving care required by human infants, if they are to develop normally, is still an expensive luxury requiring ratios of adults to young not very different from those prevailing in natural families, and a stability of personnel difficult to achieve in an institutional setting. Even in highly affluent industrial societies, there is still no good, efficient, cheap substitute for mothers (Bowlby, 1969).

The similarity of the human mother—infant bond with that found in other primates is striking. Even the most solitary of the higher primates, the orangutan, has prolonged mother—young ties, and in many of the highly social monkey societies, both arboreal and terrestrial, matrilines of kin-related females and their descendants form the core structure of the group, even determining the relative status of the males in the group (Kummer, 1971). Even in specific emotional needs for close body contact, human infants follow the basic primate pattern of inborn grasping reflexes of both hands and feet. Deprivation of such contact produces similar psychopathological symptoms in monkeys, ranging from thumb sucking to severe depression and total inability to interact in normal social settings (Harlow and Harlow, 1965).

PRIMATE MATING SYSTEMS

With rare exceptions, such as the orangutan, social ties for primates extend well beyond mother and infant. Most primates are social creatures living in groups of 10 to a 100 (or even more) individuals, often biologically related to each other. In some cases, the core of a primate troop is formed by a few related females and their offspring, with adult males moving in and out of the troop. Young monkeys and apes undergo a process of socialization wherein, after infancy, they become increasingly independent of their mothers and begin to interact more and more with other animals in their troop, both young and adults. Indeed, playing with age-mates seems an essential feature for the normal development of most monkeys and apes, as shown by the Harlows (1965) for the rhesus monkey. Infant monkeys deprived of their mothers show developmental retardation but later exposure to age-mates undoes much of the damage. Those deprived of both mother and age-mates become socially incompetent and psychotic to the point of being incapable of reproducing. Males are unable to mount females; females become inept mothers.

Man, like almost all other primates, normally lives in groups that consist of members of both sexes and of all ages. Until the advent of larger and more complex societies in the last few thousand years, the basic human groups that made up the small-scale "primitive" societies resembled their primate counterparts in that they consisted of individuals who were either biologically related to each other or who mated with each other. They were held together by kin selection as other primate societies, but reciprocity played a much bigger role in human sociality than among other primates.

Where primate societies differ a great deal from one another is in the relationship of males to both females and offspring. In nearly all primate species, adult males—or at least some of them—stay in constant proximity to females and young, presumably making some contribution to their fitness, other than inseminating females. Frequently, that contribution consists of defending the group against predators. This is especially true of the more terrestrial species (like baboons and macaques) where the males are much bigger and better armed (with long canine teeth) than the females (Kummer, 1971). Indeed, the strong sexual dimorphism of terrestrial primates is undoubtedly an adaptation to the need for defense against canid and felid predators.

Most primate species, however, are more promiscuous than man; that is, they do not form stable pair-bonds between individual adult males and females. There are some exceptions. Gibbons and siamangs (the smallest of the four main types of anthropoid apes and the most unmanlike) form stable monogamous unions and live in territorial nuclear families consisting of parents and one or two of their joint offspring. Stable monogamy is unusual among primates, however. More common, but still far from the general rule, is polygyny. A number of species, such as the hamadryas baboon, the langur, the gelada and the patas monkey have family units made up of a single adult male, several females and their young. "Their young" is used here somewhat loosely; although males attempt to monopolize their females, the latter are not adverse to an occasional sneak copulation with a bachelor male on the fringe of the group. Still, the dominant male who controls a harem typically reproduces most.

The nature of the pair-bond differs from one species to another. In the African hamadryas baboon, for example, the male adopts young females and forcibly herds adult females to his group, keeping them close to him by means of threats and neck bites (Kummer, 1968, 1971). However, among the Indian langurs, males steal harems from each other, often trying to kill the offspring of their predecessor after taking over a group of females (Hrdy, 1977).

This relatively stable type of polygyny, where one male comes close to monopolizing copulations with a harem of females, is not the general primate pattern. In most species, there is no stable pair-mating of either the monogamous or the polygynous type. Promiscuity is a matter of degree. Some species, like the chimpanzee, come close to complete promiscuity: a female in oestrus will copulate with any adult male in the vicinity (with the probable exception of her sons), and males do not show any jealousy toward each other, although juveniles sometimes harass copulating adults (van Lawick-Goodall, 1971). In other species, such as the anubis baboon, females in oestrus form a temporary "consort" relationship with one of the more dominant males in the multi-male troop. Before the peak of their oestrus, they often copulate with younger, nondominant males, and they may even change mates during the couple of days of their peak oestrus. Males sometimes try to snatch away a female in oestrus from each other, "consort" relationships typically lasting from a few hours to a few days (Washburn and De Vore, 1961a, 1961b).

Naturally, the outcome of such loose mating arrangements is that paternity is of little if any social consequence in many primate societies. That is, in many primate species, fathers have no special social relationship to their offspring, although they may live in close spatial proximity to them—along with several other adult males. The several males may pool their resources in repelling predators, thus contributing to the fitness of their own offspring, as well as that of their partners. It may also be that, in some species, coalitions of dominant males tend to be biologically related (although this remains to be firmly established) and that, therefore, the infants of the troop will often be at least nephews and cousins if not children. However, chimpanzees, gorillas and many monkeys do not have recognizable sociological fathers.

There are two striking features about primate mating systems. They vary greatly from species to species, even between very closely related species, such as the hamadryas and the anubis baboon; yet, within the species, the mating pattern is relatively set and invariant, even under a wide array of environmental conditions, ranging from the wild to zoos. When fundamental aspects of the social structure of a particular species, such as the sex ratio, are disturbed in captivity, monkeys do not readily adjust; instead bloody pandemonium often breaks out. The classic example was the famous episode in London Zoo in which hamadryas baboons lashed out at each other, leaving several dead, when they were put together in an unnatural group that comprised too few females (Zuckerman, 1932).

Experiments in the wild by Kummer (1971) have shown that, in the hamadryas baboon, it is the herding behavior of the male that largely determines the mating system of that species. Manipulations of environmental conditions, and comparisons between the behavior of male and female hamadryas baboons, anubis baboons and hybrids gave a strong indication that the herding behavior of the male hamadryas is under a genetic program, while that of the female hamadryas is not. When female hamadryas are released in anubis troops, they do not attach themselves to a male and, conversely, when a female anubis is released among hamadryas baboons, she is quickly herded by a male and starts behaving like a hamadryas female. Male hamadryas baboons, however, retain their herding behavior under a wide range of environmental conditions.

HUMAN MATING: WHAT IS NORMAL?

What of human mating systems? Is it not reasonable to hypothesize that they too are, within yet to be ascertained limits, genetically programmed? Anthropologists and sociologists have long emphasized the diversity of human sexual behavior and, in recent years, it has become fashionable to regard "alternative life-styles" as matters of capricious personal preference that could be scripted and rescripted with almost random interchangeable casts of actors (Laws and Schwartz, 1977). I suggest that a close and dispassionate examination of how humans actually behave (as distinguished from their verbal reports about their behavior) reveals a far narrower range of sexual and mating behavior than is often claimed for our species. We have definite genetic constraints on our bedroom repertoire.

The basic question here is: What is the range of "normalcy" in human sexual behavior? To be sure, man is sufficiently intelligent and imaginative to play sexual games covering a wide spectrum indeed. Some people so condition themselves that they can only reach orgasm through pain; others through extreme forms of humiliation; others yet through exotic fetishes or zoophilia. Without being judgmental, such behaviors are clearly not normal in the sense that they would appeal to many people in many societies. Indeed, I expect that they would be judged abnormal in practically all societies. The mere fact that some people "do it" does not make a behavior normal.

An exotic example will sufficiently prove the point. The following tidbit of Melanesian ethnography should gladden the cultural relativist's heart, for it illustrates how wide the range of human sexual behavior is. The cast of characters consists of cannibals from the eastern highlands of New Guinea in the district of Kogu; the account of the orgiastic feast is by the anthropologist who studied them in the early 1950s (Berndt, 1962, p. 283); and the events described are not out of the ordinary for that particular society. Here is Berndt's verbatim description from his field notes:

> Shooting continued until they reached Arufanu, near Agura, where several Tiroka men and a number of women were killed. The remaining Tiroka people disappeared into the bush and escaped home. Groups of Agura, Moiife, and Kogu men and women gathered around the corpses to cut them up. Most assembled at Arufanu, where more corpses were available for cutting. Here Unapina of Kogu selected the corpse of a young woman named Pazuna; finding her attractive, he knelt between her legs and pulling them to his thighs began to copulate, cutting the body as he did so. A Koga woman, Aria, came up, and said to him, "You are taking a long time. You are only pretending to cut. All the time you copulate." But having ejaculated he began again, at the same time slowly cutting off the woman's breasts. By this time Aria, a *nenafu* [cross-cousin] of his, became impatient and set to work on the corpse herself with her bamboo knife. She began to cut across the corpse's belly, but Unapina was so intent on copulating that he did not notice how near her knife was. Aria, for her part, was careless. She cut further in and across, hacking away at the flesh; and since Unapina's penis was in the woman's vagina, she cut most of it off. Unapina fell

back crying, blood flowing from the stump of his penis. Aria blamed him for what had happened. "You sit there copulating, not bothering to cut her up properly. This woman is dead, ready to be cut up for eating. I told you about it, but you continued copulating. Thus I cut off your penis!" Unapina replied, "I looked at this Kamano woman; she was a good woman. I looked at her vulva, and I liked it; that is why I copulated. But now you have cut off my penis! What shall I do?" Aria removed the end of the penis she had cut off, popped it into her mouth, and ate it, and then continued with the cutting. Unapina was helped back to his house, where he rested. Ovens were made and the meat cooked, amid dancing and singing. Unapina was given the woman's vulva and surrounding flesh to eat.

The cutting of the penis was, of course, an unfortunate accident in an episode of good clean fun by New Guinea highlands standards; but Kogu women are routinely gang-raped, before and after death—dismembered alive limb by limb and eaten (Berndt, 1962, pp. 285–286). Sick relatives and acquaintances are killed so that their meat can be enjoyed before it is wasted away by disease (pp. 278–279). A special culinary delicacy is putrid human meat cooked with its maggots (pp. 272–273). The Kogu are clearly not the sort of chaps most people in most cultures would want their daughters to marry.

Yet, all this behavior, while admittedly beyond the normal range, is still quite recognizeably and uniquely human. First, it is not altogether unknown in other cultures. It is not very different from the sexual fantasies (some of which he apparently enacted) of the Marquis de Sade, a refined aristocrat and recognized master of 18th century French literature, or from the behavior of SS guards in German concentration camps who, as great animal lovers, fed their watchdogs the flesh of prisoners. No chimpanzee can come close to matching these feats. Second—and this is really the clincher that forces us to admit New Guineans in our august human company—these cannibals observe uniquely human proprieties. They consider it bad form either to copulate with or to eat their children and their parents. They carefully grade their ferocity depending on degree of relatedness and amity. In short, they have incest taboos, practicing kin selection and reciprocity through complex symbolic communication. In Berndt's remarkably antiseptic analysis (p. 288): "We can speak of the structural aspect of cannibalism insofar as it symbolizes 'ingroup solidarity' as against 'outgroup hostility,' underlining the segmentary nature of the social units involved." Humans kill, rape and eat each other in uniquely human ways, we should be reassured to know.

A striking characteristic of human sexual behavior is its frequency and duration. On the whole, we do rather a lot of it, and we take our time about it. Such statements are meaningless, of course, except by comparison with other species. Compared to most other species we are sexy.

This is true by either of two criteria of sexiness: we invest a lot of time and energy in sex, with only a small fraction of our copulations resulting in procreation. The average human copulates from a few hundred to a few thousand times in a lifetime, leaving only two or three offspring. The coitus–offspring ratio is thus of the order of 1,000 to one. This is hardly a marvel of reproductive efficiency. By contrast, many invertebrates and lower vertebrates (such as fishes) mate only once in a lifetime. They may invest an enormous amount of energy in producing the gametes, but fertilization is a one-shot affair. More complex animals, especially mammals and birds, typically mate repeatedly over several breeding seasons, but, still, sex for nearly all of them is a temporally restricted activity. Generally, environmental factors limit mating to a definite, circumscribed season; even in species where there is no birth synchrony, females are only sexually receptive for a small portion of their lifetime and copulations are often quick, efficient and perfunctory. Many birds and some mammals have elaborate courtship displays, especially the ones that form stable pair-bonds, but, once the bond is established, they get down to the serious business of fertilization and reproduction without much further ado.

The "quickie" is definitely not for our species. The males of our species are ready and willing to mate most of the time, are capable of several copulations a day at their prime, regardless of season, are easily aroused, and willing to devote much time and energy in the pursuit of copulations. Our females are slower to arouse—more selective and less promiscuous—but they are capable of copulating any time, even when infertile or already pregnant. Oestrus is vestigial. Human females do not unmistakably go in heat, as do other primates with their alluringly swelled genitalia, and they have no obvious means of advertising their fertility, but they are not adverse to mating with the right partner at almost any time, except perhaps a few hours before and after childbirth. Female orgasms may also be a human monopoly.

Both sexes are not only ready and willing to mate often; they mate with affect. That is, they make a lot of fuss over it. To be sure, we are capable of quick sex without affect (males somewhat more readily than females), but neither sex finds Erica Jong's "zipless fuck" much fun, at least not as a steady diet. Human sex is typically preceded by courtship lasting days or longer, surrounded by complex and extraneous stimuli and activities such as drinking, eating, music, sport and play, and accompanied by a great deal of affect. Satisfactory coitus is not only preceded by elaborate foreplay; coitus itself is prolonged by most mammalian standards. Not only do we have the intelligence to enhance the fun of sex by making an elaborate game of it and by multiplying almost at will the sources of stimulation, but we also seek to establish complex, long-lasting relationships that go well beyond the mechanics of coitus. We tend to "fall in love" and become involved—often when we consciously try not to.

We are not the only sexy animal. Some species beat us in some respects. The penis of the dog swells after intromission to lock itself in the vagina of the bitch, and canine coitus may last hours, a feat that humans can only match with much practice. Many felids (members of the cat family) have vast numbers of quick copulations in rapid succession, but only when a female is in heat. Lions, for instance, are capable of having a hundred copulations a day and it has been estimated that it takes about 3,000 to produce a litter of cubs. The king of beasts indeed! Not only do lions and other cats have a royal ball; they do it in full view of other animals much to the embarrassment of zoo directors, and they vociferously meow their way through it, much to the annoyance of human insomniacs. Most of these sexy mammals, incidentally, share with man relative immunity to predation from other species (Eaton, 1978). Such seems to be the main ecological precondition for the luxury of reproductively inefficient but enjoyable sex. Animals continuously on the lookout for predators are quick about their sex, because sex is at least temporarily incapacitating.

WHY IS SEX SUCH FUN?

If one has to be at or near the apex of a food chain to belong to those privileged few species that have good and frequent sex, the question still remains why some animals, man included, develop such energetically wasteful methods of reproduction. Why, in short, did sex become such extravagantly good fun in those species, even at the cost of inefficient reproduction? To humans, the question may appear stupid, because we often tend to assume that good sex is an end in itself, and because we often engage in *deliberately* nonreproductive sex. But, of course, purely recreational sex is an evolutionary blind alley. Good sex must have evolved for a good evolutionary reason. The answer is that sexy species tend to be not only top predators who need not fear rude interruptions—but also polygynous species with strong male competition for access to females (Eaton, 1978). Sexual endurance then becomes a useful way for females to assess male vigor and thus to maximize their fitness. Male perseverance in courtship is also a useful test for the female of the male's propensity to parental investment, if such is needed. At the risk of disappointing human romantics, pleasurable sex is merely a means to an evolutionary end, not an end in itself.

Where does all this leave us? We may not be able to do it as often as the lion or as long as the dog, but we are by far the sexiest of primates (as well we should, being the only fully predatory primate). All in all, if we consider that we can and do do it all the time, even when infertile and pregnant; that we make inordinate fuss over it; that we consume so much time and energy on it; and that we develop so much of our precious culture around it, we must be the most obsessively sexual animal around. This is so much the case that, for humans, attempts to repress sexuality lead to new heights in sexual obsession.

One of the many things we do with sex is transform it into a type of recreation. That is, pleasure is not only a by-product of sex; we deliberately engage in sex as a form of *play behavior*. Fully half of the 39 societies in the Murdock and White (1969) sample on which Broude and Greene (1976) found information engaged in prolonged foreplay (kissing, caressing, fondling) before intercourse. We often make a conscious game of sex; we experiment with it; we enjoy the chase; we seek variety. The propensity to be playful is showed by many of the more intelligent animals (monkeys, apes, canids and felids) and man clearly has the mental capacity to turn almost anything into a game. But, besides the intellectual prerequisites for sexiness, we also evolved the extremely high coitus–offspring ratio that enables us to play sexual games at minimum fitness cost. We can, in short, afford to enjoy leisurely, experimental sex, because our bedroom antics only minimally affect our reproductive success.

True, Western societies may be more sexually obsessed than other human groups. Societies on the verge of famine may be more concerned with food than with sex. No doubt, eroticism is subject to some cultural and environmental variation. The same is true of other primates, incidentally, which become notoriously sexier in zoos with an assured food supply and no predation risk, than in the wild. Still, we evolved as uniquely sexy animals, a fact long recognized by Freud and countless others, intuitively known to all of us, but only comprehensible within the framework of evolutionary theory.

CHOICE OF SEX OBJECTS

Like all other animals, we are selected to mate with "sex objects" with whom we are likely to produce offspring. If we are male, that means women past menarche and before menopause. If we are female, that means men, preferably young and vigorous ones, though an older one will do if he has valuable resources to offer. In the absence of such sex objects as will increase our fitness, we may satisfy our sex urge through masturbation, homosexuality, pederasty, even bestiality, but these are *pis-aller;* they are poor substitutes for the "real thing." As we tend to be a rather sexy species with a constant sex urge and a fertile imagination, we may engage in more such biologically futile sexual behavior than many other animals; however, none of the behaviors just mentioned is uniquely human. Other animals, too, masturbate when they have the necessary dexterity; attempt copulation with sexually immature or unreceptive conspecifics; mount a same-sex individual; or might occasionally make a "mistake" in species.[2]

None of these acts can, therefore, be regarded as outside the range of normalcy so long as their fitness cost remains minimal, as it does in a species with a coitus–offspring ratio as high as ours. The male prisoner, for instance, who engages in homosexual acts in the absence of sexually accessible women is not acting in a biologically aberrant manner, since his behavior does not substantially detract from his fitness. Much human homosexuality, incidentally, is of this episodic and circumstantial nature. This is especially true of societies in which homosexuality is a socially acceptable form of behavior. In these societies, such as ancient Greece or some Arabic countries, certain forms of homosexuality or pederasty are or were accepted under some circumstances, but not as a complete substitute for heterosexuality and reproduction (Davenport, 1976). In fact, a fairly substantial minority of societies practice *and* tolerate homosexuality as a secondary form of sexual behavior. In 29 of the 70 societies of the Murdock and White (1969) sample for which Broude and Greene (1976) found sufficient data, homosexuality was present and not uncommon; it was absent or rare in the remaining 41 societies. One-fifth of the cultures in that sample accepted or ignored homosexuality, about one-tenth had no concept of homosexuality, and the remaining two-thirds ridiculed, scorned or punished it.

Exclusive homosexuality is a relatively rare phenomenon (Hoffman, 1976; Kinsey et al., 1948, 1953). Quite a few women in American society, for example, who claim to have adopted lesbianism as their "lifestyle," have one or more children, and so have a number of male professed homosexuals. It remains to be *demonstrated* that professed homosexuals have, in fact, fewer children as a group than professed heterosexuals. Even if they did, there are conceivable circumstances under which homosexuality *could* be a strategy to maximize inclusive fitness, as has been suggested by some sociobiologists, such as Wilson (1978). Among the eusocial insects, the vast majority of females increase their fitness by foregoing their own reproduction and caring for one of their sisters' brood. (Of course, worker termites, bees and ants are sexually inactive rather than lesbian.) If human homosexuals could be shown to forego their own reproduction to benefit close relatives, the kin selection hypothesis of human homosexuality would be supported.

At present, there is little evidence of such kin altruism among homosexuals, nor, indeed, are there good data of the extent to which they curtail their own reproduction. We simply cannot *assume* that they do, because we know that many so-called homosexuals are in fact bisexuals. Alan P. Bell and M. S. Weinberg (1978) report that one-fifth of their sample of male homosexuals and one-third of the lesbians had been married, and that over half of both male and female homosexuals who had been married had one or more children. The rare cases of exclusive homosexuality are indeed biologically puzzling and may be considered the type of "mistake" that occurs in nature under atypical environmental conditions. Without pretending to have an answer to the problem, I would suggest that perhaps we should look for a phenomenon akin to imprinting in early conditioning. Although the development of exclusive homosexuality is undoubtedly very complex, it may not be *in principle* different from the behavior of chicks who are made to follow a soccer ball if that is the only moving object in their environment after they hatch. In any case, I see no more reason to postulate the existence of a gene or genes for homosexuality than that of a gene for soccer-ball-following behavior in chicks.

In all societies, then, the overwhelming majority of people are preferentially heterosexual, although in most of them there is also some incidence of masturbation, in many of them of homosexuality, and in some of them of bestiality. If any society ever institutionalized any of the latter forms of sexuality in preference to heterosexuality, it has not survived to tell the tale.

PAIR-BONDING

Another feature of our sexual behavior is that we are not a promiscuous animal. Neither are we rigidly monogamous, as are some animals, such as geese and foxes, that mate once for life. The vast majority of humans have more than one sexual relationship in their lives and even the most puritanical cultures are often unsuccessful in their attempts to enforce rigid monogamy and to eliminate premarital and extramarital sex. Of the 141 societies in the Broude and Greene (1976) sample, nearly half (44.7 percent) are tolerant of female premarital intercourse, and only one-fourth (25.5 percent) *strongly* disapprove of it and put great emphasis on female virginity at marriage. However, equally significantly, we are far from randomly promiscuous. Sex, for humans, is not a casual activity. It is accompanied by powerful emotions of love, jealousy, dominance and competition, and it is most satisfyingly engaged in pairs of individuals whose relationship and commitment to each other extend far beyond copulation. Man, in short, is a pair-bonding animal. He forms relatively stable relationships that imply considerable emotional involvement *and* material cooperation—with a clear sexual division of labor.

The cultural relativist will object that I am merely projecting my cultural values. To prove this point, he will produce numerous examples that seem to contravene what I just stated. Let us examine the empirical evidence, including the exceptions. All known human societies recognize the existence of the sexual pair-bond and give it formal sanction in the form of marriage. With only a handful of exceptions presently to be examined, married pairs are expected not only to copulate with each other, but to cooperate in the raising of offspring and to extend each other material help. That is, marriage in virtually all societies is a mutual aid contract involving a whole set ,f obligations that often go much beyond the immediate nuclear family and that are extended to larger kin groups. There is nearly always some presumption of permanence but also, interestingly, provisions for divorce do exist under specified conditions.

All, or nearly all, cultures recognize the importance of the pair-bond as the ideal way of regulating the domestic economy for the purpose of rearing children. At the same time, all or nearly all cultures recognize (some reluctantly, some matter-of-factly) that a human pair-bond is sometimes best dissolved. (Even the Catholic Church, one of the most rigidly monogamous organizations in the world, admits that possibility.)

Like other animals who form stable sexual pair-bonds, we do so because it gives an adaptive advantage in raising our young. Human infants are born highly immature and dependent, and their nurturance is a long, energetically costly venture best achieved by having the parents cooperate in the task, albeit with a preponderant female contribution. That is why we form pair-bonds—*but asymmetrically binding ones.* Females seek stabler bonds than males, because the male always has the option of inseminating other females at minimal cost to himself, whereas the female has a clear interest in garnering as much of her mate's resources as contributes to her fitness and that of her offspring.

There are at least two main conditions that facilitate our forming pair-bonds. One is the virtual disappearance of oestrus in the human female and, consequently, her year-round sexual receptivity. The second is our sexiness, that is, our *reproductively* inefficient sexual behavior. Nearly all human sex, as we have seen, is reproductively gratuitous, so it must have another function. The reader might suggest "fun," but there is no evolutionary reason why we should have a good time. The fun of sex is merely a means to an adaptive end. Besides, our sexiness is not conducive to a great deal of promiscuity, as one might expect if fun were a function of sexiness. The most satisfying sex is love, that is, an affective relationship with one primary partner, involving much beyond copulation, lasting reasonably long periods (preferably several years, i.e., long enough to produce and raise a child). Sexiness is thus a way of cementing the pair-bond (Wilson, 1978). We copulate a lot, preferably with a loved one, and we get much satisfaction out of it, because it binds us to do other fitness-enhancing things together, especially exchange mutually beneficial goods and services. It is no accident that courtship, marriage and love relationships, in nearly all human societies, involve the exchange of gifts and services, often ritualized in such institutions as the bridewealth, the dowry or "bride service."

However, as we have already noted, there is a fundamental asymmetry in the pair-bond. Females invest more in offspring, have less of an incentive to be promiscuous, and have a greater concern to bind a male to themselves than vice versa. Males and females, in short, have different reproductive strategies. Therefore, courtship (the rituals preceding the formation of a pair-bond) is primarily a method by which females assess and choose males and whereby males woo females. A woman subjects her suitors to tests that enable her to make the best possible choice of a provider—a mate likely to contribute maximally to her fitness. A man seeks to convince his prospective mates that he qualifies, but since he can also increase his fitness by being fickle, he will seek to deceive women. Thus, courtship is an elaborate exercise whereby men seek to deceive women and women subject men to subtle and multiple tests to detect deception. The object of the game is to form a reproductively successful pair-bond.

Abundant evidence supports the fundamental asymmetry of the human pair-bond: the dual standard of sexual morality found in many cultures; the high incidence of polygyny compared to polyandry; the slower sexual arousal of women compared to men (premature ejaculation is the main male sexual malfunction); and the much greater instability of male homosexual relationships compared to lesbian ones—to mention only a few indicators of an overwhelmingly consistent pattern of asymmetry in human sexual behavior. We shall return to this basic point presently, as we examine the universal characteristics of human marriage and family structure.

CHARACTERISTICS OF HUMAN MARRIAGE AND FAMILY

Marriage, it will be objected, is a cultural institution. Therefore it is wrong to confuse it with sex. After all, much sex takes place outside of marriage, and conversely, sex is only a small part of marriage. Here I shall argue that, while this is all true, marriage is nevertheless the cultural codification of a biological program. Marriage is the socially sanctioned pair-bond for the avowed social purpose of procreation. What is the evidence for this interpretation? I suggest that the following facts, taken together, make any other interpretation difficult to sustain. Some of these generalizations have a few exceptions to which we shall turn later, but, often, as we will see, the exceptions confirm rather than invalidate the rule. To avoid the tediousness of repeating "nearly all," I shall, for the moment, present the following facts as unqualified empirical generalizations.

1. Sometimes marriage merely sanctions an already established pair-bond; sometimes it precedes its establishment, occasionally by several years in the case of child marriages. The presumption, however, is that partners in marriage will establish such a bond *for purposes of procreation*. The childless marriage is an anomaly, and childlessness is one of the most generally accepted causes for the dissolution of a marriage. Marriage systems that are accompanied by the payment of "bridewealth" to the family of the bride generally provide for the return of all or most of the bridewealth in cases of childlessness, showing that the so-called bridewealth is in fact intended to be childwealth. At the very least, marriage partners are normally supposed to *try* having children, so that the nonconsummation of marriage and the cessation of sexual intercourse are common grounds for divorce. Indeed, there is often an *explicit* cultural recognition that regular sexual relations is the *sine qua non* of marriage.

2. Marriage invariably involves much more than mere copulation. It is also an agreement to cooperate, at a minimum between the spouses, but quite commonly with wider groups of kinsmen in the "extended" family. Marriage, in short, sanctions both kin selection for the maximization of inclusive fitness, and complex systems of reciprocity between spouses and their respective kin groups. Sex is culturally defined as a necessary but not a sufficient condition for marriage, for marriage is explicitly, or at least implicitly, conceived as legally recognized kin selection and reciprocity.

3. No human society successfully restricts sex to marriage. A few attempt to do so by stigmatizing nonmarital sex. Many more express various degrees of chagrin at different forms of nonmarital sex, but have the good sense of not trying to suppress the irrepressible. Some societies are quite tolerant of *some* forms of nonmarital sex, especially the premarital variety, but no society condones promiscuity or regards it as normal. Many cultures recognize that the establishment of a pair-bond is a delicate and complicated matter and allow the unmated considerable license in trying out potential mates; but once a pair-bond has been established, and especially once the pair has produced offspring, social pressures are toward the maintenance of the bond and its regularization through marriage. Most cultures distinguish quite

readily between people who are paired and those who are not; they associate reproduction with stable pair mating; and they reinforce the stability of pair-bonds through a set of prescriptions and proscriptions.

4. Most cultures recognize that males and females have different reproductive interests and strategies, and institutionalize a double standard of sexual morality (Broude and Greene, 1976; van den Berghe and Barash, 1977). A greater measure of sexual freedom is generally granted to men than to women. This is especially true of extramarital relations (as distinguished from premarital relations, which are sometimes equally permitted to both sexes). An extremely common way to regulate the greater sexual leeway given to men without threatening the stability of offspring-producing unions is, of course, polygyny. Of 853 societies in the Murdock (1967) sample, 83.5 percent permit or prefer polygyny, compared to only 0.5 percent that permit polyandry (and, then, only under very special conditions). A number of large societies have become increasingly monogamous, *de jure* if not *de facto*, in recent centuries, but the double standard flourishes even in nominally monogamous societies. In the Murdock (1967) sample, 137 societies (16.0 percent of the total) are legally monogamous.

Until the spread of Christianity, prescriptively monogamous societies were exotic exceptions. In agrarian, horticultural and pastorialist societies polygyny is generally preferred, although the sex ratio typically restricts polygyny to only a minority of the older men. In hunting and gathering societies, polygyny is generally permitted but limited to only a small minority of men having two or at most three wives. Statistically, monogamy is the most frequent arrangement in most societies, but the vast majority of societies allow and indeed encourage polygyny or have done so until recently, when they were conquered by monogamous societies.

5. All cultures have a division of labor by sex, both in the society at large, and in its constituent family units. The specific tasks done by men and women vary from society to society, depending on the particular group's technology, mode of production and a vast array of ecological conditions, but there are some clear uniformities. In nearly all cultures, men make some contribution to the upkeep of their mates and offspring, but it is always women who do the bulk of the child rearing in early childhood, at least until the ages of five or six. Women nearly always play an important role in the system of production, as do men, and there is often extensive food sharing between men and women. However, women are largely confined to those activities closer to home that do not interfere with child care. Besides food preparation and cooking, and a variety of crafts such as weaving, pottery making and basketry, this has generally meant gathering wild foods, small-

scale horticulture and some forms of fishing. Men, on the other hand, have nearly monopolized hunting, long-distance fishing and warring (D'Andrade, 1966; van den Berghe, 1973a).

6. Practically all human societies have proscribed incestuous relations, both in and out of marriage, between siblings, and between parents and offspring. With few exceptions, sexual relations are also forbidden between uncles and nieces, aunts and nephews, and grandparents and grandchildren. On the other hand, a great many societies not only permit but prefer and even prescribe marriage between first cousins (Murdock, 1959; Lévi-Strauss, 1969). In biological terms, this means that sex is typically forbidden between individuals who share a fourth or more of their genes by common descent—generally permitted between people who are related by a factor of one-eighth or less.

7. Mated couples and their offspring generally share a home which is a defended territory. Outsiders only enter it by permission, and according to a ritual that is remarkably similar across cultures (van den Berghe, 1977). The husband does not necessarily live under the same roof as the wife. Indeed, in many polygynous societies, each wife has a semi-independent household of her own within her husband's larger compound. These family territories often comprise much larger groups of relatives than the nuclear family of mates and offspring. For example, sets of brothers and their respective wives and children may live within the same compound. Most commonly, however, nuclear families form clearly bounded territorial subunits within these extended families. In some cultures, the husband may be absent for extended periods on war or hunting expeditions, on sea voyages or the like, but, at a minimum, the mother and her subadult offspring constitute the minimum core of a territorially defended home.

8. The family, like larger human groups, is a hierarchically organized group. Males are dominant over females, and females over children, both inside the family, and in the society at large. In addition to kin selection and reciprocity, human families are held together by a considerable degree of coercion. Parent–child conflicts are often resolved by coercion. Typically the woman has a greater "say" within the family than in the public sphere outside it; some families in many societies are female led, especially in the absence of an adult male. Formal jural authority, however, is almost always vested in a male, not necessarily the husband-father. (In matrilineal societies, a woman's brother or maternal uncle plays that role.) Preadolescent children are practically never given legal or actual responsibility over adults of either sex. Seniority, as determined by birth order, is a commonly used device to establish authority relations within both nuclear and extended families.

We see that diversity in human family arrangements, while real enough, is, in fact, circumscribed by definite biological parameters. The human family has a number of species-wide characteristics that make it recognizably human and unlike family groups in other species. We have, in short, a specifically human system of mating and reproduction peculiarly well suited to our reproduction. Human family systems are flexible, to be sure, but much of that diversity is not the result of arbitrary cultural variation. It is *adaptive* variation in response to ecological conditions.

At this point, it is instructive to examine closely the exceptions to the above generalizations, for, as we shall see, the exceptions tend to confirm rather than invalidate my argument. Human marriage and kinship arrangements, although always expressed in a cultural idiom and susceptible to a considerable measure of cultural change, fall far short of being culturally arbitrary and random. They evolved, both biologically and culturally, because they turned out to be successful ways of raising babies.

CELIBACY

While monogamy or limited polygyny is statistically the most common mating arrangement of humans, other possibilities are at least possible and have been tried on a more or less temporary basis by individuals or even by small experimental groups. Three principal such alternatives are celibacy, polyandry and promiscuity. Obviously no entire society has ever adopted celibacy and survived very long. Temporary celibacy, however, typically in the form of postponement of marriage beyond puberty, is quite common, especially for males. In most human societies, males marry later than females, partly because their maturation is slower, partly because older males with more resources take more than their share of nubile women. This is especially true in polygynous societies. Typically, the more men are polygynous in a given society, the greater the age difference between husbands and wives. Indeed, given an approximately equal sex ratio, this mean difference in age of marriage between males and females is the main factor making extensive polygyny possible. (Higher male mortality, principally through warfare, can also make its contribution to polygyny, but preindustrial societies do not have large, nonaccidental mortality differences by sex in the younger age groups. The slightly higher mortality of males through disease is made up for by female mortality in childbirth.)

The temporary celibacy of young men in polygynous societies is rarely absolute, however. While it often postpones the establishment of a stable pair-bond and the procreation of children, it often does not preclude dalliance with unmarried girls, adultery with younger wives of older men, or the rape or seduction of women conquered in warfare. Thus, what sometimes looks like temporary celibacy is, in fact, temporary promiscuity. These young men often devote themselves to warfare during their unmarried years and sometimes homosexuality is tolerated during that period. In any case, postponement of marriage is clearly defined as temporary and does not in any sense undermine the norm of marriage. Indeed, in the case of polygyny, it contributes to its maintenance.

Some groups of both men and women in large, complex societies have for a variety of motives established monosexual, celibate communities. Most have been religious orders of monks and nuns, mostly in the Christian, Buddhist and Hindu traditions, and some have lasted for centuries, by continuously recruiting new members. Those utopian communities, however, have always been limited to a small proportion of the population. Furthermore, they have often not been lifelong arrangements for their members. Many of these communities, for example, have served as schools for the young before reproductive age; all but a handful of the pupils leave shortly after puberty to marry. Sometimes, members join late in life, after a normal reproductive period, as is commonly the case in the Hindu and Buddhist traditions.

Even priesthoods are seldom celibate. Some religious traditions, such as branches of Orthodox Christianity restrict compulsory celibacy to the *higher* clergy, which means older men. The Catholic Church is exceptional in trying to impose celibacy on its entire clergy and it has met with very limited success. Until the Renaissance, priestly celibacy was observed in the breach and the Church unofficially tolerated what it officially proscribed. In more recent times, attempts by the Church to maintain an unbending stand on priestly celibacy have led to massive defections and serious recruitment problems. Celibacy, however saintly, goes against most people's grain.

PROMISCUITY

At the opposite end of the sexual spectrum, promiscuity does not work very well either, although it has been repeatedly tried, both by individuals at certain phases of their lives, often in early adulthood, and by utopian groups seeking to eliminate sexual jealousy, to broaden the scope of their experiences, to establish sexual equality, to eliminate the double standard, to relieve marital boredom, to dispense with the institution of marriage or to reach sexual satiety. There are, of course, also the special cases of promiscuity for gain or prostitution, and religiously inspired promiscuity or so-called "temple prostitution." Interestingly, most of these forms of organized promiscuity are relatively recent developments of complex, stratified, urban societies in the last few millenia.

Prostitution, contrary to the old adage, is *not* the world's oldest profession. The priesthood is.

When we characterize the human species as *relatively* nonpromiscuous, the statement is only meaningful in comparison with other species. We are certainly promiscuous enough to make some degree of mate swapping possible and even appealing as a temporary diversion from matrimony, or as an experimental stage prior to it. The statement should also be qualified by sex. There is abundant cross-cultural evidence that males are more promiscuous than females for fundamental reasons of asymmetrical parental investment to which we will return later.

Small-scale, stateless, classless societies apparently cannot afford the luxury of systematic promiscuity. Sometimes, some "primitive" societies in Polynesia and elsewhere have been misrepresented as sexually permissive and promiscuous (Davenport, 1976). There is also a long tradition in Western thought to consider man naturally promiscuous and restrained from being so only through arbitrary, repressive and irksome social constraints. So-called primitive promiscuousness is often presented as a paradisiacal state of grace and innocence from which "civilized" man has fallen. This is romantic nonsense. What these supposedly promiscuous societies typically show is not the absence of marriage and pair-bonding, but a degree of premarital permissiveness in which young people have marital "try-outs." For a couple of years, young adults form less stable unions until they find a well-suited partner for marriage, but even during these premarital try-outs they form romantic pair-bonds, are far from totally promiscuous, and experience jealousy.

Let us return, then, to genuine promiscuity: to indiscriminate sex without either affect or jealousy. No human society in historical memory has come close to it. Highly self-selected groups that have tried to institutionalize it have not only remained tiny minorities—they have been highly unsuccessful. They have either broken up in a matter of months, or reverted to more conventional forms of pair-bonding. Typically, individuals who try promiscuity quickly find out that they do not like it.

Again, we must dispel some mythology here. Many "communal" living groups eager to project an image of daring nonconformity have pretended to be promiscuous, or have been thought to be so in the larger society. In actual practice, they very seldom are. Some are polygynous; some are monogamous; very few are promiscuous, and, if they are they do not last. Before long, they are rent asunder by sexual jealousy and conflicts, which is another way of saying that their attempt at promiscuity has failed. Incidentally, these communal groups also find it extraordinarily difficult to institutionalize sexual equality between men and women. This failure has been well documented for the Israeli *Kibbutzim* (Tiger and Shepher, 1975), but other even more radical experiments have been equally unsuccessful in altering male dominance and gender roles. Only monosexual communities achieve sexual equality—by eliminating one of the sexes altogether.

What is especially striking about human experiments in promiscuity or, at least, in reducing the significance of pair-bonding is not only how unstable and unsatisfying they prove to be despite expectations to the contrary, but also how hard one must work at making them work at all, however briefly. Far from being spontaneous, would-be promiscuous groups are hidebound by as many if not more rules and proscriptions than the "straights" they so condescendingly look down upon. Studies of "swinging" and "group marriage" show this very clearly (Bartell, 1971; Constantine and Constantine, 1973).

Group marriage—the simultaneous marriage of several men with several women—is a rare ethnographic curiosity. In some remote Himalayan districts of Uttar Pradesh, in Northern India, some families are "polygynandrous," to use Majumdar's (1960) word. That is, several men join together in a single extended family and share several wives. These people live under marginal ecological conditions. Agricultural land is scarce, and families made up of several productive men are more economically secure. Furthermore, the co-husbands are brothers, and thus contribute directly to each other's fitness by sharing wives as well as other resources. Finally, even there, group marriage is the exception rather than the rule. The kind of group marriage reported by Majumdar is an ecological adaptation to marginal agriculture, not an experiment in promiscuity. As such, it bears only superficial resemblance with contemporary experiments with group marriage in Western societies, where there is a deliberate endeavor to minimize the importance of the pair-bond.

Experimental group marriages in the United States were best studied by the Constantines (1973) who, while committed to group marriage as an alternative, were honest enough not to distort their data. They studied 26 groups; six were triads (five of which were made up of two women and one man); 16 were tetrads made up mostly of previously established couples; two groups included five persons; and two included six. It is doubtful that the five polygynous triads can be meaningfully lumped together with the other groups. At least, they are quite unproblematic: we already know that, far from being anomalous in our species, polygyny is quite common and highly desired in over 80 percent of the world's societies. Altogether, 104 adults were included, mostly young, highly educated, middle-class Americans, who between them had 69 children.

What did the authors find? Broadly, that group marriage does not work, though the Constantines themselves refuse to draw that conclusion from their data. Well over half of these groups (58 percent) lasted less than a year. Only five of the 26 groups were still intact at the time of their writing, and, of these, only two had survived more than four years of communal living. None of the 21 extinct groups had survived more than four years, and only three had been together more than two years. The more people were involved, the longer the odds for success. This result is hardly surprising. Quite apart from any special problems which group marriage may encounter, one would expect a low probability of success simply from the odds of regular monogamous couples. The latter have about a 2/3 chance of staying together. In a foursome of two men and two women who have *four* possible heterosexual relationships that can turn sour, the odds of success fall to $(2/3)^4$, or 16/81, that is, under 20 percent. With three persons of each sex, the odds would drop to $(2/3)^9$; if only for statistical reasons, it takes a gambler to undertake such an arrangement.

The actual situation is probably even less promising than this simple statistical calculation would suggest. Even if this mechanical computation of odds from monogamous unions were the whole answer to the instability of group marriages, however, the likelihood of successfully raising joint offspring under such an arrangement would be so low as to be strongly selected against. The Constantines' data clearly support that conclusion. Of the 69 children involved, 67 were children of existing or previous dyadic marriages, *not* children of the group marriage. By the ultimate criterion of success for a sexual living, group—reproduction—group-marriage is a resounding failure. The more, the sorrier.

It will be immediately objected that the adults involved had socioeconomic characteristics that made them unlikely to have many children anyway. The point, however, is that nearly all of the relatively few children they had were the outcome of a standard pair-bond. Presumably, they made special efforts to make their group marriages sterile outside their primary pair-bonds. The reason why they did is left totally unexplored by the Constantines, but I suggest that the participants had all kinds of reservations about their arrangements, and that they anticipated failure in many cases. Men must have been particularly eager to avoid having to sort out messy paternity problems if the group should break up. Whatever the motivations, there was little if any ambiguity who was whose child. The children themselves clearly identified their biological parents by the Constantines' own account, and had a concept of a standard nuclear family within the "group marriage." The latter was regarded by the children as a kind of extended family, quite distinct from both the outside world *and* the parents—offspring group. This was true even though the group's ideology militated against nuclear family recognition, leading to some verbal hedging in the issue.

Not only did the "group marriages" break down, in fact, into conventional pair-bonds for purposes of reproduction. The Constantines also report that, in most cases, there was no indifferent mating within the group. Despite an *ideology* of sexual liberation, including bisexuality and group sex, very little of either took place. Homosexual behavior was almost completely absent within the groups (except for a bit of male-encouraged "lesbianism" in male-dominated triads). Although several groups had tried group sex, by and large they did not like it and practiced it only rarely—some never went into it at all.

In all groups, all men had had some sex with all the women, and the Constantines make much of this "finding," hastening to add that sex was not part of their definition of a "multilateral marriage." This, however, is a bit of semantic casuistry. We know that there are many communal groups that are not *sexually* communistic, so, presumably, the only reason to call some of them "multilateral marriages" is that they *are* so. Indeed, this is congruent with the use of the term "marriage" to mean a relationship that, though not limited to sex, necessarily includes it. So the Constantines' finding is no finding at all. It was implicitly, if not explicitly, built into their definition of multilateral or group marriage.

Despite the fact that these groups were explicitly established on a sexually communal basis, their sexual communism was difficult to maintain, as repeatedly suggested by the Constantines' data. Half of the groups enforced rigid rules of rotation, usually with a twice-a-week bed switch. Some groups only paired off after a painstaking group discussion each time. Spontaneity seems to have been the rarest arrangement. Indeed, the Constantines mention that group marriages seem bound by more explicit and formal rules of all kinds than conventional monogamous couples, an indication of how hard they have to work at making a go of it. Many of the persons involved in these group marriages recognize what the Constantines call a "primary pair-bond" that takes precedence over the other relationships. So we are really back at preferential monogamy, certainly for reproductive purposes, with a little "meaningful" sex on the side. Even so, four-fifths of the Constantines' respondents report feelings of jealousy. I suspect that the remaining fifth did not want to admit it.

So, with how much of the daring experiment are we left? It seldom happens; when it does, it does not last long, and almost never produces children. Finally, a closer look of the participants' behavior reveals, in fact, something very close to either polygyny or conventional monogamy, with a clear nuclear family structure within the larger group.

What do 26 groups of upper-middle-class Americans tell us? By themselves not much. Their failure can be ascribed to the deadweight of tradition, the hang-ups of their upbringing, the pressures of the larger society or any number of *ad hoc* cultural explanations that social scientists are so quick to advance to salvage the cultural determinist thesis. The cultural determinists, however, cannot have it both ways. If highly self-selected groups of highly motivated people cannot make their behavior conform to their sexual ideology, try as they may, and at considerable cost to themselves, then their failure begs for a better explanation than that conventional morality triumphs in the end. This is doubly true if their actual behavior bears a striking resemblance to that of countless other humans in numerous other societies that have quite different values and ideologies.

The longest-lasting experiment in group marriage on record is that of the famous Oneida community (Carden, 1969; Kephart, 1976; Muncy, 1973). Started in the 1830s as a religious movement by a highly devout, intellectually creative, socially daring and sexually vigorous gentleman by the name of John Humphrey Noyes, the community did not settle in Oneida, New York, until 1847. There it existed as a religious communist utopia until 1881, when it disbanded as a community and incorporated as a highly successful business corporation that still thrives today. At its peak, the community had over 500 members; it collectively owned hundreds of acres of land, raised most of its food, manufactured steel traps for sale to the outside world, and was as prosperous, hard-working and efficiently organized as any group of red-blooded Americans around them.

Ideologically, although they were fundamentalistic Christians, the Oneidans were as radical as any counterculture drop-outs of the 1960s. All property, even clothing and children's toys, was held in common. All living, eating and working was communal: a central building, Mansion House (still standing) sheltered all adults, but each person had his or her individual sleeping room. No family groups were allowed. Children were raised communally and were supposed to treat all adults as their parents. Adults, in turn, were to show universal love equally to all members. Romantic love was regarded as selfish and monogamy harmful to good community feelings. Oneida was supposed to be a completely egalitarian society, even for women.

How did it work out in practice? Economic communism presented, it seems, few if any problems. Personal property was easily renounced. For a brief period, children were allowed individual dolls, but an end was put to that in a big doll-burning ceremony. Sexual equality simply did not work. The women were excluded from most positions of influence and authority and conformed very much to the sexual division of labor prevailing in the larger society around them. There were obviously no economic class distinctions within the community, but the community was completely autocratically run by Noyes, seconded by a few of the older men. Noyes imposed all his ideas on his followers. There was not even a pretence of democracy. In theory, the hierarchy was one of religious worthiness, according to the principle of "ascending fellowship," based on approximation of the ethical standards set by Noyes. In practice, it was a male-dominated, age-graded society, with Noyes as the ruling patriarch.

Had it not been for Noyes' extraordinary notions of sex, eugenics and child-raising ("stirpiculture" as he called it), the Oneidans would not have enjoyed the notoriety they did. (Not that they minded that notoriety, for they obligingly ran conducted tours for titillated sensation seekers on Sundays, apparently making tourism a profitable economic sideline.) Noyes was, by all accounts, a worthy but virile gentleman, who, in his monogamous younger life, had the misfortune of losing four children through stillbirth. He was genuinely concerned about "excessive" reproduction with its deleterious effects on women; he imposed on his followers a uniquely imaginative solution: *coitus reservatus,* i.e., intercourse without ejaculation, *not coitus interruptus,* for, in line with the sexual ideas of his time, he thought that the spending of semen had a debilitating effect on men. Only in intercourse with women past the menopause, were his followers allowed to ejaculate, an exception that no doubt gave the older women an unexpected attraction.

Since Noyes was also against monogamy and "special love" between two individuals, he advocated "free love" (his term, by the way), and "complex marriage." Any member of the community could practice *coitus reservatus* with any other member of the opposite sex. Soon, however, this was surrounded by a little ritual. A man (for, almost invariably it seems, the man initiated the request) would let a go-between, usually an older woman, know that he wanted to sleep with a particular woman. The latter was free to refuse, and would transmit her answer through the go-between. If the answer was yes, the couple would spend the night in either her or his private room. This was all perfectly proper, so long as no "special love" formed, as evidenced by too frequent or lengthy cohabitation by the same people. The go-betweens, it may be supposed, policed the rule of no pair-bonding, all under the ever-vigilant eye of Noyes.

The extraordinary thing is that such a bizarre system worked at all. Yet, to some extent it did, although I suspect that what started out as *coitus reservatus,* often ended as *coitus interruptus.* In any case, for 20 years, from 1848 to 1868, Noyes imposed a ban on having children. During that period, there were about 135 children in Oneida, but most of them were already born when their parents joined the community. During that 20-year period, only one or two children a year were born in the community, a tribute to the self-control of the men and the leadership qualities of Noyes.

Then, concerned with the future of the community, Noyes changed his mind about having chiidren, introducing another extraordinary experiment in child-licensing. He thought that only the worthiest people ought to be allowed to reproduce, and, then, only by special permission. He therefore set up a committee, controlled by himself of course, to which members could apply for a child permit. This experiment was in effect for ten years, during which 53 women and 38 men were allowed to have children; 62 children were born. Of these births, a dozen or so were apparently unplanned and unlicensed. The men chosen as fathers were on the average considerably older than the women, and the ratio of 38 men to 53 women indicates that the system operated polygynously. (The system also worked quite well from the viewpoint of Noyes' fitness: Noyes and his son Theodore had 12 children between them.) Apparently, all children knew who their parents were, and identified with them. Parents and children were allowed contact with each other, but only "in moderation," since "special" parental love was regarded as selfish.

By the late 1870s, dissent and discord were rife in the community. Just as it had been held together by the iron hand of Noyes, the community disintegrated through a crisis apparently brought about by the behavior of the aging despot. It seems that Noyes was increasingly arrogating himself "first husband" rights over the community's pubescent girls. A group of younger men led by one Towner, threatened to bring charges of statutory rape against him; Noyes left Oneida in 1879 to escape prosecution. Within a few months, on January 1, 1881, the community officially disbanded and incorporated itself as a joint stock company, Oneida Ltd. Many members continued to live in the vicinity, but as conventional families and mere stockholders in the Company. For half a century, the Company (which is still the largest manufacturer of stainless steel tableware in the United States and has net sales of around $100 million a year) was managed by John Humphrey Noyes' son, Pierrepont. He was succeeded by P. T. Noyes, a grandson of John Humphrey. Mansion House is still kept in good repair as a combination tourist attraction and Community Center for the remnants of the people who claim some historical connection with that extraordinary utopia that failed.

Much like in the kibbutz, the economic aspects of Oneida utopianism worked rather well. Oneida was a genuinely communistic, classless group, which successfully abolished private property. But then, so are, to all intents and purposes, hundreds of the world's "primitive" societies. Like the kibbutz, and like more recent attempts at "group marriage," Oneida failed to eliminate all the following: the sexual division of labor; the dominance of adults and males over children and women; the sexual pair-bond; and parent-child ties. The "complex marriage" experiment of the Oneidans worked only for a limited time, in a limited way, and under considerable strain. It disguised what was, in fact, something fairly close to a polygynous system dominated by the leader and a few of the older men who had preferential access to the young more nubile girls, while the young men were encouraged to consort with the older postmenopausal women. In both cases, this was rationalized under the principle of "ascending fellowship." The young were to become worthier by associating with the older who had already achieved higher levels of spiritual achievements. A democracy, sexual or otherwise, Oneida most assuredly was not.

Group marriage is an attempt to institutionalize "meaningful," emotionally involved sex with several partners, without jealousy, and on terms of equality for both men and women. "Swinging" is a less ambitious experiment. No attempt at communal living is involved, and sex is deliberately reduced to pure recreation (Bartell, 1971). With such modest aims, swinging is probably more common than group marriage, but hardly any more successful. Swinging is different from group marriage in that participants try to maintain their pair-bond with a single individual while knowingly swapping spouses. While group marriage endeavors to keep together groups of people who are all sexually and emotionally involved with each other, swinging is an attempt to divorce sex from emotional involvement. As one might expect from the greater promiscuity of males, men almost invariably pressure their wives into swinging. Far from making for more sexual spontaneity, swinging is highly constrained by formal rules. Mating is often done by drawing lots rather than by a choice growing out of mutual attraction and the rules of the game call for sex without involvement. Even with all these arbitrary rules and safeguards against the disruption of existing pair-bonds between spouses, swinging often leads to the formation of new bonds. The family that swings together typically does not stay together.

What these "alternative life-styles" teach us is that humans, most especially females, do not find sex without emotional involvement satisfying; that repeated sex with the same person is difficult to sustain without involvement; and that emotionally involved sex with several partners simultaneously is most unlikely to result either in a stable group or in satisfied members, except in the form of limited polygyny. Frequency and variety of orgasm bears little if any relationship to human happiness—or even satisfaction. This seems even truer for women than for men.

Of course, limited experiments by highly atypical minorities in a single society do not tell us a great deal by themselves. The fact remains, however, that no self-reproducing human society known to science has ever institutionalized promiscuity, group marriage or swinging as the most common form of mating. Many societies have tolerated these practices under some restricted and well-defined conditions. Orgiastic religious rituals, for example, are not uncommon: Africans have their fertility cults; Germans their *Fasching;* American businessmen their office Christmas parties. All these events, however, are temporally circumscribed and clearly bracketed from normal existence. They are carefully defined interludes, the seeming licenciousness of which is in fact constrained by rules, lest they disrupt the social order. They are most assuredly and explicitly *not* the usual way of doing things. The exceptions confirm rather than invalidate our statements about human matings. We are *capable* of being promiscuous on occasions, and we might even temporarily enjoy it for a change, especially if we are male, but we dare not produce offspring and organize a society on random, indiscriminate mating.

PROSTITUTION

An examination of prostitution leads us to the same conclusion. Prostitution is sexual promiscuity for gain. It is fashionable in some circles, especially among some political radicals, militant feminists, and prostitutes, to extend the definition of prostitution to almost any sexual relationship, in and out of marriage (Erich Goode, 1978). By such loose definitions, prostitution is, of course, universal. Here I am restricting my meaning to the conventional one. A prostitute is a person who indiscriminately exchanges sexual services for gain and without emotional involvement. So defined, prostitutes are only found in stratified, politically centralized societies, and, indeed, mostly in the more complex urban societies. The professional whore is an urban amenity, thriving on a very special set of conditions that are far from universal in our species.

Yet, the characteristics of prostitution closely fit what we *do* know of human sexuality and mating. First, prostitution is an overwhelmingly female occupation. Male prostitutes not only are far fewer and found only in a few societies, but they cater almost exclusively to other males; that is, such prostitutes specialize in the homosexual trade. We have seen that the female of the human species, as well as of nearly all species, is the biologically scarce resource. At any given time, the number of males looking for opportunities to mate is always greater than the number of females. Females are much choosier about mating, because their investment and therefore risks are much greater. A male prostitute would have to be an extraordinary paragon of manly virtues to find many women knocking at his door, and would draw a most unappetizing clientele of last resort. Within limits, most males are quite willing to donate their sperm for the asking. The male prostitute, unless he caters to homosexuals, is an economic redundancy, constantly undercut by eager amateur competition.

The same is often said of female prostitutes, but this is largely male wishful thinking, or a hooker's rationalization when the trade is slow. While it is true that physically fit and/or economically secure men have little difficulty finding mates, many men simply do not get as much sex as they would like. Furthermore, the preliminaries of human courtship are sufficiently lengthy and costly to make mating with a nonprostitute either unlikely (for instance, for the transient male in town for a three-day convention) or not worth the candle. The irrefutable proof of all this is the irrepressibility of prostitution in any city of any size, anywhere in the world. (Some communist societies claim to have eliminated prostitution, but, then, as they also claim to have eliminated inequality and class distinctions, one has to take this assertion with a lump of salt.)[3]

Beyond the sex ratio of those involved in prostitution, it is interesting to examine the prostitute's adjustment to "the life." Notwithstanding the myth of the "happy hooker," prostitutes who actually enjoy their line of work are few and far between. Many enjoy the material rewards of the trade; they may appreciate the relative ease with which they earn money compared to their sisters in factories or offices; the more successful call girls may even luxuriate in the indolence and extravagant life-style made possible by their earnings. Very few, however, enjoy promiscuity or find prostitution a desirable way of life, apart from the easy money, the flexible hours and the tax shelters (Adelman and Hall, 1972; Ellis and Abarnabel, 1973; Wells, 1970).

The prostitute's need for an emotionally satisfying pair-bond is often so intense that, contrary to her economic interest, she sometimes falls prey to pimps, in the full knowledge that she is being exploited and abused. The pimp–prostitute relationship is completely baffling and self-defeating from a rational, economic perspective: the prostitute is in "the life" because of material gains, yet she often surrenders these gains to a parasitic pimp. Why? Simply because the pimp is the only man willing to establish at least the *semblance* of a normal pair-bond with her.[4] She can pretend to believe his promises of marriage and the fullfilment of her dreams of decorous retirement as owner of a nice little boutique or hair-dressing parlor.

Another adjustment of the prostitute to uncongenial promiscuity is the clear separation of intercourse from involvement. One simply does not become emotionally involved with a "John." This often takes the form of little ritualistic denials of some acts regarded as marks of affection in normal sexual relationships. The same woman who routinely performs fellatio with customers will reserve kissing for her pimp, for example. Since emotional involvement naturally accompanies sex, sex without emotion can be rationalized as not having taken place, or, at least, as not affecting one's fidelity to a loved one. The pimp may be a poor imitation of a fiancé, but, then, whores can't be choosers.

POLYANDRY

Polyandry, the stable union of a woman with several men, is extremely rare. Indeed, polyandry is quite uncommon among vertebrates in general, being regularly found only in a handful of bird species, such as Tasmanian native hens, spotted sandpipers, jacanas and phalaropes (Jenni, 1974)—unknown among nonhuman mammals. In the handful of human societies that practice it (four in a Murdock sample of 565 societies), it is traceable to very special conditions (Peter, 1963). First, even in those exceptional cases, polyandry is almost never the sole or even the preferred form of marriage. It is typically found alongside monogamy and even polygyny. Second, in several of the few cases of polyandry, a woman marries a set of brothers. Co-husbands thus have a reasonable assurance that their common wife's children are at least nephews, if not children, and that their parental investment is not wasted on nonrelatives. Third, polyandry is often a response to an unusual scarcity of women, or to ecological conditions so adverse as to require the labor of several men (often brothers) to support one woman and her offspring (Majumdar, 1960). The Eskimo groups that permitted polyandry, for instance, also practiced female infanticide as a population control device in an extremely harsh environment. In a few groups of the Indian subcontinent, one finds polygyny, monogamy and polyandry coexisting in a hierarchical system that encourages hypergamy: women are expected to marry men of a status equal to or higher than their own. The result is that upper-status men tend to be polygynous and lower status men polyandrous. Since women marry "up," there is a scarcity of them at the bottom of the hierarchy and a glut at the top.

MALE AND FEMALE REPRODUCTIVE STRATEGIES

Our thesis is that pair-bonding in humans, in the form of limited polygyny and/or monogamy, is, as in other species, a fitness maximization strategy for the parents. Pair-bonding is a mechanism favoring paternal investment, and the latter, in turn, will be selected for to the extent that the offspring (and, therefore, parental fitness) benefit by it. Unless the father's presence is beneficial to the offspring, why should he wish to stay around instead of increasing his fitness by siring other children with other women? The reproductive game is, however, quite different for men and women because of the asymmetrically greater investment of the female in the offspring. Since women have more at stake, and since their reproductive mistakes are far costlier, they have developed strategies (such as coyness and slower erotic arousal compared to men) to resist seduction and to capture and retain a man in a cooperative pair-bond with themselves. Trading sexual favors (generally in short supply for men) against support for themselves and their offspring is one of the most basic female strategies, a strategy that becomes especially tricky and chancy when a woman seeks to get a man to support another man's children. Men also have an interest in contributing to the fitness of their offspring, and, hence, can be lured into stable relationships.

However, for men, there are two countervailing factors that encourage a more promiscuous behavior. First, men can never be as sure of their paternity as women can be of their maternity. Any factor lowering the probability of paternity demonstrably shakes the human pair-bond. Second, even pair-mated men have a marginal advantage in trying to inseminate and then abandon a woman—a fate which women obviously seek to avoid, even by means of abortion if everything else fails. (The high fitness cost of abortion makes it a strategy of last resort.) The "illegitimate" offspring of a man may have lower fitness if he abandons it, but so long as there is some probability of survival for the offspring, the man is ahead in the genetic game. In short, men will seek to parasitize women if given a chance and women will develop counterstrategies to avoid being parasitized: long courtships, material tokens of affection, bridewealth payments, careful withholding and dispensation of sexual favors, in the last extremity infanticide, and, increasingly, contraception and abortion.

The competing cultural explanation for the greater promiscuity and sexual aggressiveness of males compared to females does not stand up to close examination. Girls and boys are indeed socialized to play very different sexual roles. But why is there cross-cultural consistency in socialization for distinct sexual roles? Notwithstanding Margaret Mead's (1935, 1949) unconvincing attempt to support the thesis that all or nearly all differences in temperament and behavior between males and females are the product of arbitrary socialization, and that cultures vary randomly in the roles they assign to each sex, the ethnographic data clearly show the opposite (D'Andrade, 1966; Stephens, 1963; van den Berghe, 1973a). There is some variability in the details of what is considered feminine and masculine in different cultures, but there are also fundamental consistencies.

For instance, Broude and Greene (1976) found that in over three-fourths (76.9 percent) of the 65 societies in the Murdock and White (1969) sample for which the relevant data were available, men were "forward in sexual overtures." In half of these societies (50.8 percent), male sexual aggressiveness was mostly verbal and sometimes solicited by women, but in a fourth of them (26.2 percent) male aggressiveness was regularly physical—to the point of rape. In only 9.2 percent of these cultures were men sexually shy or diffident. Indeed rape was accepted or only mildly ridiculed or disapproved in over half (55 percent) of the societies in the sample.

Even Margaret Mead, the late grande dame of feminist anthropology, was forced to concede that there is no androgynous society. In *all* societies, a person's sex is a matter of great social consequence and an essential basis for differentiating behavior.

If all cultures recognize the importance of a person's sex; if they define maleness and femaleness in much the same way (allowing for differences of detail and emphasis); if attempts at introducing androgyny as a social norm are so unsuccessful, there must be a good reason behind this seeming "sexist" obstinacy. I am suggesting that a culture (or a parent) that socializes children to live in an androgynous society would be at a severe disadvantage. Under preindustrial conditions, such a possibility never arose at all. Under industrial conditions, androgyny, although no longer impossible, would still be costly, difficult and therefore unlikely. Even at the prosaic level of the division of labor by sex within the simple American nuclear family, most couples who concertedly tried equal distribution of tasks report failure, especially when children are involved. Indeed, it appears somewhat easier to *reverse* some aspects of conventional sexual roles than to keep the roles sexually undifferentiated.

Greater male promiscuity is widely recognized cross-culturally in sexual double standards. Some cultures have more of a double standard than others (often for reasons traceable to the structure of their social organization, such as the greater male control over female sexuality in patrilineal compared to matrilineal societies), but the *direction* of the double standard is almost invariably toward greater leniency for males. Broude and Greene (1976) coded 116 societies from the Murdock and White (1969) standard cross-cultural sample. They found that almost two-thirds of them (65.5 percent) were more permissive of extramarital intercourse for men than for women. About one-tenth (11.2 percent) were equally tolerant of marital infidelity for both sexes, and nearly a fourth (23.3 percent) disapproved it equally for men and women. *Not a single society,* however, was more lenient of female extramarital dalliance.

Given that consistency in cultural norms across a wide range of societies, it is far more plausible that the norms *reflect* biological differences than that they should *cause* behavioral differences. The behavior of homosexuals confirms that conclusion. At least in Western societies—the only ones in which homosexuality has been extensively studied—male homosexuals are *conspicuously* more promiscuous than lesbians (Hoffman, 1976). Homosexual behavior is about equally and generally condemned in both sexes, yet the sex differences remain. Of course, it might still be argued that the cultural norms of male promiscuity carry over from "straight" to "gay" society, but that is really stretching the cultural argument to the breaking point. Indeed in Western societies where homosexual communities have been forced by social stigmatization to create little countercultures of their own, which stridently reject the morality of the dominant society, why should they make it such a point to retain the double standard? Quite the opposite is true: many male homosexuals deplore the promiscuity of the male "gay" world, actively seeking more stable relationships. Most fail however.

POLYGYNY AND THE SYSTEM OF PRODUCTION

Empirical evidence overwhelmingly supports the analysis of human mating and reproduction in terms of differential sexual calculus of fitness for men and women. For example, let us examine the incidence and distribution of polygyny. Hunting and gathering societies are stateless, produce very little surplus, and do not have class differences. In these societies, polygyny is typically permitted but quite limited. Only a few men have more than one wife, and then only two or three. Women in these societies often contribute the bulk of the caloric intake in the diet through their food-gathering activities and, hence, are no big burden on men. Men contribute mostly valuable animal protein to the diet. Since men do not greatly vary in the resources they have to offer (except in their relative skills as hunters), they also have few opportunities to monopolize more than their share of women.

In simple agricultural societies, sometimes called "horticultural" (Lenski and Lenski, 1978), the resource picture changes. Some surplus accumulation is now possible, and with it at least incipient states and class distinctions. Polygyny becomes more widespread and more extensive. Up to 20 or 25 percent of the men, especially the older ones, have several wives, and political leaders begin to form large harems. In many of these societies, women do much agricultural work, and thus contribute greatly to subsistence. They are no great economic burdens on men, and may even be an asset. Thus, polygyny is potentially within the reach of many men.

Table 1 clearly shows the close relationship between polygyny and agriculture, and more particularly the kind of tropical horticulture where women do a lot of agricultural work. In a sample of 130 societies in Africa (the continent where polygyny is still most extensively practiced), all but one of the 88 societies where women contribute an equal or

Table 1. Agriculture and Polygyny in Africa[a][b]

Sexual Division of Labor and System of Production	Monogamous Societies	Polygynous Societies	Total Societies
Agriculture, Women Do Most Work	0	25	25
Agriculture, Men and Women Work Equally	1	62	63
Agriculture, Men Do Most Work	5	22	27
No Agriculture (Hunting and Gathering)	3	12	15
Total Societies	9	121	130

[a] Numbers refer to number of societies.
[b] Sources: Murdock (1957); Clignet (1970).

greater share of agricultural labor compared to the men are polygynous. Conversely, all but one of nine monogamous societies are either hunting and gathering societies or agricultural societies where men do most of the productive work.

Political leaders in horticultural societies begin to claim more than their share of women, but economic class differences are still not pronounced enough to debar most freemen from polygyny. Many of these societies also have some form of slavery, a contributing factor to polygyny, as female captives are taken on as secondary wives. The typical situation is one in which polygyny is a privilege of mature, middle-aged men. Marriage is often subject to payment of "bridewealth," especially in patrilineal societies, and older men, by controlling the economic resources necessary to the acquisition of wives, force young men to postpone marriage or at least to remain monogamous for a while, in order to acquire junior wives for themselves in later life. Much the same conditions prevail in many pastoralist societies.

Indeed, it is precisely this association between polygyny and age of husbands that makes extensive polygyny possible despite an approximately equal sex ratio in most human societies. The older husbands are in relation to their wives in a given society, the more wives married men can, on the average, have. Women, in effect, are put into marital circulation earlier than men—a practice facilitated by the sexual bimaturism of our species. The extent of polygyny practiced in some societies is shown by the sub-Sahara African data in Table 2. Since nearly all traditional sub-Saharan African societies strongly prefer polygyny, and since Africa is the last continent where polygyny is still extensively practiced, the African data are the best available to study the demographic effect of

Table 2. Incidence of Polygyny in Selected African Countries[a]

Countries	Date	Married Women per 100 Married Men	Married Women per 100 Polygynous Men
Lesotho	1936	114	218
Botswana	1946	112	201
Swaziland	1936	168	307
South Africa	1921	112	216
Zambia	1947	122	211
Tanzania	1934	117	219
Kenya	1951	236	283
Sudan	1945	199	253
Zaire	1947–1948	131–144	224–273
Guinea	1950	159	245
Cameroon	1942	152	?
Togo	1931	131–157	?
Upper Volta	1951	190	233
Nigeria	1950	155	237
Ghana	1909–1939	190–218	?
	1945	160	252
Sierra Leone	1945	304	325
Gambia	1951	184	276

[a] Sources: Dorjahn (1954); Clignet (1970).

polygyny. With the exception of the Southern African territories where the European and Christian influence has been the strongest, most African countries have an average of 150 to 200 married women per 100 married men. *Polygynously* married men have between two and three wives on the average in most countries.

A special, but quite common form of polygyny is sororal polygyny, a system wherein co-wives are sisters. Nearly half of the world's polygynous societies practice or even prefer sororal polygyny. Kin selection provides again a plausible explanation for sororal polygyny. Just as, in the rare cases of polyandry, it contributes to the inclusive fitness of co-husbands to be brothers, the same is true if co-wives are sisters. Children of co-wives then become nephews and nieces, and half-siblings raise their coefficient of relatedness from ¼ to ⅜ by virtue of the fact that they are also first cousins.

Sororal polygyny can only contribute to the inclusive fitness of co-wives to the extent that they are in a position to help each other and their respective children. This condition is most likely to prevail if they live close to each other; one would, therefore, expect sororal polygyny to favor co-wives sharing a common residence. Indeed, this is precisely what happens, as shown in Table 3. In some 9/10 of societies where

Table 3. Sororal Polygyny and Residence of Co-Wives [a]

	Preferential Sororal Polygyny		No Preferential Sororal Polygyny		Total Societies	
	N	%	N	%	N	%
Co-wives Share Common Dwelling	12	92.3	9	36.0	21	55.3
Co-wives Do Not Share Common Dwelling	1	7.7	16	64.0	17	44.7
Total Societies	13	100.0	25	100.0	38	100.0

[a] Source: Murdock and White (1969).

sororal polygyny is preferred, co-wives share a common dwelling, compared to only a third of societies were co-wives are not siblings.

Complex agrarian societies are much more clearly stratified in economic and social classes and are far more politically centralized. In many of these societies, the role of women in production is not as great as in technologically simpler horticultural societies, and, hence, polygyny becomes more of a economic burden on the ordinary peasant. The combination of this factor with the concentration of wealth in the hands of the upper classes makes polygyny in agrarian societies a privilege of the wealthy and powerful to an even great degree than in horticultural societies. Some agrarian societies, like preindustrial Japan and Christian Europe, even became legally monogamous.

In industrial societies, polygyny has clearly been on the decline. All industrial societies are legally monogamous, but even more or less clandestine forms of polygyny (such as concubinage, which was common in the slave societies of the Western Hemisphere until the mid-19th century, or in the class-stratified societies of Europe) seem to have become much rarer. This is due in part to the lesser contribution of women to the productive system of industrial societies, and thus to the increasing burden they represent for men if women are not gainfully employed. Children also become much more of an economic liability and less of an economic asset and, therefore, the optimum fitness strategy is no longer to produce as many children as possible, but to produce a few highly fit ones into whom one invests vast resources. The fitness value of additional wives to a man declines steeply if he only intends to have two or three children! Finally, if women are gainfully employed, it will typically be outside the home. This, in turn, will have a double effect: it will decrease her dependence on a man and thus her willingness to share a man with other women; and it will interfere with her reproduction and will thus lower her fitness value to a prospective husband. In short, polygyny with unemployed women is an expensive luxury in industrial societies, particularly for men who only want a few children; as for employed women, they are neither much inclined toward reproduction nor willing to become junior wives.

The analysis of human mating and reproduction in terms of biological fitness and differential parental investment for men and women fits actual behavior remarkably well. Nevertheless, as a model for human behavior, natural selection is repellent to many social scientists who argue not only that the model is mechanistic and "antihumanistic," but also that it is irrelevant because humans are self-conscious animals with an ability to modify their behavior at will.

It would be foolish to contest that man is a self-conscious animal with great behavioral flexibility and an ability to modify his environment through man-made technology. But it is equally foolish to deny that man acts within biological parameters and, indeed, that his consciousness includes an understanding of the kind of animal he is. We have the intelligence to be *consciously* engaged in a mating and reproductive calculus of fitness; we need no biology course to do so in our daily life. True, the mating game is often hidden under a heavy crust of ideology. I doubt, however, that there is a human culture where the social implications of differential parental investment for men and women are not at least dimly understood by a majority of both sexes. Certainly, the average American high school senior is aware that "a girl can't be too careful," and that "boys are only after one thing."

My argument is *not* that biology is destiny in a rigid, immutable way. There is no such thing as rigid genetic determinism even for other animals. Higher vertebrates have the capacity to modify many aspects of their behavior, including their mating behavior, in response to changed environmental conditions. For example, male hoary marmots behave as philandering husbands and disinterested fathers where ecological conditions permit dense concentrations; they become doting parents in isolated circumstances where other adults are few and far between (Barash, 1975). For man, who now has the technological ability drastically and consciously to modify his environment, the possibilities for change are all the greater. Nevertheless, any successful attempt to change our behavior must take our biological nature into consideration. If we should decide to disregard, for example, sex differences, or the requirements of child-rearing, we should be prepared to anticipate the consequences and pay the costs. The issue is not that we are incapable of change, even drastic change. Rather, I am arguing that few cultures and few groups deliberately choose to buck their biology at great cost in fitness.

THE KIBBUTZ: A UTOPIAN EXPERIMENT

Let us now examine closely a concerted attempt to alter a conventional system of mating, reproduction and child-rearing. One of the longest lasting and largest-scale experiments in social utopia has been the Israeli kibbutz. As might be expected, kibbutzim have been extensively studied by social scientists (Spiro, 1956, 1958; Tiger and Shepher, 1975). The kibbutz was conceived as, in all basic respects, an anti-*shtetl*.[5] The shtetl was an urban settlement; the kibbutz was to be agricultural. The shtetl was part of a capitalist system based on private property of the means of production; the kibbutz was to be socialist, with all means of production owned in common and private property reduced to a few personal effects. Inheritance of property was to be totally abolished. The merchants and craftsmen of the shtetl were to become collective farmers. The patriarchal family was to be abolished. Marriage was not to be formally sanctioned and children were to be reared communally from infancy to liberate women for productive work. All inequalities were to be abolished.[6] This was obviously true of inequalities of birth, education, wealth and power, but true sexual equality was to be established as well. The division of labor by sex would disappear. Every member of the kibbutz would become eligible for every job; the less desirable service and maintenance tasks would be assumed in rotation. All decisions would be taken and all officers elected by a weekly general assembly of all members. The presumably more desirable and authoritative jobs in administration would be subject to yearly elections and instant recall. Finally, where the shtetl had been a theocratically ruled community with the rabbi as the guardian of orthodoxy, morals and learning, the kibbutz was to be a non-kosher secular society with no institutionalized religion in any shape or form.[7]

Kibbutzim now number about 250 in Israel, and include some three percent of the country's Jewish population of about three million. The experiment is now almost 70 years old, and some older kibbutzim have been in continuous existence for over half a century. New ones continue to be formed, often by groups of army veterans of both sexes (women are subject to military service in Israel) who have served together as a military unit. Though some kibbutzim are conspicuously more economically successful than others, most of them endure (often with outside subsidies) and have little difficulty in maintaining their membership. As membership is completely voluntary, and as one can withdraw at any time, there is some attrition, but new members also join, and the kibbutz birth rate is higher than that of the rest of the Azkenazic Jewish population of Israel, from which kibbutzniks are overwhelmingly (93 percent) drawn.

Broadly speaking, the kibbutz has been one of those rare utopian ventures that can be said to work by the criteria of longevity, stability of membership and ability to reproduce biologically. Several qualifications have to be made, however. The kibbutz is far from a self-sufficient society; it is only a small, highly self-selected sector of a society. It draws its members overwhelmingly from well-educated, ideologically committed Azkenazim, and its members are greatly overrepresented in the leading echelons of Israeli military and civilian society. Kibbutzniks, although they would reject the label, have, in fact, become something close to a collective elite in Israeli society, and are widely perceived and even resented as such by outsiders. Also, many, if not most, kibbutzim have been heavily supported by the Israeli government, by outside donations, and by the labor of volunteers from overseas. Some have now attained economic self-sufficiency, and are able to provide for their members an adequate though still somewhat austere standard of living, but many remain subsidized enterprises. Indeed, they are frequently located more for strategic considerations (as front-line Jewish settlements along a hostile frontier with the Arab states) than for economic ones, and the test of economic self-sufficiency is probably not the most appropriate to judge their success. In any case, they are very atypical of human communities in general—and of Israeli society in particular.

Our interest in the kibbutz lies in the utopian attempt to eliminate the family as a child-rearing group and to abolish sexual inequality and the sexual division of labor. Interestingly, the kibbutz's "venture in utopia" (to use Spiro's phrase) succeeded in every major respect, but these. Private property and inheritance were eliminated; so were class distinctions. In many ways, the kibbutz recreated the type of small-scale, acephalous, classless community found in many "primitive" societies. The kibbutz is a kind of primitive community utilizing modern technology. But where it attempted to deviate from the model of the traditional peasant village, namely in its mating and reproductive system, it failed, as clearly documented by Tiger and Shepher (1975).

Let us dissect the elements of that failure. Kibbutzim seem no less male dominated than Israeli society as a whole. Women attend general assembly meetings almost as much as men because attendance is defined as a civic duty. (Interestingly, general assembly is held on Saturday, and performs many of the same functions as would a religious service in a traditional community.) However, women talk much less, and less often than men at these assemblies. They seldom get elected to chairmanships of important committees or to executive functions in the kibbutz. They are grossly underrepresented in primary production tasks, especially when they have children, and they nearly monopolize service occupations (in the collective laundry, kitchen and dining room), as well as child care and education in the "children's houses." Men, on the other hand, run kibbutz administration, run and maintain machinery and work in the fields and other productive enterprises, with the auxiliary help of unmarried, childless women (such as foreign volunteers). In both its division of labor and its distribution of power in running community affairs, the kibbutz is clearly male dominated and very conventional, despite considerable ideological commitment to make it different.

The most glaring failure of the kibbutz experiment was its attempt to ignore or minimize marital, parental and kin ties, and to provide communal child care from infancy. Despite statements to the contrary, the family is alive and well in the kibbutz. To be sure, the kibbutz continues to give little or no official sanction to marital and kin ties. Membership is not hereditary. Children of members have to be voted in at age 18 and are accepted as individuals. Married couples too are treated as individuals rather than as units. In practice, however, one accommodation after another had to be made to familial relationships, leading to a *de facto* recognition of the family. Living quarters are allocated on the basis of whether an individual is pair-bonded or not, and while unmarried couples are allowed to live together without stigma, the vast majority of kibbutz adults get married and stay married. Kibbutzim now even go as far as financing and organizing the wedding party!

Everybody in the kibbutz is, of course, well aware of marital and kin ties between members, and in some of the older kibbutzim which now have many second- and third-generation members, there are even extended families linking dozens of members and forming patterns of political alliances. Meals are taken in a common dining hall, but family groupings reconstitute themselves at separate tables, especially for the more leisurely evening meal. Kin selection is obviously at work, and everyone recognizes it, indeed, by now, accepts it as inevitable.

The most unconventional (and costly) aspect of the kibbutz experiment was in child-rearing. In recent years, an increasing number of kibbutzim have given up on communal child-rearing, allowing parents and children to live together again under the same roof. For several decades, however, most kibbutzim raised their children in age-segregated "children's houses." Small groups of eight to 12 children, within a year or so of each other in age, slept, ate, played and went to school in a single building, under the supervision of three adults (almost invariably women). Each kibbutz had ten or 12 such large and well-appointed houses, catering for tightly knit little groups of children who changed house from year to year as they grew up, but retained their integrity as a group. For military security, these children's houses typically formed a circle in the middle of the kibbutz, with direct access to well-equipped underground shelters. In effect, each children's house was a miniature boarding school, which catered to a single grade, from the infant nursery through the primary school grades. (For high school, kibbutzniks attend special institutions run by one of the kibbutz federations and shared by several kibbutzim in the region.)

At first, the motivation for creating the children's houses was both ideological and economic. This arrangement, it was thought, would deemphasize parental ties and contribute to sexual equality, also freeing women for productive labor and providing children with a better environment than was possible in the Spartan early years of the kibbutz movement. The economic benefits soon proved illusory. Of course, it would have been cheap to provide primitive day-care centers for children, but kibbutz members, typically coming from intellectual urban middle-class milieux, wanted nothing but the best for their children. And the best was very expensive. It meant, among other things, an adult–child ratio in the children's houses not very different from that of a normal family. It also meant that, in practice, only women were suited for the job, requiring quite a number of them to do it well. (The rationale of freeing female labor for production also partly motivated the communal laundry and eating facilities, but these too became largely women's monopolies, so that few women were "freed" for primary production after all these service jobs were filled. There, too, acceptable quality of service turned out to be costly and female labor intensive.)

Without a doubt, kibbutz education is first-rate. The children are happy, well adjusted, energetic and intellectually alert. In competition with other Israeli children, they do conspicuously well, as shown by their overrepresentation in such demanding milieux as the universities and the fighter pilot program in the armed forces. The kibbutz, as a great collective Jewish mother, lavishes enormous resources on its children, and dotes on them at least as much as individual parents would. The results, from the viewpoint of the children, are impressive. Lavish surrogate parental care is an expensive but effective substitute for the real thing— at least when provided by females.

The big drawback to communal child care was that parents, especially mothers, did not like it. The intent had never been to separate parents from children altogether. From the beginning, parents saw their children daily. Over the years, pressure mounted, overwhelmingly from women, to have more and more contact with their children, at first after work in the evening, but increasingly during "the hour of love" in the middle of the day. This further restricted mothers to jobs within easy running distance of the children's houses. The *metaplot* (women in charge of the children's houses) increasingly complained of meddling mothers interfering with their routines. It was also found, that even though mothers made the best metaplots, no woman could be entrusted with a group containing one of her *own* children, for fear of favoritism. This imposed an additional constraint on the system.

Finally, the kibbutz federations gave in to their members' pressure, and allowed individual kibbutzim to return to more conventional family groups where parents and children would sleep under the same roof. More and more kibbutzim are converting their children's houses into mere day-care centers at the pre-school level, and primary schools thereafter. And, as resources allow, new more spacious housing units are replacing the Spartan little two-room flats previously allocated to married couples, so as to accommodate the children in reconstituted nuclear families. Kin selection triumphs after half a century of ineffective suppression. Lest the change be interpreted as a sinister male chauvinist plot to put women in their place, let it be emphasized that the reversion to standard family groups was overwhelmingly a response to the mounting dissatisfaction of *women* (Tiger and Shepher, 1975).

DIVORCE, ADOPTION, ADULTERY

In many societies, there are some families that do not conform to the model of cohabiting spouses and offspring. Divorce typically separates children from one of their parents, usually the father. Adoption ensures that a number of children are reared by nonparents. Marital infidelity reduces the probability of paternity. Unmarried mothers often raise children by themselves. There are also some ethnographic curiosities such as the Nayar of India where the nominal husband went off to war after marriage and left his wife to live with a succession of lovers (Gough, 1959, 1968). The point is not that these various arrangements are impossible, but rather that no entire society, so far as we know, ever institutionalized any of them as the ideal way of raising children. Indeed, the opposite is true: where these atypical cases are found, they are usually defined as undesirable or at least only the best of a bad bargain.

Divorce is generally seen as an unfortunate failure or worse, and is less likely when young children are affected. In societies where paternal investment is heavy (such as many patrilineal societies), divorces are usually initiated by the husband, especially when children are involved. Women with children have more to lose by divorce than men who are then free to start a new family while reducing their investment in the old one. The former wife is left to fend for herself and her children, to fall back on her kinsmen, or to find another man willing to assume the responsibility for another man's children. As any divorcée with children knows, this is no easy task.

Adoption is usually considered as a less than ideal substitute in case of sterility, or, alternatively, it often involves orphaned or abandoned relatives. In ancient Greece and Rome, in India and in China, for example, there was a distinct preference for the adoption of close agnates (Goody, 1976) and in Japan young men are adopted in families that lack a male heir so that they can marry a daughter and thus perpetuate the patrilineage. Even in industrial societies where the adoption of strangers is more likely, adoption agencies generally attempt to match the phenotype of the child with that of the adoptive parents; in the United States, for example, transracial adoptions are discouraged by both whites and blacks.

Adultery is widely condemned, especially on the part of women. The reason for the double standard is obvious: insofar as the husband contributes to the fitness of his wife's offspring, cuckoldry is the ultimate dirty trick that his wife can play on him. She parasitizes his parental investment. Male adultery, on the other hand, so long as it does not appreciably affect paternal investment, is of much less concern to the wife. Male adultery, from the point of view of the married couple, is principally the other woman's problem if she is unmarried, and another man's problem if she is married. Unlike female adultery, which tends to be regarded as reprehensible in itself, male adultery becomes so principally if it threatens the existing pair-bond. Indeed, female adultery is often a cause for divorce for the male who cannot abide the prospect of being parasitized, while male adultery is frequently tolerated by women so long as the pair-bond is not broken. One-night stands by philandering husbands are of little consequence to many wives, and even longstanding affairs (which are typically sterile) are often accepted by wives in preference to divorce and loss of paternal investment in her offspring.

MATRIFOCAL FAMILIES

Patterns of "matrifocal" families, as they have been called in the United States (Frazier, 1948), also fit the paradigm of biological fitness. Family units in which an adult female is the central figure are not evidence of matriarchy, or even of an unusually high status for women. If anything, the opposite is true. They are a symptom of social disorganization and are found mostly in slave or former slave societies (as in the Caribbean, or among American and Brazilian blacks), or among uprooted, geographically mobile urban proletarians. In the societies where matrifocal families are found, they may be fatalistically accepted as inevitable, given the prevailing conditions, but they are not considered an ideal state of affairs. Women lead matrifocal families not through design, but because the desertion of their mates left them no other option, short of abandoning their children. It is well known that in the societies where matrifocal families occur with some frequency, children suffer compared to those in "unbroken" families.

The matrifocal family, then, is merely a semi-institutionalized, atypical pattern recognized by the people involved as an inferior alternative to a monogamous or stable polygynous union. Some social conditions of extreme disruption foster the abandonment of women with children, but these conditions merely aggravate a natural tendency: in most societies, men are more likely to abandon their children than women. The more unstable social conditions are (in terms of likelihood of migration, anonymity of large cities, family disruption through chattel slavery and the like), the more likely men are to desert their mates. This is true simply because, under those conditions, they are more likely "to get away with it." This asymmetry in the behavior of men and women is traceable to the asymmetry in parental investment. Women invest more in their children than men; since the female contribution to the fitness of children, especially in early infancy, is far more crucial than the male one, women are biologically selected to have a much higher threshold of child abandonment than males. Men can fairly reliably expect their former mates *not* to abandon their common children, but women cannot be nearly as sure. If the male abandons his children to their mother, their fitness may be substantially reduced, assuming that he was a good father before. Still, it will often be a good bet for him to start a new family with another mate if his earlier brood can reliably be expected to survive well enough to reproduce. Even if worse comes to worse and the children die, the man still has a large reproductive potential to start on a new brood. A woman, on the other hand, is much more limited in the number of children she can produce, and loss of already produced offspring therefore affects her fitness much more. She can therefore be expected to continue her parental investment after abandonment by her mate. If pregnant, she may cut her losses and have an abortion in order to improve her chances of forming a stable pair-bond with another man, but she will rarely resort to infanticide or to gross neglect of her children, except under circumstances where infanticide of a young, sickly or handicapped child substantially increases the fitness of her other children, or her own ability to raise fitter children with another man.

INCEST AVOIDANCE

Incest and incest taboos have long fascinated social scientists and need to be looked at more closely.[8] Several of the early anthropologists assumed that incest taboos in humans were the cultural expression of a biological predisposition. Some went as far as to suggest that the mechanism for incest avoidance was erotic disinterest resulting from familiarity in childhood (Westermarck, 1891). Then, it became fashionable to ridicule these views (Cohen, 1978). Two main objections were advanced against them. One was that, if incest avoidance were natural, then why should there be powerful taboos against something we would not do anyway? Freud was perhaps the most prominent proponent of the view that incest taboos are there to block a powerful desire to commit incest. The evidence for his theory of the Oedipus complex remains elusive, however. The fact is that, although many societies do have strong incest taboos, a substantial number do not, and that incestuous relations seem uncommon even in societies that do not have strong taboos (Fox, 1967; Meillassoux, 1977; Firth, 1936). There are some societies, for example, where the notion of incest seems so ludicrous or incongruous as to require no strong sanctions against it. Sexual bantering between grandparents and grandchildren, for instance, is expected behavior in some cultures.

The second objection to the biological theory of incest avoidance is even more beside the point than the first one. If the reason for incest avoidance is the deleterious effect of inbreeding, the argument goes, then humans must have known about it for thousands of years. Since many societies still know nothing about Mendelian genetics and yet practice incest avoidance, the biological explanation is untenable. This reasoning is, of course, a complete *non sequitur.* Organisms are selected to behave in ways that increase their fitness, quite irrespective of whether they are consciously aware that this is the case. That man has achieved a measure of self-consciousness in the analysis of his conduct does not by any means imply that he is always clearly aware of all the reasons for all of his behavior.

Notwithstanding the insubstantial character of the objections to the biological theory of incest avoidance, most anthropologists have, for several decades, adopted a cultural explanation of incest avoidance. Only recently, has there been an incipient shift back to the earlier theories (Fox, 1967; Parker, 1976). The leading, or at least the most eloquent, advocate of the cultural theory of incest avoidance is Lévi-Strauss (1969). Incest taboos are rooted in the biology of mating, but they are also cultural and unique to man. They, therefore, constitute the passage of man from nature to culture. The incest taboo, by forcing men to swap sisters for spouses, started humans on systems of reciprocity that are at the basis of all human societies. The incest taboo is the very foundation of human society: it is what makes man so fundamentally unlike other animals.

But does it? It is true that, so far as we know, only man has incest *taboos*—that is, explicit rules against close inbreeding. However, most other animals also have mechanisms that make close inbreeding unlikely. Often, simple physical dispersal of one or both sexes at some time between birth and the onset of reproduction has that effect. We are then far from alone in practicing incest *avoidance,* although we may well be alone in knowing that we do. As is often the case, comparison of our behavior with that of other species shows us to be not as different and unique as we first believed. We have already suggested a general formulation to explain widespread avoidance of close inbreeding in many species. Some inbreeding reinforces kin selection in species where social cooperation enhances inclusive fitness, but, the more inbred a population is, the more the adaptive advantages of sexual reproduction itself are negated. Therefore, every animal population tends to an equilibrium between inbreeding and outbreeding at or near a point where the benefits of both are maximized and the costs minimized. That equilibrium point will, of course, vary, depending on many environmental conditions.

Humans are no exceptions. The small-scale societies that relied primarily on kin selection and reciprocity for their social cohesion were fairly highly inbred, and many of them created explicit rules of preferential cousin marriage. Yet, no human society went to the extreme of practicing inbreeding with parents, children or siblings. Indeed, very few societies permit sexual relations between relatives who share even one-fourth of their genes by common descent (half siblings, grand-parents–grandchildren, uncles–nieces and aunts–nephews). The threshold of relatedness where mating becomes permissible in many human societies seems to be below one-fourth.

The exceptions to close incest are themselves instructive. There are three well-known cases of institutionalized brother–sister incest and all three are extraordinarily alike. In the Hawaiian, Incan and Egyptian royal family, the king has, at least in certain periods, been permitted or even expected to marry his sister. In Ptolemaic Egypt and in Hawaii, brother–sister incest was even extended to other high ranking noblemen, but in all three cases, brother–sister incest was taboo for all but a privileged handful. Why the exception for royalty? The answer that is usually given is this: to preserve the purity of the royal line (which, in the Incan and Egyptian cases, claimed divine descent from celestial bodies). But purity for what? A more prosaic explanation is that dynastic incest restricted the number of legitimate claimants on the most important resource in those societies, supreme political power. The possible reduction in biological fitness of one's children-nephews was more than made up for by the monopolistic retention of extraordinary resources, especially when those resources gave one access to innumerable lesser wives and concubines who, although they could not bear future kings, could certainly bear children. Dynastic incest was thus a cultural innovation enabling the high aristocracy to keep the state business in the most intimate family circle, *and* to sire any number of "lesser" children on the side.

Lévi-Strauss is only partly wrong, however. While our species is far from unique in practicing incest avoidance, it is, to the best of our knowledge, unique in having explicit rules of incest taboos. These rules are, of course, cultural and, as we have just seen, they are subject to a measure of flexibility to suit the special circumstances and interests of royal families. It is manifestly true that all human societies have not only incest taboos, but also rules of endogamy and exogamy that prescribe, proscribe or suggest who is a suitable mate and who is not. It is also true that these systems of rules are often such as to encourage, or indeed force, groups of kinsmen to swap women among them, and thus to create larger societies bonded by complex ties of reciprocity. That is the core of Lévi-Strauss's argument, and that much of it holds up. His, as we shall see in Chapter 4, is a theory of exogamy, not a theory of incest avoidance.

However, culture is emphatically not the antithesis of nature, as Lévi-Strauss, ever so prone to find dualistic oppositions everywhere, would have us believe. Culture, in this respect as in so many others, grew out of nature, not to overrule it, but to add on to it. The incest taboo was not the great leap from nature to culture, but it probably contributed to the creation of more complex societies based not only on kin selection, but increasingly on reciprocity. Where Lévi-Strauss saw a leap and a hiatus, there was in fact smooth growth and continuity in an evolutionary process toward ever more complex human societies.

FAMILIARITY BREEDS CHASTITY?

If the basis for incest avoidance is biological, what then is the specific mechanism that makes it work? Recent ethnographic studies from China and Israel give at least a tentative answer to that question (Parker, 1976; Shepher, 1971; Wolf, 1966). Both cases are at first puzzling because, although they do not involve relatives, sexual inhibitions similar to those of incest avoidance are present. In neither case is there a social norm that the people concerned should not marry or have sexual relations. In fact, in one of the cases, there is a definite norm that they should marry and have sex, and, in the other, no norm one way or the other. Yet, in both cases, the individuals concerned find it difficult to establish normal sexual relations, and their stated reason for avoiding each other sexually is that they know each other too well and look upon each other as siblings.

The first case concerns the Chinese institution of child marriage with bride adoption. It had long been customary in prerevolutionary China for poor families to give away infant daughters to be adopted in better off families. The infant girl would then be married to a son of the adoptive family, the marriage being consummated when the children reached puberty. Meanwhile, the child-spouses were raised together in the same household. To his surprise, Wolf (1966) found that in 17 out of the 19 cases of child marriage he encountered in the Taiwanese village he studied, the young people concerned refused to consummate the marriage on reaching adolescence, despite parental pressure that they should. In the two cases where the marriages had been consummated, the child-brides had been separated from their husbands until the age of eight and eleven, respectively.

The second case is better documented yet and brings us back to that remarkable experiment, the kibbutz. A number of investigators had more or less casually reported what every kibbutznik is aware of: that children raised in the same intimate small group in the same "children's house" never marry or even have sexual relations with each other (Spiro, 1958). Shepher (1971) investigated the question systematically. He discovered that out of a total of 2769 marriages involving kibbutzniks, only 14 came from the same kibbutz small group. A closer examination of these 14 exceptions revealed that in only five of those cases had the spouses been raised together before the age of six, and then never for longer than two of these six years of early childhood. Cultural norms are neutral or even slightly favorable to intermarriage within the kibbitz, yet the communal child-rearing system institutionalized in the kibbutz has the unintended consequence of making the kibbutz age peer group almost entirely exogamous. Young kibbutzniks reared together typically have extremely strong ties to each other; indeed, they regularly report that they feel toward each other as brothers and sisters.

Further evidence for the old "familiarity-breeds-sexual-disinterest" thesis comes from clinical cases of actual brother-sister incest. Weinberg (1963) who studied incest in the United States reports that out of 37 cases of sibling incest, 31 were transitory attachments, and that in all six cases of a stable bond, the siblings had been separated from early childhood.

Where does this evidence lead us? Obviously, incest avoidance is not the effect of a mysterious gene that makes us recognize and thus avoid close kin, since unrelated people raised together in infancy regularly avoid each other, while siblings separated in infancy sometimes do form attachments. Does not this point to a cultural explanation? No, because the avoidance clearly operates in the total absence of norms to that effect, or even against cultural norms that marriage should take place. This leaves the "negative imprinting" hypothesis suggested by Shepher (1971), according to which we are genetically predisposed not to be erotically aroused by those with whom we have been in intimate contact during a critical period of early infancy, probably between the ages of two and six. Under natural conditions, this mechanism of propinquity-based avoidance would have the effect of making sexual relations within the nuclear family extremely rare. The proximate mechanism for incest avoidance, according to this plausible hypothesis, is not avoidance of recognized kin, but its practical effect is that.

Incidentally, this hypothesis is also congruent with what we know of outbreeding in many other species: spatial dispersion of one or both sexes at birth or at any rate before sexual maturity is the rule. Simple mechanisms of spatial propinquity or dispersal seem to account for outbreeding in most species. In simpler organisms like fish and amphibians where parental care is nil or minimal and where the young disperse soon after hatching, spatial dispersal, in and of itself, would ensure outbreeding. For birds and mammals where siblings are reared together, dispersal may be the result of parental exclusion or negative sexual imprinting against each other. Different species probably have different proximate mechanisms, but they all result in a substantial measure of outbreeding.[9]

SEX AND CULTURE

If we have dwelt on exceptional cases in our systems of mating and reproduction it has been to stress that these exceptions themselves fit quite well within the explanatory framework we have advanced. They confirm rather than invalidate the theory. It may be objected that the theory is so broad and so flexible that, by explaining everything, it explains nothing. To that I reply that the theory is capable of generating any number of falsifiable hypotheses. Many of the statements that I have made are empirically falsifiable and, indeed, need to be put to more rigorous testing than they have so far. A number of these statements are based, for lack of better data, on more or less impressionistic evidence, rather than on solid statistics. The field is wide open to scientific investigation. Very possibly, some of the above statements will be shown to be incorrect.

Natural selection theory is precise enough to specify changes in conditions such as would modify the generalizations. For example, the modern technology of reliable contraception and the consequent lowering in fertility substantially reduce the sexual disparity in parental investment. We can therefore expect that behavioral differences between men and women in their sexual behavior will also be reduced. Indeed, we have evidence that such a change is already taking place. Modern technology changes the environmental conditions of human mating and reproduction. Behavior, being adaptive to environmental changes, therefore also changes, and culture enables us to change quite fast. But we change in directions that are biologically predictable. Previously derived empirical generalizations have to be modified, but the theory still holds.

The evolutionary thinking underlying natural selection theory is uncongenial to most social scientists who have been conditioned to explain human behavior almost exclusively in culturally deterministic terms. At the risk of belaboring what should by now be obvious, I do not deny that human culture is important. Culture is a way our species has of adapting fast to changes in the environment, including those changes that have been induced by culture itself. But culture does not happen in a biological vacuum. It is part and parcel of a process of biological evolution, and, therefore, is bounded by biological parameters. Humans are quite adaptable, but not randomly or infinitely so.

As Davenport (1976) has suggested, a double process took place with the development of human culture: the socialization of sex (in the sense that everywhere sex is subject to a series of cultural rules and restrictions) and the sexualization of culture (insofar as every culture is bounded by the imperatives of mating and reproduction, and makes kinship and marriage a basic feature of social organization). Being the good cultural anthropologist that he is, Davenport stresses the socialization of sex at the expense of the sexualization of culture.[10] Both are, however, the two inextricably intertwined aspects of the same reality, which, in the final analysis, is rooted in biology. Unless one accepts the biological foundation of culture, how else is one to explain that *all* human societies are organized, at least partially, on the basis of mating and reproduction? It is, of course, quite true that sex takes place within a social matrix, but as Beach (1976a) points out, this is also true of other animals, indeed of all social animals, for kin selection is the most fundamental basis of animal societies. Human culture is a species-specific idiom for expressing mating and reproduction.

Natural selection theory is not a theory of rigid genetic determinism as social scientists sometimes misrepresent it to be. It is a theory of the interplay of genotype and environment, an environment which, for humans, includes culture. The burden is now on the cultural determinists to show that their *narrower* explanatory framework for human behavior provides us with a better "fit" to the data than the broader framework suggested here. I seek to integrate the paradigm of biological evolution with what the social sciences have discovered about the behavior of our species. It is for those who would like to resist this ambitious undertaking to show that we would do better by disregarding the fact that we are animals.

NOTES

1. Interestingly, even though the sociobiological paradigm is fully compatible in all basic respects with Marxism, Marxists have been in the front line of attack against sociobiology, proclaiming it a racist and reactionary product of capitalism. Of course, Marxism itself was an intellectual product of a capitalist society and a direct outgrowth of

classical economics and laissez-faire liberalism. Both Marx and Darwin owed a heavy debt to such leading intellectual figures of early British capitalism as Malthus, Ricardo and Adam Smith.

2. Beach's (1976a) *caveat* concerning comparisons of homosexual behavior between humans and nonhumans is well taken, however. Behaviors that look superficially alike may, and indeed often do, have a different ontogeny and phylogeny in different species, even sometimes in closely related species. A complicating factor in interpreting homosexuality in primates is that, in many primate species (including *Homo sapiens*), there is a considerable overlap between sexual arousal behavior and dominance behavior. Many primates "present" to, and are mounted by, each other, irrespective of sex. They use superficially sexual-looking signals to mark dominance and submission, the subordinate animal playing the female role irrespective of sex, and vice versa. The dominant animal mounts the subordinate one, irrespective of the sex of either, but the mountings have a clearly perfunctory, nonsexual character. Erection, intromission and ejaculation are absent in males, and females present both in and out of oestrus.

Humans, too, use sexual signals or symbols to express dominance and submission, and, of course, sexual relations have a clear component of dominance–subjection. Indeed, it is difficult to have a stable sexual relationship in which dominance is totally absent. As examples of sexual symbolism to express dominance, many words for sexual intercourse have double meanings, as in "getting screwed,""getting the shaft," "being fucked," and so on. The same is true in other European languages (e.g., "se faire avoir," "se faire posséder," "va te faire foutre" in French).

Beach (1976a) concludes that homosexual behavior in animals and man is not homologous because, in animals, homosexual behavior is generally a correct response to a correct signal given by a wrong-sexed signaller. For example, if a male animal gives a female signal, it will elicit a male response from another male, and vice versa. Human homosexuality is different, claims Beach, because most lesbians are not attracted to masculine women, nor most male homosexuals to feminine men. In view of the fact that human homosexual relationships very frequently fall into a dominance order in which the subordinate partner plays the female role, and the dominant partner the male role, I find Beach's conclusion dubious. It is true that individuals can shift from the active to the passive role, but so can and do monkeys, depending on their dominance order in the troop.

3. For Cuba, the assertion that the Castro regime has greatly reduced prostitution is undoubtedly accurate; but that is the result, not so much of Communism, as of the special role of pre-Communist Havana as the gambling den, playground and brothel of dollar-heavy American businessmen and *mafiosi*. Soviet advisers are probably paragons of virtue by comparison, if only because they do not have any rubles to throw around, but my guess is that they can still find a *chica* with whom to spend the night.

4. The pimp, however, is not a universal accompaniment of the prostitute. In fact, he seems to be largely a Western institution, in Europe and North America. In Latin America, Africa and the Middle East, prostitutes often do not have pimps. In some of these societies, the prostitute is the captive inmate of a brothel where she is kept virtually as a chattel. A lesbian relationship to the madam or another inmate may then replace the pimp. In some other societies, the term prostitute has sometimes been loosely applied to what are in effect entertainers and courtesans supported by a succession of lovers, with whom they maintain at least the pretense of an affective relationship. This is, of course, not real prostitution, however much it may deviate from that society's standards of respectability.

5. The shtetl was the Jewish quarter of Eastern European cities, especially in the Tzarist empire.

6. Age inequality is the exception. One only becomes a member of a kibbutz at age 18. Until then, one is treated as a child and disfranchised.
7. A few orthodox Jews have founded some religious kibbutzim, organized in a small federation of their own, but they make up only 2.5 percent of the 100,000 people in the kibbutz movement. The mainstream remains firmly secular and even anticlerical.
8. Shepher (1979) gives the best review of the voluminous literature on incest which, from Westermarck to Lévi-Strauss via Malinowski and Freud, spans nearly a century of heated debate between the protagonists of various theories. The theories hitherto advanced give, at best, partial explanations; Shepher presents a synthesis anchored in sociobiology, which parallels in every essential respect the conclusions I arrived at semi-independently. (The two manuscripts were written simultaneously, and we exchanged them when they were being copy-edited for publication. Each of us was, of course, well aware of the other's previous work and we had verbal exchanges on this and many other topics.) Shepher's main contribution is probably his insistence that we must distinguish between mother—son, father—daughter and brother—sister incest, for each of which he suggests a slightly different evolutionary scenario. In this, he followed through on Fox's (1962, 1967) suggestions.
9. Some species, especially species long domesticated by man, such as the dog, are reported not to have any incest avoidance. Whether this is because domestication physically prevents spatial dispersal or because thousands of generations of *un*natural (and often highly incestuous) selection by man have extinguished mechanisms for outbreeding is not clear. Any animals that have long been domesticated have, by definition, been bred to contribute to human fitness, often at great cost to their own fitness. This is the very opposite of natural selection, and this is why long-domesticated species cannot be expected to conform to natural selection. The increasing domestication of more and more plants and animals, combined with the reduction of both the number of species and their genetic diversity present serious problems for our evolutionary future. We become increasingly dependent on fewer and fewer species of decreasing fitness. The ultimate rationale for conservation not only of species but of genetic diversity within species is not our esthetic enjoyment or our sentimental attachment to other creatures, but our eventual survivability as a highly parasitic species.
10. Davenport, in common with many other social scientists, overstresses sex as such, which, biologically, is merely a means to reproduction. This strong emphasis on sex (or on its repression) is an unusual feature of Western societies, including their social scientists. In many other societies, sex is taken much more casually as a means to an end rather than as an end in itself. With the increasingly reliable divorce between sex and reproduction made possible by modern contraceptive technology, the hedonistic emphasis on recreational sex as well as the sanctimonious condemnations of it are ever more salient in contemporary Western societies.

SUPPLEMENTARY READINGS

Since the application of sociobiology to human behavior is so recent, there is, at present (1979), relatively little textbook material on the subject. In addition to the works cited in the Supplementary Readings for Chapter 2, there are two collections of articles edited by Fox (1975) and by Chagnon and Irons (1979) that bear on human sociobiology. So does Wilson's (1978) latest book, Shepher's (1979) work on incest and a couple of recent articles in the *American Anthropologist* (Barkow, 1978a; Dyson-Hudson and Smith, 1978). The main (but rather shallow) critique of the human application of sociobiology is Sahlins (1976), who was in turn ably refuted by Alexander (1977). There is, of course, an immense literature on human sexual behavior. See *inter alia,* Gagnon and Simon (1973), Ellis and Abarnabel (1973), Kinsey et al. (1948, 1953), Masters and Johnson (1966), for some important sources of data. Nearly all the literature on human sexuality singularly lacks theoretical coherence.

THE SOCIOCULTURE
OF MARRIAGE AND KINSHIP

For humans, mating and reproduction do not simply happen. They are the outcome of complex interactions between individuals who are *conscious* of belonging to organized groups and who behave according to a system of *learned rules* communicated through *symbolic language*. In those human characteristics lies the claim of the social sciences for an identity separate from the natural sciences. It will be the aim of this chapter to show that, while culture is indeed important and allows humans to respond quite flexibly to their environment, humans nevertheless continue to behave in species-specific ways. It is quite true that in some respects we are unlike any other species; but it is inadequate to let the statement stop there, for if culture were all-powerful in determining our behavior, then there would not be much left of our common humanity except our physical morphology. Yet, we behave in recognizably human ways that are, within admittedly broad limits, predictable across cultures. Underlying cultural diversity, there is human nature. Culture is a set of variations on the human theme. The variations are not infinite; nor are they all arbitrary and capricious. Some, like musical, artistic and literary creation, may indeed be fanciful flights of the human spirit, but many are fine-tuned adaptations to environmental conditions.

Naturally, when a native is asked why he behaves in a certain way, he will invoke the rules governing that behavior in his particular culture.

Social and cultural anthropologists have, by and large, accepted the validity of such an answer, on the theory that the native always knows best. What the native, and the anthropologist after him, does is give a *proximal* cause for the behavior in question. The answer is correct as far as it goes, but it begs another question. To be sure, a particular form of behavior is often explainable in an immediate sense through the learning experience of the individual. He has indeed learned his sex identity from his parents; picked up sexual lore from his playmates; and adopted prevailing attitudes around him about marriage, the family, incest and so on. These are all proximal, ontogenic explanations for behavior. But, in any organism, ontogeny and phylogeny are *complementary,* not conflicting levels of explanation. The phylogenic level of explanation I have stressed so far is a more *distal* explanation than the cultural, ontogenic level that has characterized the social sciences to date.

The question is thus not who is right and who is wrong, but the level of explanation sought. Sociobiology does very poorly in explaining conscious motivations of individuals, and the detailed cultural idiom through which a behavior is expressed, such as the ceremonies of a wedding ritual. On the other hand, I shall try to show that sociobiology goes a long way in accounting for basic structural features of human societies.

Specifically, we will see that human systems of kinship and marriage conform to only a few basic types. Underlying a great deal of variety in detail, human societies share much of their basic structure of kinship and marriage. The variations, while they attest to our versatility in adapting to a wide range of environmental conditions, are themselves not random but adaptive.

First let us recapitulate what we said of the three main bases of human sociality: kin selection, reciprocity and coercion. Generally, the simpler and the less differentiated a society's social organization, technology and system of production, the greater kin selection looms in relation to reciprocity and coercion. All human societies are organized in part on the basis of kin selection, but, in the simpler societies, kin selection, along with the patterns of reciprocity that surround mating (and, therefore, indirectly determine kin relations), is tantamount to the social charter by which individuals regulate their interactions. As societies become more complex, kin selection continues to operate, but reciprocity becomes more complex and extends well beyond systems of marriage, and coercion, especially coercion of people other than kinsmen or spouses, plays an ever-increasing role. Kin selection, in short, does not completely explain the sociality of any human society, but the simpler the society, the more it explains. Even in the simplest human societies, however, reciprocity is important, particularly the very special (and probably the oldest) kind of reciprocity involved in systems of marriage.

DESCENT AND ALLIANCE

All of this is "old hat" to anthropologists who, for generations, have been concerned with kinship and marriage as the principal bases of simpler human societies. This even led to two distinct approaches to the study of such societies, known respectively as "descent" and "alliance" theory, depending on whether one put the analytical stress on kinship or on marriage (Fox, 1967). In practice, most anthropologists readily grant that both are important. However, most anthropologists also consider kinship and marriage to be, first and last, cultural institutions, and this is where the basis of their disagreement with a sociobiological approach lies (Sahlins, 1976; Schneider, 1965; Pasternak, 1976). The outstanding exceptions are Robin Fox (1967, 1975), and Meyer Fortes (1953, 1959, 1969). Fortes categorically states that solidarity is closely linked with kin relatedness. Indeed he formulates his "Axiom of Amity" in terms fully compatible with sociobiology: "Where kinship is demonstrable or assumed . . . there amity must prevail!" (Fortes, 1969).

Of course, human kinship and marriage are cultural phenomena insofar as they are subject to systems of consciously recognized and symbolically expressed rules that regulate behavior. My only disagreement with the accepted view is that I reject the implicit assumption that, because marriage and kinship are cultural, therefore they are *purely* cultural and can only be understood in their own cultural, normative terms. To explain culture purely in terms of culture is to explain nothing. It is no explanation of a particular group's structure of marriage and kinship to give that group's rules of descent, residence, marriage, inheritance and so on. The rules are, at best, a native's description of behavior. Sometimes the description is a fairly accurate model of the way people actually behave; sometimes it is not. Sometimes the rules reported by the anthropologist are indeed a native model for behavior; more often, the rules are the anthropologist's inferences from observed behavior, or from the natives' reports of the way they ought to behave, reinterpreted through the anthropologist's own analytical categories.

Apart from all these thorny problems of what the rules really are, whose rules they are, and whether the rules actually reflect behavior, it clearly begs the question to try to explain human mating and reproduction in terms of the cultural norms surrounding these activities. For then the questions become these: If other animals mate and reproduce without rules, why don't humans do the same? Why is it that *all* human societies have rules about mating and reproduction? Why do all human societies organize around kinship and marriage?

I have already answered these questions in Chapter 3. The modalities of our behavior are indeed importantly shaped by the cultural rules we invent for ourselves; but the rules themselves reflect an underlying biological reality. Human behavior in general, and mating and reproductive behavior in particular, are thus *both* cultural and biological, *both* genetically and environmentally determined, and it makes no sense to dissociate one aspect from the other. What we call kinship and marriage in humans is the cultural expression of our biologically predisposed system of mating and reproduction. We set up societies around mating and reproduction and we cook up rules of conduct about them because it was adaptive for us to do so. The few groups foolish enough to do otherwise failed to survive in competition with those that did. This may not remain true for all time, but it has been true everywhere so far; and "everywhere so far" is all the data we have with which to construct an explanatory social science.

RULES OF DESCENT

One of the things about which all human societies have rules is descent or filiation. We might as well start here, as rules of descent are often invoked in refutation of sociobiology (Sahlins, 1976). Biologically, we have, of course, two parents, four grandparents, eight great-grandparents and so on. Does it not stand to reason, then, that all societies should recognize this? Yet, only 36 percent of a sample of 857 societies have "bilateral" descent as the anthropologists call this way of taking into account all lines of descent (Murdock, 1967).[1] The others have opted for officially recognizing or stressing one line of descent. In 47 percent of the cases, they recognize the male line (patrilineal descent); and in 14 percent, the female line (matrilineal descent). This leaves three percent of the societies with "double" descent, a combination of patrilineal and matrilineal descent. The reader might ask how "double" descent differs from "bilateral" descent. Under bilateral descent, all lines of descent are recognized, whereas in double descent only two are: the line of the father, father's father and so on, and that of the mother, mother's mother and so on. Thus, double descent excludes two out of four grandparents, six out of eight great-grandparents, 14 out of 16 great-great-grandparents and so on.

These four possibilities—bilateral, patrilineal, matrilineal and double descent—exhaust the list. All known human societies fall more or less clearly under one of these, though some may show features of more than one type. (For instance, although American society is overwhelmingly bilateral, we generally transmit surnames patrilineally.) The fundamental choice is even more limited than this list would suggest. In fact, there are only two double options: either one can choose to recognize all lines of descent or one opts for a single line. If one chooses one, then one has the choice of the male or the female line. Double descent is only a rare special case that simply combines (but usually for different purposes) patrilineal and matrilineal descent.

We must stress here that the *logical* possibilities are numerous. First, one need not recognize any line of descent at all. If one chooses to pay attention to descent, there are many possible rules. One could, for instance, decide to recognize all of one's father's ancestors, but not one's mother's, or vice versa. Or one could decide to trace descent through one's mother, mother's father, mother's father's mother and so on. One could, but no one does. To be sure, some of the other rules would be more complex, but complexity of rules has never stopped humans. Chess is much more complex than tic-tac-toe, yet chess can be played with delight for a lifetime whereas tic-tac-toe becomes boring after ten minutes when it becomes obvious that, unless one partner blunders, every game must be a draw. Why, then, this narrow range of choices out of many other possibilities?

First, why a rule of descent at all? We already suggested the answer: because of kin selection. Then, why is not bilateral descent the obvious solution for all societies since it conforms most closely to biological relatedness? If unilineal descent (either patrilineal or matrilineal) is so common, there must be a big advantage in it which overrules the genetic cost of short-changing some relatives. Why favor some relatives over others on a basis other than degree of relatedness, as one does under unilineal descent? The answer is obvious, and has long been discovered by anthropologists.

BILATERAL VERSUS UNILINEAL DESCENT

Once one decides on unilineal descent, every person in a society automatically belongs to a single, nonoverlapping kin group of potentially very large size. Such a group is called a *clan* when the common ancestor is unknown or mythical, and a *lineage* when the actual descent can be traced. A clan typically is subdivided into a number of constituent lineages and each lineage can in turn be subdivided, depending on the number of generations one goes back in tracing common descent. The whole society thus becomes a pyramidal structure of clans, lineages, sublineages, sub-sublineages, and so on, in which every individual native to the society has a place—and only *one* place. A person belongs to only one kin group at each level, e.g., clan *A,* lineage *a,* sublineage a_1 and so on. In such a system, it becomes quite clear who belongs to which kin group; no one can belong to more than one since no one can have more than one father, one father's father and so on, or one mother, one mother's mother and so on. Since everyone born into a society perforce belongs to one and only one descent group, the kin groups have clear boundaries, stable membership, and the clear potential for organizing for all kinds of purposes as kin groups against other kin groups. Furthermore, there is, in theory, no size limit to the kin group. Unilineal kin groups often run into the hundreds, commonly into the thousands, occasionally into the millions.

Consider the alternative: bilaterality is quite nice as far as it goes. It enables one to be nepotistic toward all of one's relatives, to the degree that one is related to them. This is kin selection pure and simple. But there is a catch to it. Beyond first cousins, kin selection becomes very weak and groups of first cousins are typically smallish. Another problem is that only full siblings have identical sets of relatives. Groups of first cousins would be very difficult to organize because different groups would compete for our loyalty. My group of first cousins would only overlap by one-half, on the average, with that of any of my first cousins, since first cousins, barring inbreeding, only share one-half of their ancestors. The problems of organizing kinsmen for collective action in bilateral descent societies are immediately apparent. Only full siblings can form unambiguous, mutually exclusive groups, as indeed they often do in bilateral descent societies; but such groups are of necessity very limited in size, and thus ineffective for many collective purposes.

The stark dilemma is the following: Either one follows kin selection pure and simple and opts for bilateral descent, but then the scale on which stable groups of kinsmen can collectively organize and cooperate is effectively limited to sets of full siblings; alternatively, one has to jettison most of one's kin in order to organize into larger groups with some of one's kin, if necessary, against other kinsmen. Unilineal descent is a trade-off between kin selection and reciprocity. It still utilizes the principle of kinship to organize a society. Indeed, unilineal descent is the simplest and the most common device for organizing large collectivities on the basis of kinship. But unilineal descent increases the scope of reciprocity in human interaction. Unilineal descent is, in fact, a social contract between a particular category of relatives to gang up against all others, including, if necessary, other relatives. Unilineal descent, then, is an adaptive response to societies that were under pressure to increase the size of their cooperative groups (as indeed most human groups must have been for thousands of years) without abandoning kin selection altogether.

If this interpretation is correct, then one would expect bilateral descent to be most prevalent in two opposite kinds of societies: (1) large-scale, industrial societies where reciprocity and coercion have become the principal bases for organizing large collectivities, and where, therefore, the incentive to create large unilineal kin groups is not great; and,

(2) small, stateless, egalitarian societies that create little or no storable surplus production and where kin selection is maximally operative. Unilineal descent societies, on the other hand, should be most prevalent in the societies of intermediate size and complexity, where kin selection still plays an important role, but where competitive pressures from other societies fosters the formation of larger cooperative groups. Schema I summarizes evolutionary trends in kinship and other aspects of social organization (see pp. 94–95).

The data strongly support the hypothesis, as shown in Table 1. Of the small hunting and gathering societies, 65.6 percent (61 out of 93) have bilateral descent, and so do nearly all of the industrial societies of Europe and America. (Japan is still patrilineal, but the lineages are weak as corporate groups and the society shows signs of slowly becoming more bilateral.) By comparison, only 34.1 percent (86 out of 252) of the horticultural societies, 25.3 percent (19 out of 75) of the pastoralist societies and 32.8 percent (38 out of 116) of the agricultural societies have bilateral descent (Aberle, 1961).[2]

The contrast between bilateral descent and unilineal descent societies, however, is not as clear-cut as was hitherto implied. When it is said that a society "opts" for unilineal descent, it does not mean that its members do not know that they are also related to many people outside their clan or lineage. The opposite is true. People are not only aware of kin ties outside their unilineal descent group, but they act nepotistically on them. The relatives outside the descent group are thus not systematically excluded from all relationships; they only take second place to lineage members for *certain specified purposes,* such as inheritance of property or military alliance. Clearly, in a unilineal descent system, conflicting loyalties between different categories of kin inside and outside the lineage occur, and one may have to prefer a distant relative within the lineage over a close one outside it. Typically, however, unilineal descent does

Table 1. Rule of Descent and Production Technology [a]

Rule of Descent	Production Technology									
	Hunting and Gathering		Horticulture		Pastoralism		Plow Agriculture		Total	
	N	%	N	%	N	%	N	%	N	%
Bilateral	61	65.6	86	34.1	19	25.3	38	32.8	204	38.1
Unilineal	32	34.4	166	65.9	56	74.7	78	67.2	332	61.9
Total	93	100.0	252	100.0	75	100.0	116	100.0	536	100.0

[a] Source: Murdock (1957).

not prevent good relations between kinsmen belonging to different descent groups or only does so on rare and special occasions.

In fact, several mechanisms foster good relations between the constituent clans and lineages of a society, and thereby facilitate kin selection between close relatives belonging to different descent groups. By far, the most important of these mechanisms is *exogamy*. Most unilineal descent societies prohibit marriage (and generally sexual relations as well) between members of the same clan and lineage. But most societies also tend to be *endogamous* at the societal level, which until recently were fairly small ethnic groups or "tribes" of a few hundred or at most a few thousand people. Since it is expected that you marry within your ethnic group but outside your own clan and lineage, it follows that you must seek a spouse in another clan of your "tribe." This, as we shall see in greater detail later, is precisely what takes place in the majority of preliterate societies.

Unilineal descent societies, then, are typically made up of clans whose men swap women for mates.[3] The result of several generations of clan exogamy within endogamous populations of a few thousand people or less is clear. One ends up marrying relatives, since practically everyone in the society is a kinsman, whether inside one's own clan or not. Most societies are quite aware of consanguineal marriages; in fact, a great many even specify that you *should* marry certain categories of relative. We will return to marriage systems and their significance later. The important point here is that marriage rules in a great many societies, probably in the vast majority of preliterate societies beyond the *simplest* ones, involved people who, even though they belonged to different unilineal descent groups, were relatives and knew each other to be such. Ties of marriage and ties of kinship, then, overlap sufficiently in these societies that they should be regarded as mutually reinforcing. In other words, I am suggesting that, in unilineal descent societies, marriage rules and systems serve the ends of kin selection. Relatives who are "lost" through the principle of unilineal descent are "recaptured" as spouses and in-laws. More about that later.

PATRILINEAL VERSUS MATRILINEAL DESCENT

The next interesting question regarding rules of descent is why there should be many more patrilineal societies than matrilineal ones. In a sample of 564 societies, patrilineal societies outnumber matrilineal ones by 248 to 84—nearly three to one (Aberle, 1961a). Why preference for patriliny? Hartung (1976) gives a twofold sociobiological explanation. One has to do with the fact that the Y chromosome, which determines

Schema 1. Evolutionary Synopsis of Social and Kinship Organization [a]

	Overall Level of Complexity				
	Simplest	Low Intermediate	High Intermediate	Complex	Most Complex
SOCIAL ORGANIZATION VARIABLES					
System of Production	Hunting, fishing, gathering	Swidden horticulture	Advanced horticulture	Agrarian	Industrial
Population Size	40–100	100–10,000	10,000–100,000	100,000–300,000,000	5,000,000–300,000,000
Population Density per km²	less than 1	1–20	20–100	50–500	50–500
Political System	Stateless	Incipient chieftainship	Small states	Bureaucratized states	Highly bureaucratized states
Stratification	Mostly by age and sex	Incipient status differences and slavery	Extensive class distinctions and slavery	Elaborate and rigid class order and slavery	Flexible class distinctions. No slavery
KINSHIP ORGANIZATION VARIABLES					
Type of Family	Nuclear or limitedly extended	Extended	Extended	Extended or stem	Nuclear
Rule of Residence	Flexible	Virilocal, less commonly uxorilocal	Virilocal, less commonly uxorilocal	Virilocal	Neolocal

Rule of Descent	Bilateral or patrilineal	Unilineal (Patri- or matrilineal)	Unilineal (Patri- or matrilineal)	Patrilineal or bilateral	Bilateral
Inheritance of Property and Authority	Little to inherit	Unilineal (Patri- or matrilineal)	Unilineal (Patri- or matrilineal)	Patrilineal, sometimes primogeniture	Bilateral
Marriage Type	Limited polygyny	Extensive polygyny	Extensive polygyny	Upper class polygyny, peasant monogamy	Monogamy
Marriage Rules	Few and flexible, except for incest taboos	Prescriptive exogamy, often with cross-cousins	Prescriptive exogamy, preferential class isogamy or hypergamy	Prescriptive exogamy, often status group endogamy	Preferential class isogamy, but few pre-scriptions or proscriptions other than incest taboos
Choice of Marriage Partners	Partners often choose each other from fair range of candidates; some input by kinsmen	Marriages arranged between lineage groups from limited range of candidates: little or no input by partners	Marriages arranged between lineage groups from limited range of candidates; little or no input by partners	Marriages arranged by parents from fair range of candidates; some input by partners	Partners choose each other from wide range of candidates; limited input by parents
Exchange of Goods and Services at Marriage	Gift exchange, sometimes "bride service"	Bridewealth	Bridewealth	Gift exchange and/or dowry	Gifts to spouse

[a] Note: The above schema is to be treated flexibly. The categories overlap; the numbers are rough orders of magnitude; and, for any given cell, a number of "exceptions" can be produced. The schema is merely a gross first approximation of how human systems of kinship and marriage co-evolved with increasing size and complexity of society.

maleness, has no homolog. That is, in a diploid male individual, it is not matched with another Y chromosome, as all other 22 pairs of chromosomes are, and indeed as the X chromosome is in females. (Females are XX, while males are XY.) Since the Y chromosome has no homolog, it cannot crossover, as presumably do all other chromosomes, including X in females. Only males can produce Y chromosomes and that Y chromosome, in the absence of crossing over, is presumably passed on intact in the male line. A man's son's son has a replica of his grandfather's Y chromosome. The same cannot be said of the X chromosome of a woman's daughter's daughter, because of the possibility of a crossover at each generation between the two X chromosomes that it takes to produce a female. It follows that a man has a somewhat higher assurance of sharing genes with his descendants in the male line than a woman has with her female line descendants.

This argument is ingenious but not very convincing—at least not to me. First, we are talking of one chromosome out of 46, only accounting for a small fraction of all the genes transmitted. Second, the Y chromosome is much shorter than the X chromosome and probably has far fewer genes, perhaps none except those that control maleness. (It is the absence on the Y chromosome of many genes on the X chromosome that produces the high incidence in males of such deleterious sex-linked recessive genes as color blindness and hemophilia. The apparent paucity of genetic material on the Y chromosome may well be the principal cause of the higher age-specific mortality of human males compared to females.) Thus, with few genes, the Y chromosome, while it is passed on intact, accounts for little of the genetic material. Third, and this is the clincher, the slight edge that the Y chromosome gives males in probability of relatedness with male-line offspring is obviously offset by the probability of paternity itself, which is always short of a certainty, in some societies very short indeed.

The second of Hartung's argument is more convincing. It has to do with variation in reproductive success which, in man as in most species, is greater for males than for females. Males and females necessarily have an equal number of offspring on the average, but the variation is greater for males than for females. More men than women have no children, but men are also capable of having many more offspring than women. Obviously, the more polygynous a society is, the greater male variation in reproductive success becomes. It follows from this sex differential in reproductive success that, if resources (both material—like land and livestock—and social—like knowledge) can contribute to reproduction, as they very often do, there is an incentive to invest and pass on these resources in the male line, because this is where these resources can give the greater reproductive return. Stated simply, a daughter's reproductive success is less affected by poverty than a son's; so, if you have resources to invest and pass on, you are well advised to favor sons. While this applies to both mothers and fathers, the simplest way to translate that principle into a clear-cut social rule is patrilineal inheritance of property (including social property such as trade secrets, knowledge about the environment and so on).

There is much to support this interpretation of patrilineal inheritance (typically found in patrilineal descent societies). The main form in which wealth is "invested" in societies of the intermediate range of complexity (that is, those largely nonliterate societies living from herding and simple agriculture, but with little or no social stratification, urbanization and political centralization) is in the acquisition of wives. Those are also the societies, as we have seen, where unilineal descent is most prevalent: 61 percent of a sample of 857 societies are unilineal (Murdock, 1967), but for horticultural and pastoralist societies, the percentage rises to 68 and 75 percent, respectively. In the vast majority of cases, the bulk of the goods and services that are transferred as part of the marriage transaction passes from the lineage of the groom to that of the bride. Such property is referred to as "bridewealth" or "brideprice." In over two-thirds (67.4 percent) of the societies in the above sample, the groom or his kin transfers goods or services to the bride's kin group. In about one-fourth (23.8 percent) of all societies no exchange of goods or services takes place at marriage and, in 6.2 percent of the cases, there is a reciprocal exchange between the kin groups of the bride and of the groom (Table 2).

As shown in Table 3, there is a clear association between the institution of bridewealth and patriliny. Over two-thirds (71.4 percent) of the patrilineal societies sanction marriage through substantial bridewealth payments compared to only 36.7 percent of matrilineal societies and 32.0 percent of double and bilateral descent societies. Conversely, in only 12.2 percent of the patrilineal societies does marriage take place in

Table 2. Exchange of Goods and Services at Marriage [a]

	Number of Societies	Percent
No Exchange	205	23.8
Reciprocal Exchange Between Groom's and Bride's Kin	53	6.2
Groom's Kin Pays	580	67.4
Bride's Kin Pays	22	2.6
Total	860	100.0

[a] Source: Murdock (1967).

Table 3. Rule of Descent and Exchange of Goods at Marriage [a]

	Patriliny		Matriliny		Nonunilineal Descent		Total	
	N	%	N	%	N	%	N	%
Substantial Bridewealth	288	71.8	44	36.7	74	22.0	406	47.4
Other Exchanges of Goods and Services	64	16.0	26	21.7	110	32.7	200	23.3
No Significant Exchange	49	12.2	50	41.6	152	45.3	251	29.3
Total	401	100.0	120	100.0	336	100.0	857	100.0

[a] Source: Murdock (1967).

the absence of any significant exchange of goods or services; this is the case in two-fifths (41.6 percent) of matrilineal societies and nearly half (45.3 percent) of nonunilineal societies. Since the often conscious intent of bridewealth is to compensate a kin group for the loss of the reproductive power of one of its women, its association with patriliny is not surprising. In bilateral descent societies, there is no large corporate kin group that needs to be compensated; and in matrilineal societies the woman's offspring belong to the mother's lineage. In a patrilineal system, the lineage of the woman surrenders jural claim to her offspring to her husband's patrilineage.

The association between bridewealth payments and agriculture is shown in Table 4. Only one-fifth (20.5 percent) of societies without agriculture have substantial bridewealth payment, compared to over two-fifths (43.6 percent) of societies where agriculture is present. Finally, Table 5 shows the close association between the institution of bridewealth and the nonsororal variety of polygyny which is characteristic of patrilineal societies. Over two-thirds (68.0 percent) of societies that preferentially practice nonsororal polygyny have substantial bridewealth payments, compared to only 15.4 percent of societies with preferential sororal polygyny, and 23.7 percent of monogamous societies or societies where polygyny is limited.

In short, one of the first forms of investment of wealth, as soon as surplus could be created through agriculture and animal domestication, has been matrimonial. Men and their male kinsmen in patrilineal descent societies have invested in women to secure access to and control of the reproductive power of as many of them as possible. Women are the ultimate scarce resource for men. The institution of bridewealth converts, in effect, production into reproduction.

Table 4. Agriculture and Exchange of Goods at Marriage [a]

	No Agriculture		Agriculture		Total	
	N	%	N	%	N	%
Substantial Bridewealth	9	20.5	61	43.6	70	38.0
Other Exchanges of Goods and Services	22	50.0	50	35.7	72	39.2
No Significant Exchange	13	29.5	29	20.7	42	22.8
Total	44	100.0	140	100.0	184	100.0

[a] Source: Murdock and White (1969).

Table 5. Polygyny and Exchange of Goods at Marriage [a]

	Monogamy or Limited Polygyny		Sororal Polygyny Preferred		Nonsororal Polygyny		Total	
	N	%	N	%	N	%	N	%
Substantial Bridewealth	14	23.7	2	15.4	17	68.0	33	34
Other Exchanges of Goods and Services	28	47.5	3	23.1	7	28.0	38	39.0
No Significant Exchanges	17	28.8	8	61.5	1	4.0	26	26.0
Total	59	100.0	13	100.0	25	100.0	97	100.0

[a] Source: Murdock and White (1969).

The case of the dowry, where it is the woman who brings property into the marriage, is exceptional and more characteristic of complex, highly stratified societies, such as those of Europe and Asia. Only 2.6 percent of the societies in the Murdock (1967) sample had the institution of dowry. As women are the scarce resource for men rather than vice versa, it makes little sense for women to "buy" men, unless they can improve their fitness by catching a high-status male. Indeed, in the few societies where the dowry exists, such as much of Europe and China until recently, it is most prevalent in the upper classes, and its effect is to secure for women a husband of equal or higher status. Furthermore, the dowry does not so much transfer property from the kin group of the bride to that of the groom, as from the bride's parents to the bride. In that sense, the dowry is *not* the opposite of the bridewealth, but a means of passing property on to daughters before one's death (Goody, 1976; Goody and Tambiah, 1973). It is thus an investment in the fitness of daughters.

Even in the more complex societies that do not have bridewealth, the bulk of the productive property, such as land, money and livestock, tends to be inherited by males rather than females, or, at least, so it was until comparatively recent times. In bilateral descent European societies, for instance, until the 19th century, it was a son who typically inherited the throne or the family business, farm, trade or occupation, sometimes through a rule of primogeniture. Even today in Europe and America where a family's investment in the next generation increasingly takes the form of quality advanced education, there is still a strikingly asymmetrical investment in sons rather than daughters. The same is true, and to an even greater degree, in "developing" countries of Asia and Africa (Clignet and Foster, 1966; van den Berghe, 1973b).

In most societies, then, where there is enough wealth to be transferred from generation to generation, males receive more than women. Let us return to the "intermediate" level societies that most strikingly confirm Hartung's hypothesis. Even though these transfers of goods and services at marriage have generally been called "bridewealth" by anthropologists, a closer look at them reveals that what is being invested in is not women as such, but the women's reproductive power. The ritual payments would be more aptly called "childwealth." This is shown by such common provisions as return of all or much of the bridewealth in case of barrenness. In the minds of the natives, then, wealth is clearly being converted into reproduction, overwhelmingly the reproduction of males. A wife is, first and foremost, a child-maker.

Since nearly all these intermediate level societies have preferential polygyny, the association between wealth and the reproduction of males is very strong indeed. In the Murdock (1967) sample of 862 societies, 83 percent are polygynous, less than 0.5 percent are polyandrous and 16 percent are monogamous. Monogamous societies are characteristically either very simple or very complex. The incidence of polygyny is highest in the intermediate level horticultural and pastoralist societies. In polygynous societies, there are two main correlates of how many wives a man has. One is age and the other is political or economic status. As those societies are also strongly age-stratified, age and status go together. Older men have had more time to accumulate wealth and hold position of greater authority; therefore they tend to appropriate more than their share of women.

Not only is wealth in these societies being converted by men into the reproductive power of women. The women, once acquired, are often kept within the family. They are frequently passed on between close male relatives, such as brothers or father and son. A common custom is the *levirate,* whereby a man inherits the widow of his deceased brother.

In some societies, a son inherits his father's widows (with the exception of his own mother). These practices have often been represented by anthropologists as a humane social security system for widows, and they may indeed have that effect; but, equally clearly, they foster the inclusive fitness of men.

In sum, intermediate level societies show that, as soon as wealth could be accumulated and transferred, the first use to which it was put was reproductive. Given that women are reproductively the scarce resource and that men have no ceiling on the number of offspring they can have, it is no surprise that, in the vast majority of societies, wealth has been used by men to acquire the reproductive power of as many women as they could muster. Hence, the close association between wealth and polygyny. In a few societies, to be sure, women have used wealth (in the form of dowry) to marry men, but *not* to marry as many men as they could. One husband is quite enough to maximize a woman's reproductive potential. Rather, dowry has been used to attract the best possible husband, typically a wealthy, high-status one. The dowry is mostly found in complex, highly stratified societies, and, even in these societies, it is often not a generalized phenomenon. It is of greatest significance to the upper classes. Through the bait of a dowry, upper-status women (and their fathers) can ensnare upper-status men against stiff competition by lower-status women who are quite happy to be had for free.

How does all this relate to patrilineal descent? After all, it pays for men to reproduce whether they live in a patrilineal or a matrilineal society, and the institution of the bridewealth is by no means *restricted* to patrilineal societies. Interestingly, however, there is a strong correlation between the *amount* of the bridewealth (relative to a particular society's system of production and level of wealth) and patriliny. Many matrilineal societies also exchange goods and services on marriage, but the amount involved is typically much lower, and there tends to be more *reciprocal* exchange of gifts between the kinsmen of the bride and of the groom. In patrilineal societies, the transfer of wealth is not only larger on the average, but much more overwhelmingly unidirectional: goods and services move from the patrilineage of the groom to that of the bride. The male kinsmen of the bride, in turn, recirculate that wealth to acquire women for themselves.

The reason for this disparity between patrilineal and matrilineal societies is apparent. Even in matrilineal societies, it makes good reproductive sense for men to use wealth in order to acquire women, but there is a "catch" to it. In matrilineal societies, inheritance of wealth, political office and other resources is mostly between males but through the female line, i.e., between mother's brother and sister's son. Much of a man's resources are thus diverted from his own direct reproduction and from the reproduction of his children to that of his sisters and his sisters' children. In matrilineal societies, the men maximize their inclusive fitness more indirectly than in patrilineal societies. The simplest, most obvious solution for a man with material or social resources to maximize his inclusive fitness is to invest in (and pass on his property to) his sons. This, in turn, is best done in patrilineal societies. Sons are better than daughters because daughters can be expected to reproduce anyway, whereas sons are more likely to benefit if wealth can buy them extra wives. And obviously sons are better than sister's sons because they are twice as highly related to one. Hence, patrilineal descent.

MATRILINEAL SOCIETIES AND PATERNITY

This raises the next interesting question: why, then, are there any matrilineal societies at all? After all, there are far too many of them to dismiss them as unlikely aberrations. Not only that, but matrilineal societies were probably once more common than they are now. A number of matrilineal societies have been observed to change in the direction of patrilineal organization, and a number of presently patrilineal societies still show remnants of matriliny. For instance, traditional Judaism has given rise to a strongly patriarchal and patrilineal social organization; yet the ritual criterion of who is Jew is matrilineal. The reverse case of a patrilineal society becoming matrilineal has never been documented (Murdock, 1949).

Matrilineal societies thus seem to have been selected against, at least in the last few millenia, but they were probably more common in the past. Indeed, it is an old theory of early anthropology that the primeval form of human social organization was not only matrilineal but also matriarchal (Morgan, 1877; Bachofen, 1861; Westermarck, 1891). Although there are many myths of matriarchy, both among contemporary feminists and sundry natives, there is not a single documented case of a matriarchal society. Nor does it seem likely that matrilineal organization was the prototype of human societies. Extrapolating backward from contemporary hunters and gatherers (admittedly a risky and speculative venture, because of many important differences between them and earlier hunters and gatherers), bilateral descent seems a more likely candidate for the primeval human society. Of the 101 such societies in the Murdock (1957) sample of 564, 61 percent have bilateral descent, and only 13 percent are matrilineal. Horticultural and pastoralist societies are 18 percent matrilineal (Aberle, 1961a), and matriliny is most likely to be found in simple horticultural societies (Schneider and Gough, 1961).

Over two-thirds (67.9 percent) of the 84 matrilineal societies in the Murdock (1957) sample are horticultural.

Before answering the question of why matrilineal societies should have arisen at all, let us take a closer look at them. There are two striking facts about them. One, they are remarkably like one another in their basic social structure, even in widely different parts of the world (Schneider and Gough, 1961). Matrilineal organization thus appears to have been independently reinvented many times and to have hit on the same solutions to the same problems. Two, matrilineal societies are *not* simply the mirror image of patrilineal societies. In all known matrilineal societies, it is men who are in ultimate jural authority, much the same as in patrilineal societies, but the transmission of authority is between mother's brother and sister's son. In the absence of such relatives, the transfer is between the nearest matrilineal relatives, e.g., a mother's mother's brother and a sister's sister's son.

In both matrilineal and patrilineal societies, thus, it is men who rule, but in the former, men invest their resources and pass on the bulk of their property and authority to uterine nephews (sister's sons) rather than to their own children. Why this seemingly strange arrangement? And why should this peculiar system have been independently invented everywhere? Theoretically, the simplest matrilineal counterpart of a patrilineal system would be one in which women are in authority and in which material, social and political resources are passed from mother to daughter. Such a system must be unviable because, as far as we know, it does not exist anywhere. Male dominance seems to have been a first condition that matrilineal societies had to satisfy to survive.

If males were dominant, however, why did they not invest principally in their own offspring rather than in their sisters' children? The answer, of course, is that many did, and that is why patrilineal societies are so common. But what of those who did not, establishing matrilineal societies? What conditions would lead one to expect men to care more for uterine nephews than for their own children in seeming violation of the principles of kin selection? The answer, of course, is a low probability of paternity (Alexander, 1974, 1975; Greene, 1978). If a man cannot be sure that his wives' children are also his own, then he might indeed be better advised to invest in uterine nephews, because he has the assurance that he is related to his sister.

Theoretically, uterine nephews become a better bet than putative offspring when the probability of paternity falls below .25, i.e., when there is less than a one-in-four chance that a wife's children are also her husband's. This can be simply demonstrated: a man is related to his children by a factor of .5, and to his full sister's children by a factor of .25.

However, his sister may only be a half-sister; therefore, a man's nephews may only be related to him by a factor of .125. It takes a probability of paternity of less than .25 to reduce the average relatedness of a putative offspring to a value lower than that of a uterine nephew by a half-sister ($.5 \times .25 = .125$).

Leaving aside the practical problem of computing a probability of paternity, it is clear that men in most societies are concerned about paternity, and that they are much surer of it in some societies than in others. There are a few societies where people have been alleged not to be aware of the role of men in conception (Malinowski, 1929), but, in many societies, men are not only concerned about paternity—they constantly put it to the test of physical resemblance. In any case, the sociobiological argument does not hinge on men being conscious of and concerned about paternity; it merely requires that they preferentially invest, consciously or not, in those categories of relatives with whom they have the highest probability of being related.

The ethnographic facts tend to support the sociobiological hypothesis. Matrilineal societies can be inferred to have lower probabilities of paternity than patrilineal ones because they are characterized by a higher incidence of divorce and adultery (Clignet, 1970; Schneider and Gough, 1961). Patrilineal societies not only have lower rates of these things; they are notorious for taking active steps to control the sexual behavior of wives, thus raising the probability of paternity (Fox, 1967; Gluckman, 1950). Adultery is more severely punished, though often as a civil offense against property, subject to compensatory damages to the husband, rather than as a criminal offense. (What matters is often not the *sexual* transgression as such, as the potential damage of cuckoldry to the husband's parental investment.) Women may be physically isolated from men, other than their husband and their husband's kin, as they are in many Muslim societies that keep women in *purdah*. In the extreme cases of some African societies, girls are subject to such painful attempts at controlling their sexuality as clitoridectomy and infibulation.[4] Furthermore, as we will see presently, nearly all patrilineal societies [96.5 percent in the Murdock (1967) sample] have virilocal residence, a system wherein married women live under the constant surveillance of their in-laws, often, in the first instance, their mothers-in-law, but also their husbands' agnates.

By contrast, paternity, and therefore the sexual behavior of women and the marital bond itself, are much less consequential in matrilineal societies, especially the ones that are uxorilocal as well. In such societies, divorce is easy and frequent, and husbands are often regarded, in Harris' words (1977, p. 62), as "temporary sojourners with sexual privileges." The Navajo, whom we shall examine in Chapter 5, are a case in point.

Another condition presumably associated with a lowered probability of paternity is the type of warfare frequently found in matrilineal societies. Ember and Ember (1971) and Harris (1977) note that, while small-scale, stateless, patrilineal societies also engage in chronic warfare, their warfare tends to be "internal"—among neighboring, culturally related groups. Matrilineal societies, on the other hand, are characterized more by "external" warfare between geographically and culturally distant groups. Men often stay away on remote war expeditions for long periods of time, a condition notoriously conducive to cuckoldry. Some patrilineal and bilaterial societies, especially the larger and more complex ones, also engage in external warfare, but they often attempt to police the sexuality of the women left behind by means of chastity belts, confinement under the watch of eunuchs, watchful eyes of mothers-in-law and similar measures.

Statistical data in support of the above generalizations are still scanty. Broude and Greene (1976) had sufficient data to code the frequency of female extramarital sex for only 56 of the 186 societies in the Murdock and White (1969) standard cross-cultural sample. As an indirect measure of probability of paternity, frequency of female extramarital sex can be predicted to be greatest in matrilineal societies and lowest in patrilineal societies, with bilateral descent societies in between. Table 6 supports that prediction although the small number of cases makes conclusions tentative. Marital fidelity seems much more exceptional in matrilineal societies than in patrilineal ones. Only one-tenth or so of the matrilineal societies generally practice marital fidelity, compared to one-third of patrilineal societies. Conversely, rampant infidelity is the norm in only one-tenth of patrilineal societies compared to one-fourth of matrilineal ones.

Table 6. Frequency of Extramarital Sex and Rule of Descent [a]

Frequency of Female Extramarital Sex	Rule of Descent							
	Matrilineal		Bilateral or Double		Patrilineal		Total	
	N	%	N	%	N	%	N	%
Universal	2	25.0	2	7.7	2	10.0	6	11.1
Moderate	5	62.5	17	65.4	11	55.0	33	61.1
Uncommon	1	12.5	7	26.9	7	35.00	15	27.8
Total	8	100.0	26	0	20	100.0	54	100.0

[a] Source: Broude and Greene (1976).

Interestingly, the pattern for *premarital* sex for women is strikingly different. Premarital sex for women is approved or tolerated by two-thirds (66.7 percent) of the bilateral or double descent societies and by over half (57.1 percent) of the patrilineal societies but by only a third (36.4 percent) of the matrilineal ones (Table 7). Actual incidence of premarital sex for women follows attitudes. It is highest in bilateral or double descent societies, and lowest in matrilineal societies (Table 8).

Why do we find these differences and why are they seemingly in the opposite direction of the data on *extramarital* sex for women? In an exogamous patrilineal society, agnates have interest in the insemination of in-marrying wives (who are often not kin) by the husband (who is a kinsman) but they have no objection in principle to their own kinswomen being premaritally inseminated, since that too contributes to their fitness. Illegitimate children may be adopted in the mother's patrilineage, in which case the lineage gains an additional member. Alternatively, the woman may marry her lover or her child will be adopted by her future husband at no cost to the woman's agnates. In a patrilineal system, female

Table 7. Rule of Descent and Attitudes Toward Female Premarital Sex [a]

Attitude Toward Female Premarital Sex	Rule of Descent							
	Matrilineal		Bilateral or Double		Patrilineal		Total	
	N	%	N	%	N	%	N	%
Approved	4	36.4	32	66.7	20	57.1	56	59.6
Disapproved	7	63.6	16	33.3	15	42.9	38	40.4
Total	11	100.0	48	100.0	35	100.0	94	100.0

[a] Source: Broude and Greene (1976).

Table 8. Rule of Descent and Frequency of Female Premarital Sex [a]

Frequency of Female Premarital Sex	Rule of Descent							
	Matrilineal		Bilateral or Double		Patrilineal		Total	
	N	%	N	%	N	%	N	%
Frequent	5	38.5	42	77.8	22	56.4	69	71.9
Rare	8	61.5	12	22.2	17	43.6	37	28.1
Total	13	100.0	54	100.0	39	100.0	106	100.0

[a] Source: Broude and Greene (1976).

virginity at marriage only becomes consequential if its absence depreciates a woman's value in the matrimonial market. If substantial bridewealth accompanies the marriage transaction, there is typically greater stress on female virginity, since the "buying" agnates want to get their money's worth. They want to avoid getting a woman already pregnant by a man who is not an agnate. (However, they often have no objection to a pregnant bride marrying her lover—one of them—since her pregnancy proves her fertility.)

The Broude and Greene (1976) data show that, where substantial bridewealth is involved in marriage, there is a lower incidence of female premarital sexuality. Premarital intercourse for girls is rare in half (48.6 percent) of the 37 societies where substantial bridewealth changes hands at marriage, compared to only a fourth (26.9 percent) of the 67 societies where no substantial bridewealth is involved.

Turning to matrilineal societies, the fitness calculus of the males who exercise control over the behavior of their kinswomen is quite different from that of male agnates. Like them, they are interested in the reproduction of their kinswomen, but, unlike them, once a woman is married they do not care much who fathers her children; her children will in any case belong in their matrilineage. Extramarital behavior of women is thus of little consequence to males in matrilineal societies. However, insofar as a husband contributes to the fitness of their nephews more than does a lover, men are interested in their sisters being married.

In other words, matrilineally related men have an interest in parasitizing their brothers-in-law for the benefit of their uterine nephews, and thus of themselves. Obviously, in order to have brothers-in-law to exploit, their sisters must marry, the sooner the better. It will be objected that agnates too parasitize their brothers-in-law, and indeed they do, but this parasitism is much less beneficial to agnates than to matrilineal related males, since uterine nephews in patrilineal societies belong to their fathers' lineage, and are thus "lost" to the agnates' kin group.

Further substantiation for the contrasting male strategy in patrilineal and matrilineal societies is provided by the Broude and Greene (1976) data on wife-sharing and rape. Patrilineal societies are least likely to practice wife-sharing, while matrilineal societies are most likely, with bilateral and double descent societies in the middle (Table 9). As for rape, matrilineal societies are most tolerant of it—patrilineal societies least tolerant; bilateral and double descent societies are, once again, in an intermediate position (Table 10). The number of cases (39) is too small to reach definitive conclusions, but the results are in the predicted direction. Both wife-sharing and rape have the effect of reducing the probability of paternity and are thus much less problematic in matrilineal than in patrilineal societies.

Table 9. Rule of Descent and Wife-Sharing [a]

| | Rule of Descent | | | | | | | |
| | Matrilineal | | Bilateral or Double | | Patrilineal | | Total | |
Wife-Sharing	N	%	N	%	N	%	N	%
Present	7	63.6	20	39.2	13	36.1	40	40.8
Absent	4	36.4	31	60.8	23	63.9	58	59.2
Total	11	100.0	51	100.0	36	100.0	98	100.0

[a] Source: Broude and Greene (1976).

Table 10. Rule of Descent and Attitudes Toward Rape [a]

| | Rule of Descent | | | | | | | |
| Attitude Toward Rape | Matrilineal | | Bilateral or Double | | Patrilineal | | Total | |
	N	%	N	%	N	%	N	%
Accepted or ridiculed	4	57.1	6	30.0	3	25.0	13	33.3
Disapproved	3	42.9	14	70.0	9	75.0	26	66.7
Total	7	100.0	20	100.0	12	100.0	39	100.0

[a] Source: Broude and Greene (1976).

Let us now summarize the arguments on contrasting male strategies of fitness maximization in patrilineal and matrilineal societies. In both types of society, women are dominated by men who set norms in an attempt to control women's reproductive behavior for maximum male fitness. In matrilineal societies, women are controlled primarily by their real or classificatory brothers (or mother's brothers), both before and after marriage. In patrilineal societies, women are controlled primarily by their fathers or other senior agnates before marriage and by their husbands or husbands' senior agnates after marriage.

In matrilineal societies, where men invest principally in their uterine nephews, men want their sisters to marry and to reproduce, but they care relatively little about their nephews' paternity (and hence, about their sisters' marital fidelity). In patrilineal societies, where men invest mostly in their own children, they care a great deal about their wives' fidelity, but are not adverse to their sisters reproducing, maritally or premaritally. Women's extramarital sexuality is controlled, but premarital sex presents little problem since no husband is yet involved. Premarital pregnancy may even be a welcome test of a woman's fertility, especially if her lover ends up marrying her.

Also supportive of the sociobiological hypothesis is the fact that men in matrilineal societies are almost invariably expected to invest most heavily in their *nearest* matrilineal kinsmen: in their uterine nephews if they have any; otherwise, in their nearest "classificatory" nephews, such as grandnephews. There is also evidence of considerable strain in matrilineal societies where changing conditions lead men to be increasingly reluctant to invest in nephews and increasingly prone to favor their own children. It remains to be proven that those are societies in which the probability of paternity is well above the theoretical .25 threshold, but modern serological techniques make the hypothesis testable in practice.

RULES OF RESIDENCE

Closely related to rules of descent are *rules of residence*. These determine who lives with whom and therefore the composition of the localized family group. Since it is obvious that until the advent of modern means of long-distance communication and in the absence of writing, one's interactions are largely limited to people who live within walking distance of one another, propinquity is a key determinant of social relations. Indeed, the spatial dimension of behavior, in man as in other species, is regulated and ritualized. This is what ethologists call territoriality and spacing, and what Hall (1969, 1973) has suggested that we call "proxemics" for humans. Until the advent of more complex societies, the rules of residence were the principal determinant of which relatives lived close to each other and therefore were in the best position to behave cooperatively.

In practically all societies, when people marry they are expected to cohabit.[5] Since rules of exogamy and incest avoidance almost invariably prevent marriage between relatives raised in the same nuclear family, and often in the larger extended family as well, clearly either the bride or the groom has to leave. The possibilities are theoretically many, but only a few are actually practiced. Both bride and groom can leave their respective families and establish a household of their own. This is considered the ideal in most industrial societies, but is otherwise a rare arrangement. Only five percent of 858 societies in the Murdock (1967) sample take that option, which anthropologists call *neolocality*. Neolocality limits the local family group to parents and unmarried children; this is called a *nuclear* family. This is convenient in industrial societies where the location of the family is in good part determined by the breadwinner's job and where monetary employment is nearly always outside the home. It is bad enough having to move from Kansas City to Buffalo when the company promotes you, or to follow the harvest of industrial crops as an agricultural laborer; it would be unthinkable to take a whole tribe of relatives with you.

For the vast majority of preindustrial societies, however, neolocality is not a sensible solution. The nuclear family is too small and too inefficient a system of production, given their technology and environment. There are obvious economies of scale and flexibilities of adaptation that give the *extended* family definite advantages. Work and hunting parties, child care, food processing and preparation, house construction, land clearing, livestock herding and war raids are so many occasions where it pays for relatives to be near at hand for convenient mutual help. The exploitation of an environment with a preindustrial, labor-intensive technology makes the nuclear family unsuitable in most cases.

VIRILOCALITY AND UXORILOCALITY

The two most likely possibilities for establishing an extended family are for the bride to join her husband and his folks, or, conversely, for the husband to join his bride and her kinsmen. In either case, this forms family groups which include more than two generations, since children of one sex now stay put with their parents after marriage. Where the men stay put, the rule is called *virilocality* (sometimes also *patrilocality)*; when women stay put, we speak of *uxorilocality* (or *matrilocality)*.[6] Together, these two rules account for 82 percent of the 858 societies in the Murdock (1967) sample. The remaining 13 percent of societies that are not neolocal, virilocal or uxorilocal are either *bilocal* or *avunculocal*. Bilocality gives the spouses some choice of whether they want to be virilocal or uxorilocal, accounting for nine percent of the societies. (Such societies are sometimes also called *ambilocal* or *utrolocal*.) Avunculocality is a rule whereby a couple settles in proximity to the groom's mother's brother, whose daughter he typically marries. This happens in four percent of the societies in the sample. Avunculocality is really a variant of uxorilocality; bilocality is a combination of virilocality and uxorilocality. We are thus left with only two basic options for preindustrial societies: virilocality and uxorilocality.

By chance, one would expect that an approximately equal number of societies would be virilocal and uxorilocal. But human societies are not organized by chance. Indeed, over five times as many societies are virilocal as are uxorilocal [69 versus 13 percent of the societies in the Murdock (1967) sample]. In fairness, one should combine uxorilocal and avunculocal societies, so that 17 percent are either, compared to 69 percent virilocal, still a one-to-four ratio. Why is the rule of residence so heavily biased toward males? Clearly, the person who stays put has the advantage of continuing to live with relatives, whereas the one who moves finds himself or herself in the lion's den of in-laws. Why should roughly four-fifths of all societies give that advantage to men? There are two elements to the answer. The first is patriliny. Societies that stress the male line of descent, and that are organized on the basis of corporate patrilineages obviously have a strong incentive to be virilocal as well, since this is the arrangement most likely to maximize propinquity between agnates. (Agnates are patrilineally related kinsmen.) Not all patrilineal societies are virilocal, but the vast majority [96 percent of the Murdock (1967) sample] are. A handful of patrilineal societies are bilocal or neolocal; *none* are uxorilocal or avunculocal (Table 11).

The rule of descent is not the whole answer, however. Descent does not entirely determine the rule of residence, as becomes clear when one looks at matrilineal, bilateral and double descent societies. If descent were all-determining, one would expect all or nearly all matrilineal societies to be either uxorilocal or avunculocal, and, in fact, only 66 percent of them are. Bilateral descent societies should, by the same logic, be either neolocal or bilocal; yet only 29 percent are. As for double descent societies, they might be expected to be bilocal, but only four percent (one out of 27) are (Table 11).

Patrilineal versus matrilineal descent does indeed predispose a society to virilocal or uxorilocal residence respectively, since 96 percent of the patrilineal and 66 percent of the matrilineal societies conform to the expectation. However, there must be a powerful attraction to virilocality (independently of patrilineal descent) since 93 percent of the double

Table 11. Rules of Descent and of Residence [a]

Rule of Residence	Rule of Descent									
	Patrilineal		Matrilineal		Double Descent		Bilateral		Total	
	N	%	N	%	N	%	N	%	N	%
Virilocal	384	96.2	18	14.8	25	92.6	161	52.0	588	68.6
Uxorilocal	0	0.0	44	36.0	0	0.0	67	21.7	111	13.0
Avunculocal	0	0.0	36	29.5	1	3.7	0	0.0	37	4.3
Bilocal	5	1.3	14	11.5	1	3.7	53	17.2	73	8.5
Neolocal	6	1.5	6	4.9	0	0.0	28	9.1	40	4.7
Duolocal	4	1.0	4	3.3	0	0.0	0	0.0	8	0.9
Total	399	100.0	122	100.0	27	100.0	309	100.0	857	100.0
% of Grand Total	46.5		14.2		3.2		36.1		100.0	

[a] Source: Murdock (1967).

descent societies, 52 percent of the bilateral descent societies and even 15 percent of the matrilineal societies have virilocal residence. We have already seen why neolocal residence is not a viable alternative in most preindustrial societies. So, the only real alternative to virilocal residence is uxori- or avunculocal. Combining these two categories, we find that they account for only 22 percent of bilateral descent societies, four percent of the double descent societies and *none* of the patrilineal societies (Table 11).

Stated differently, 45 percent of the nonpatrilineal societies are virilocal, while only nine percent of the nonmatrilineal societies are either uxorilocal or avunculocal. Even in nonpatrilineal societies, virilocality is five times as common as uxori-avunculocality. There must be other factors that make for virilocality—besides patriliny. One such factor is polygyny. If a man has several wives and is expected to cohabit with all of them as he almost invariably is, his wives must come to his place rather than vice versa. The only convenient way to combine uxorilocal residence with polygyny is to make the polygyny sororal, e.g., to restrict men to marrying a set of sisters. Sororal polygyny is indeed found fairly frequently in uxorilocal or avunculocal societies, but unrestricted polygyny is incompatible with these rules of residence. Not surprisingly, the rule of residence which puts fewest limiting conditions on polygyny can be expected to be most common.

An additional factor favoring virilocality is that virilocal residence facilitates the control over the sexual behavior of wives by husbands and their agnates. This is indeed what takes place in patrilineal societies, but even in matrilineal societies, a husband's agnates have a reproductive interest in his not being cuckolded. Or, at least, should he be cuckolded, they would rather have him cuckolded by one of themselves rather than by a nonkinsman. Marital fidelity or cuckolding by a husbands' agnates is, of course, maximized by virilocal residence, since wives live surrounded by their husbands' agnates. A woman's kinsmen, on the other hand, have no symmetrical interest in policing her husband's fidelity. They only care that she reproduce, no matter with whom. That asymmetry in the reproductive interests of a man's kinsmen and a woman's helps account for the fact that a substantial minority (15 percent) of matrilineal societies are virilocal whereas *none* of the patrilineal societies are uxorilocal.

We have examined in the last chapter the sociobiological base for human polygyny. Rules of residence, though obviously cultural, are not divorced from underlying biological conditions. It is perfectly possible for a range of cultural alternatives to develop in response to a multiplicity of environmental conditions; but, given our biological predispositions, not all alternatives are equally likely. Some are only possible under a set of limiting conditions and are therefore less likely to occur. Uxori- and avunculocality are cases in point. So is neolocality, but largely because of ecological constraints.

The picture I have drawn of rules of residence is overly schematic. In a number of societies, especially in complex industrial societies as we shall see in Chapter 6, substantial numbers of families do not conform to the "ideal" type. Not all American families, for instance, consist of father, mother and joint offspring. Some families are "broken" by divorce, and consequently many children are raised away from one of their parents, usually from their father. Other families include other relatives, but not consistently one type of relative (e.g., the husband's parents). In addition, there are many individuals who live by themselves, or who establish households with others who are neither spouses nor children. However, the monogamous nuclear family can still be said to be the norm; even many of those who do not conform to the norm expect to do so at a later stage of their life—or wish they could establish such a family.

Simpler societies usually do not have such a wide range of family types as industrial societies, but a substantial number of them permit some variation, as in the case of bilocal societies, where a young couple may decide to join either the bride's or the groom's parents, depending on who is most prosperous and can best accommodate them. This is done, for example, in a number of Andean Indian communities that have bilateral descent and bilocal (or now, increasingly, neolocal) residence. In other societies, an elaboration of basic rules is made; one of the more common of these is a combination of uxorilocality and virilocality in temporal sequence. A groom, for example, stays with his father-in-law for a certain period of time, during which he works for him as part of the marriage arrangements; when he has fulfilled his obligations to his father-in-law, usually referred to as "bride service," he takes his bride to his relatives, establishing permanent virilocal residence.

These practices are all variations on a basic theme. What is surprising is not the range of variations, but the severe constraints on these. Considering all the theoretical alternatives, strikingly few of them are actually realized. Virilocality works best. Uxori-avunculocality is a poor second and imposes limiting conditions. Neolocality is largely a luxury made possible by (or, as many would put it, a price to be paid for) an advanced technology of production.

RULES OF MARRIAGE

Man mates much like other mammals do, but he makes much more fuss about it. He surrounds mating with sets of culturally invented rules, consciously avoids mating with certain categories of kin, and differentiates casual mating from the stable pair-bond that he institutionalizes in marriage. In all of these things, human societies elaborate culturally on the kind of mating and reproductive system for which we are biologically programmed. Most basic features of human sexual and parental behavior are not unique to our species; but the specifically human twist to it all is *consciousness*. Many other species form stable pair-bonds and rarely mate with close kin, but man is aware of behaving that way, imposing self-made rules on his behavior.

A specifically human feature of mating is that mating is a basis of *reciprocity* between *groups* of people, as distinguished from simply two individuals. In no human society is marriage simply the private business of the spouses. Relatives almost always get consciously involved as indeed one might expect them to do, since their inclusive fitness is affected by the mating of kin. This is also true of other animals, but only man organizes conscious collectivities around the biological act of mating. Advanced industrial societies may seem to be exceptions to the rule, and it is true that marriage in the most complex societies has become "reprivatized" to a degree unthinkable in simpler societies. This is another consequence of the diminishing importance in industrial societies of kinship and marriage relative to other bases of sociality. There are enough other ways in which people depend on each other, or coerce one another, that marriage can become a more private affair. Even in industrial societies, however, close relatives (parents, siblings, children) typically *do* get involved to some extent when a marriage takes place. They may not determine the outcome, and they may have to accept a marriage as a *fait accompli,* but they are seldom indifferent to it.

We have suggested before that the sexual bond between male and female was, evolutionarily, the primeval form of reciprocity. In those species where the bond lasts beyond copulation, male and female cooperate to increase the fitness of their joint offspring and, by the same token, their own fitness. In these respects, then, man is not unique. He just happens to belong to a species where the successful raising of offspring has required a long-lasting pair-bond, and he has invented rules about his pair-bond as indeed about almost every conceivable aspect of his behavior. Since the successful raising of children involves economic cooperation, a division of parental responsibilities, a sexual division of labor and a great many other forms of coordinated activities between spouses, marriage contracts typically include many things beyond sexual behavior.

So far, man simply behaves like the rule-making animal that he is, but probably not very differently from the way he would without rules. The great human invention, however, is making marriage the concern not only of the spouses, but of a wider kin group. This has long been noted by anthropologists; perhaps most eloquently developed in recent times by Lévi-Strauss (1969). In his justly famous classic, *The Elementary Structures of Kinship,* Lévi-Strauss makes the incest taboo the origin of culture itself, or, as he puts it, the great leap from nature to culture. The incest taboo, while rooted in biology, is subject to cultural rules and is therefore a connecting link between nature and culture. The incest taboo, states Lévi-Strauss, forced individuals to seek mates outside their own kin group, and therefore fostered the development of exogamous kin groups swapping sisters and daughters for wives. This, in turn, favored other forms of cooperative behavior between woman-exchanging kin groups and, therefore, the rise of larger, more complex, more solidary societies.

Once the system is established, the possibilities become limitless. The simplest such woman-swapping system is where a society consists of two exogamous lineages (called *moieties,* from the French *moitié,* meaning "half") that trade women with each other. More complexly, there can be more than two such exogamous lineages in a society. Finally, there can be "generalized exchange" no longer obligating the specific wife-receiving group to reciprocate with a woman of their own. This is easily accomplished through the institution of the bridewealth. Indeed, group A which receives a wife from group B, no longer has to return the favor directly. It may not have a marriageable woman to give away. Instead it transfers to group B a set quantity of goods which group B can then use to get a woman from any other group in the system.

INCEST TABOOS

The Lévi-Straussian formulation is not only seductively elegant in its parsimony. It is a good description of what actually happens in hundreds of societies. Where I would take issue with it is in the role it ascribes to the incest taboo. Implicit in the formulation is the notion that rules of exogamy are extensions of the incest taboo. But, as some anthropologists have noted, incest prohibitions and exogamy are two very different things, despite some empirical overlap and some *prima facie* resemblance (Fox, 1967; Shepher, 1979). An incest taboo prohibits all *sexual relations* between certain categories of *individuals* defined by relationship to ego. A rule of exogamy, on the other hand, specifies that one must *marry* outside a *group,* generally a kin group.[7]

On the face of it, exogamy seems like an outgrowth of incest taboos. Indeed, the incest taboo almost universally applies to all members of the nuclear family (except, of course, for the spouses); therefore, the nuclear family has been termed an "exogamous" group. In practice, however, exogamy rules very seldom apply explicitly to the nuclear family; much more commonly, the exogamous unit is an extended kin group much larger than the nuclear family, of which the nuclear family simply happens to be a part. Not only that, but, quite commonly, an extensive rule of exogamy that prevents marriage between even distant relatives within large lineages and clans operates simultaneously and *without any conflict* with another rule that prescribes that one marry a first cousin in another exogamous lineage. Exogamy has little to do with avoidance of incest, at least not beyond members of the nuclear family; even there, it applies to the nuclear family by accident rather than by design.

Indeed, the nuclear family is defined primarily by the pair-bond between reproducing adults. To call the nuclear family an exogamous group, or the object of an incest taboo, is an absurdity when it is the sexual relationship between its breeding adults that brings such a group into existence. It happens that siblings, parents and offspring are covered by incest prohibitions. But so are, in virtually all societies, other relatives outside the nuclear family. It is therefore not the nuclear family as a group that is the object of taboos, but certain categories of relatives in and out of the nuclear family. Conversely, a rule of exogamy is frequently accompanied by an injunction to marry a close relative. It is true that relatives within the exogamous lineage are often called by the same kin terms as a parent, offspring or sibling, and are the object of similar restrictions against sexual relations, but the same is often true of relatives outside the exogamous kin group. Furthermore, these characteristics of lineages are far from universal. Sometimes, for instance, marriage between fellow clansmen is forbidden, but sexual relations are not uncommon.

The relationship between exogamy rules and incest prohibitions is best stated in the following set of propositions:

1. The individuals affected by the two sets of rules always overlap, but almost never coincide.
2. Exogamy concerns marriage, whereas incest prohibitions apply to sexual relations, and there is no society in which marriage and sexual relations are coterminous.
3. Incest taboos are purely *proscriptive,* whereas exogamy rules typically both *pro*scribe and *pre*scribe.
4. Incest taboos define, often ambiguously, which categories of individuals related to ego are proscribed, whereas exogamy rules apply to all members of clearly defined corporate groups, regardless of relationship to ego.
5. Finally, and of most importance, incest taboos have the effect of reducing close inbreeding, while exogamy rules often prescribe that you marry a cross-cousin, thus fostering a considerable amount of inbreeding.

This all adds up to a strong case against treating exogamy as an extension of incest taboos. Incest taboos are the cultural expression of a biological predisposition not to breed with close relatives. Exogamy is a purely cultural rule of marriage applied to corporate kin groups. The *cultural* significance of incest taboos has been much exaggerated in the anthropological literature. The conventional anthropological view of incest taboos is based on a fallacious argument and on an erroneous account of the facts.

The fallacious argument runs as follows: the incest taboo cannot be biologically based because, if it were instinctive, we would not need taboos. This overlooks the fact that practically everything we do, including very basic biological functions, is covered by sets of cultural rules and takes place in a cultural context and through a cultural idiom. We are indeed a cultural animal, but this is not to say that the basis of everything we do is purely cultural. We have a proper and a taboo way of doing practically everything we would naturally do or not do anyway: eat, drink, copulate, sneeze, urinate, defecate, cough. It remains to be shown that the incest taboo, *except for its biological consequences,* is any more important than, say, the taboo against belching or eating with one's left hand. The only significance of the incest taboo may be that it reflects a biological predisposition toward some degree of outbreeding.

The erroneous account of the cross-cultural facts surrounding incest taboos is based on the assumption that, in all societies, incest taboos are absolute, unequivocal as to their application and rarely violated, and that their transgression evokes a deep shudder of horror in all but a few psychopaths, and is subject to extreme sanctions, usually death by execution or induced suicide. To be sure, one finds a number of societies that are "hung up" on incest; but then, one also finds many societies that make an inordinate fuss about many other forms of sexual behavior such as sodomy, homosexuality or having sex on religious holidays. The only cross-cultural uniformity about incest, is that in all human societies close kin who share one fourth or more of their genes very seldom mate and even more rarely have children.

The cultural taboo against incest ranges from deeply internalized horror at the mere thought of it, to faint amusement at the absurdity of it. Many cultures benignly tolerate or even encourage sexual bantering and erotic play between close relatives (e.g., between grandparent and grandchild) who do not normally mate. The thought of mating between them is so ludicrous as to be the object of joking rather than sanctimonious horror. In a number of cultures, our own included, incest (especially father—daughter incest) does occur at an unknown and fairly low, but not negligible, frequency, without evoking more than mild sanctions (Weinberg, 1963). When discovered, such cases are seldom prosecuted, and there is merely an attempt by social work agencies to break up the relationship and to procure an abortion if necessary.

Even within a society, there is often lack of consensus as to which relatives are covered by incest prohibitions, and a wide range of sentiments on how reprehensible incest is. In the United States, for instance, there are almost as many legal definitions of incest as there are state jurisdictions, not to mention different canonic law definitions in various religious denominations. Provisions are even made for obtaining bureaucratic dispensations from incest rules (as in cousin marriages in the Catholic Church). Incest with close relatives is generally disapproved, of course, but individual feelings about it vary widely, from mild distaste and the position that sex between consenting adults is strictly their own business, to profound shock and horror. This range of sentiments regarding incest, incidentally, is approximately as wide as that concerning homosexuality, sodomy, group sex and other unconventional forms of sexual behavior.

What we are left with, therefore, is the statistical conclusion that very few children (almost certainly under one percent, or even one per thousand) are the product of mating between relatives who share more than one-fourth of their genes (parents−offspring, grandparents−grandchildren, uncles−nieces, aunts−nephews and siblings−half-siblings). This is true in all human societies. Many other species, as we have seen, also have mechanisms to reduce inbreeding, such as spatial dispersal. For humans, that proximate mechanism seems to be a negative imprinting in early childhood as a consequence of intimate spatial propinquity. This is the old "familiarity-kills-sexual-attraction" thesis of Westermarck (1891). Overlaying that broad *behavioral* consistency across human societies is a wide range of cultural expressions, known as incest taboos. These taboos differ in severity of sanction, seriousness of intent and extent of application, but they all have the effect of reinforcing a presumably biologically based disinclination to mate with those people who were around us during our infancy or early childhood.

The effect of incest avoidance in humans is to lower the coefficients of inbreeding of human populations. Defined as the probability that an individual in a population receives at a given locus two genes that are identical by descent, the coefficient of inbreeding *(F)* is generally around one per thousand (.001) in most contemporary, large human populations (Bodmer and Cavalli-Sforza, 1976). However, in the smaller-population isolates, which characterized mankind until recently and which are still found in various parts of the world, coefficients of inbreeding probably often exceeded one percent (.01); contemporary groups such as the Dunkers of Pennsylvania, the Samaritans of Israel and the islanders of

Tristan da Cunha (off the coast of South Africa) have coefficients in excess of .02 (Bodmer and Cavalli-Sforza, 1976).

Inbreeding is relatively high in the many human societies that practice preferential cousin marriage. Five generations of first cousin marriages would give an F value of around .15 in such a population (Lerner, 1968). After five generations of cousin marriages, any two individuals chosen at random would share an average of 30 percent of their genes by common descent, more than half-siblings in a panmictic population. Of course, no human society is as inbred as this: even where first cousins are preferred, they are not always to be had and thus many of the matings are between second or third cousins. Furthermore, many of these preferential cross-cousin marriage societies engage in continuous warfare and steal each other's women, thus making for a continuous influx of fresh genes into the population. The Yanomamö, whom we shall study in Chapter 5, are a good example of this. We may safely conclude that even small, relatively isolated, preindustrial populations that practice preferential cousin marriage have inbreeding coefficients well below .1, and probably in the .01 to .05 range.

EXOGAMY

Exogamy is quite different from incest. Exogamy has traditionally been considered a human universal, which it is if one includes the nuclear family within its purview. This is misleading, however, as we already suggested. When we speak of exogamy, we usually mean an explicit rule applied to an explicit group. There are many societies where the nuclear family, though it can readily be discovered by the anthropologist, is not a functionally or structurally important unit, but merely a subunit of much more important lineages or clans. In those societies, exogamy explicitly applies to the larger units, not to the nuclear families, although the latter are, of course, implicitly included. Or take the United States. Is there a rule of nuclear family exogamy? Only by stretching the point, I think. There is definitely a rule prohibiting sexual relations between siblings, and between parents and offspring, and this rule implies that you do not marry them either. This, however, is an incest taboo, not a rule of exogamy.

For these reasons, I prefer to restrict the meaning of exogamy to an explicit rule prohibiting *marriage* (not necessarily sexual relations, though the latter are also often included) between members of the same *kin group*, however distantly related (not simply categories of relative who may or may not belong to your own kin group). By that definition, then, exogamy is restricted to unilineal descent societies, since only these have clearly defined, mutually exclusive kin groups beyond the nuclear family. Not all unilineal descent societies have exogamous lineages and clans, but the vast majority do. Unilineal descent may be considered a necessary but not sufficient condition for exogamy.

What, then, does exogamy accomplish? Basically, all the good things that Lévi-Strauss (1969) is talking about, for his is a theory of exogamy, not of incest. Exogamy does not extend the incest taboo, for it often operates together with a rule of preferential cross-cousin marriage that results, in fact, in a fairly high degree of *inbreeding*. Instead, exogamy extends the principle of reciprocity inherent in the male−female relationship to large unilineal descent groups. Unilineal descent, we saw, was that great cultural adaptation that made one forego some relatives in order to form with other relatives larger, better organized, more stable, permanent and powerful groups that had a competitive advantage over bilaterally organized societies. The next step in social organization was to weld together several such unilineal descent groups into yet larger, more cohesive, and more powerful societies. The solution was exogamy. Force men to exchange women with other groups, and soon kin selection operates *between* unilineal descent groups. Obviously, the more such exchanges, the more relatives one can have *outside* one's own lineage and clan.

Unilineal descent combined with exogamy thus creates larger societies that are powerfully knit together by a double web of kin selection and reciprocity. *Within* the unilineal descent group, the idiom of sociality is kin selection, but reciprocity obviously also operates. *Between* the descent groups, the idiom of sociality is that special kind of reciprocity called matrimonial exchanges, but the very frequency of such exchanges also creates a web of kinship between the lineages and clans. Kin selection triumphs again! Exogamy enables one to recoup the kin selection loss inherent in unilineal descent: it makes your in-laws kinsmen as well. This is why it makes no sense to see exogamy as an extension of incest taboos.

Let us pursue the logic of this argument. If exogamy in a system of unilineal descent is meant to foster kin relatedness *between* the woman-swapping clans, then an explicit rule that one should marry a close relative outside one's own clan would make eminently good sense. Indeed, hundreds of societies have independently hit on that idea with a rule of preferential or prescriptive cross-cousin marriage![8] In the Murdock (1957) sample of 487 societies where that information is available, nearly a third (31.4 percent) prefer or prescribe cross-cousin marriage, while only 2.5 percent permit parallel cousin marriage; 9.2 percent of the societies allow marriage with any cousin, and 56.9 percent disapprove of all cousin marriage (Table 12). Unilineal descent societies are over three times more likely to approve of cousin marriage, especially of cross-

Table 12. Preferential Cousin Marriage and Rule of Descent [a]

Cousin Marriage	Rule of Descent									
	Bilateral		Patrilineal		Matrilineal		Double		Total	
	N	%	N	%	N	%	N	%	N	%
Disapproved	120	69.4	110	50.8	33	46.5	13	48.1	277	56.9
Preferential Cross-Cousin Marriage	22	12.7	82	38.0	36	50.7	14	51.9	153	31.4
Preferential Parallel Cousin Marriage	0	0.0	12	5.6	0	0.0	0	0.0	12	2.5
Any Cousin Permitted	31	17.9	12	5.6	2	2.8	0	0.0	45	9.2
Total	173	100.0	216	100.0	71	100.0	27	100.0	487	100.0

[a] Source: Murdock (1957).

cousin marriage, than are bilateral descent societies. Whereas over two-thirds (69.4 percent) of bilateral societies disapprove of all cousin marriages, only 50.8 percent of patrilineal societies and 46.5 percent of matrilineal societies do so. For the special case of cross-cousin marriage which is especially suited to unilineal societies, we find that fully half (50.7 percent) of matrilineal societies and over a third (38.0 percent) of patrilineal societies prefer it, compared to only 12.7 percent of bilateral descent societies.

Systems of cross-cousin marriage in relatively small societies raise, of course, the coefficient of inbreeding well above the human mean for larger populations that do not encourage consanguineal unions. For instance, a population in which 50 percent of matings would be between first cousins and 50 percent between second cousins (which represents about the upper limit of human inbreeding) would have a coefficient of inbreeding of .04 after one generation. Any two individuals chosen at random in such a population could expect to share some eight percent of their genes by common descent. Clearly, the kin selection advantages of inbreeding have to be balanced against the "genetic load" of reduced fitness.[8]

ENDOGAMY

The term *endogamy* has been used equivocally to mean either an explicit rule that one must marry within a defined social group or a mere statistical tendency to do so. Endogamy in the broad sense of a mere preference for, or tendency toward, in-group marriage is nearly universal. In the narrow sense of a prescription to marry within a certain group, endogamy is exceptional. From this double usage of the term ensues much confusion in the sociological and anthropological literature.

Not only are there groups out of which one should marry; there is also typically a group within which one is expected to marry. In most cases, the endogamous group is coterminous with what anthropologists have sometimes called the "tribe," the "deme" or the "ethnic group." This group would correspond to what a biologist would call a "population." Until the advent of industrial societies, endogamous human populations were fairly small, numbering typically in the hundreds or, at most, the thousands. Most marriages took place between neighboring nomadic bands or villages, or even often *within* villages. This meant, of course, that human societies have traditionally been fairly highly inbred, whether by an explicit rule of cousin marriage or merely through the small size of the breeding population.

Often endogamy (unlike exogamy) is not an explicit rule or injunction, but merely a preference or a statistical expectation. In many societies, there is no stigma, especially for men, to marry outside the usual in-group. Many polygynous societies, for instance, quite readily take over women captured from other groups. Where an explicit rule of endogamy applies, it is usually much stronger for women than for men, because women are the reproductively scarce resource, and the women's reproductive capacity is lost to the group, should they "marry out," except in the uncommon case of uxorilocal residence. A few societies have stringent rules of endogamy for both sexes. The Hindu caste system is a notorious example. Each caste *(jati)* is a strictly endogamous group and breach of the rule of endogamy is typically punished by outcasting. Strong taboos against interracial marriages in such racist societies as South Africa and the United States are other cases in point.

In most societies, however, people *tend* to marry within a certain group, or simply prefer to do so, without there being strong taboos to forbid out-marriage. It is most probable that people who live close to each other; who share the same language and culture; and who constantly interact will also intermarry. Such in-marrying groups are what we usually mean when we talk of ethnic groups or "tribes." The whole group conceives of itself, rightly or wrongly, as having a common origin and ancestry, as being a kind of super-family. It is no accident that the idiom of kinship is often extended to ethnic groups, as when fellow ethnics refer to each other as "brothers" and "sisters." Origin myths are also frequently invoked to claim common ancestry.

Large industrial societies, or indeed even complex preindustrial societies, no longer conform to this simple blueprint where the solidary ethnic group is coterminous with the entire society. Often, these large, complex societies are internally fragmented by ethnicity. This is the case for about 90 percent of the contemporary sovereign states: nearly all of them have within their body politic more than one ethnic community that regards itself as a separate people, in the sense we have just defined. Even in the most industrialized countries, ethnic sentiments of separate peoplehood are often deeply rooted and difficult to extirpate, much as many states have tried.

Before the advent of these large multiethnic states, however, the prototypical human society was a relatively small group of a few hundred or a few thousand people who shared a body of common traditions, beliefs and symbols, who constantly interacted, and who intermarried. Often, although not always, that community was also a "peace group," that is, warfare within the group was rare, or least subject to severe restrictions to limit the damage. From the sociobiological standpoint, the endogamous group is, in fact, an inbred population held together by a mixture of reciprocity and kin selection. The smaller the group, the higher the degree of kin relatedness and the higher the level of solidarity, as sociologists have long noted.

Most human societies, then, have not sought to *maximize* outbreeding; quite the opposite, they have tended to limit it, and in so doing they have continued to make kin selection an important basis of human sociality. Only in the most complex societies that are more prominently integrated by new forms of reciprocity and coercion, does the size of the endogamous group increase, and the boundaries between groups become blurred. Even in these, however, preferential endogamy does not disappear. Human societies, then, have all sought a compromise between inbreeding and outbreeding. Nearly all have proscribed inbreeding between close relatives, typically those sharing one-fourth of their genes or more. Yet, many have encouraged marriage between people related by as much as one-eighth (e.g., first cousins).

Endogamy and exogamy are often presented as a pair of opposites. Yet, this formulation is quite misleading. It is better to see them as two sides of the same coin: as a system of mutually complementary rules and expectations that maintain a sufficient level of outbreeding to minimize the appearance of harmful recessive genes in homozygous form, and a sufficient level of inbreeding to retain solidarity through kin selection. In this fundamental respect, humans are no different from other social animals, which also balance the advantages and disadvantages of outbreeding and inbreeding. The main human achievement, however, consists in manipulating rules of marriage to that effect. Preferential endogamy sets the outer limits of the solidary system. Incest avoidance makes for a certain amount of outbreeding. As for exogamy, it does not regularly lead to outbreeding as we have already seen, for it is frequently associated with rules of preferential cross-cousin marriage. Indeed as Fox

(1967) and others have stated, exogamy can be seen as a negative rule: you must not marry within a given group. A negative rule, however, calls for a positive one, since you must be able to marry *someone*. The positive rule is endogamy: marry within a certain group. It is only a small step from a general rule of marrying anyone of the opposite sex within a group, to a more specific rule that says: you must marry a particular category of persons within that group. A rule such as preferential cross-cousin marriage is thus a specification of the general principle of endogamy, which is, in turn, a logical concomitant of a rule of exogamy.

Exogamy, combined with unilineal descent, defines solidary groups within the larger endogamous group, forcing these smaller groups to swap women. By so doing, these women-exchanging groups not only establish networks of reciprocity, but also networks of kinship. Exogamy and endogamy are the two mutually reinforcing sides of the same invention: marriage rules are made to integrate more tightly larger groups of people by means of a *double network of solidary ties based on both kin selection and reciprocity.* The Book of Genesis (34:16) puts it well: "Then will we give our daughters unto you, and we will take your daughters to us, and we will dwell with you, and we will become one people."

THE SOCIOCULTURAL EVOLUTION OF KINSHIP AND MARRIAGE

Let us recapitulate the main arguments of this chapter and put them in evolutionary perspective. The smallest hunting and gathering societies of prehistoric times could survive with a very loose kind of social organization based on bilateral descent; incest avoidance between close kin; limited polygyny; shifting band composition in response to ecological constraints and no elaborate rules of marriage. It is true that many *contemporary* hunters and gatherers (insofar as any still survive) have a far more complex and rigid social organization that no longer corresponds to this schematic picture. But, then, contemporary hunting and foraging societies are often devoluted remnants of societies that have been pushed into marginal habitats by more successful competitors. That is why contemporary hunters and gatherers are not necessarily a good model of primeval man. Yet, since behavior unfortunately does not fossilize, they are the next best thing to a model of early man. And indeed, some of the present hunters and gatherers have the kind of loose social organization just described, as we will see in Chapter 5.

The quantum jump in population density made possible through the domestication of plants and animals enabled, indeed forced, human societies to become organized on a larger scale if they were to compete successfully. This was done in two big waves of cultural inventions, both so basically simple and obvious that they were independently reinvented many times—all over the globe. The first wave of cultural inventions was unilineal descent combined with exogamy. The biological bases of kin selection and pair-bonding were used to create large solidary groups of kinsmen who exchanged women, and thereby other goods, services and favors, between them. Kin selection and reciprocity had existed long before, but their effective operation had hitherto been restricted to small, loosely organized groups in the size range of 40 to 100. Now, solidary societies of thousands could easily be created to wipe out the societies of scores of individuals. Exactly when this first explosive wave of inventions in social organization took place is difficult to ascertain. Many of the contemporary "primitive" societies studied by anthropologists, though now incorporated into larger state societies, were until recently in that "intermediate" stage of cultural evolution. Usually a date of roughly 10,000 years is given for the "Neolithic Revolution," that is, for the domestication of plants and animals, but we know that the dog had been domesticated long before that, and agriculture probably developed quite slowly and unspectacularly at first. So the beginnings of the "first wave" may have antedated the Neolithic Revolution by quite a few thousand years.

The second big wave of cultural inventions making for yet bigger and more powerful societies is, of course, that which came with the state. When surplus production could be stored, it could also be appropriated by means of coercion, and larger societies could be created in which coercion was added to kin selection and reciprocity as an important basis of sociality. The rise of the state is beyond the scope of the book, though we examine state societies later, when dealing with modern industrial societies in Chapter 5.

NOTES

1. Most of the comparative data about human societies are directly or indirectly traceable to the massive compilation undertaken by George P. Murdock and his associates and named the Human Relations Area Files—HRAF (Murdock, 1949, 1957, 1967; Murdock and White, 1969). The original sample of societies was expanded in the "World Ethnographic Sample" (Murdock, 1957) and the "Ethnographic Atlas" (Murdock, 1967), and nearly all comparative work is heavily indebted to Murdock. (This includes the present author.) The number of societies varies, depending on which generation of the sample was used by the author in question, and on the number of societies for which the particular items of information are available. The Ethnographic Atlas (1967) includes some information about 1100 societies.
2. One of the problems with the HRAF data is that industrial societies are inadequately represented. Nearly all "traditional" societies in the sample are far smaller than the modern states of which they are now a part. The world of HRAF is thus suspended in a kind of atemporal ethnographic present. Most "societies" of the HRAF sample are no

longer autonomous societies, but dependent subgroups of larger societies; conversely, the modern states that determine so much of the important boundaries between contemporary societies are not taken into account.

Another problem with the HRAF data is that the various societies have not been chosen randomly, and cannot be treated as independent of one another since they have long been in contact with each other and have freely "borrowed" cultural traits from each other. Therefore, the statistical tests of significance (such as Chi Square, Tau, and so on) that are often applied to cross-cultural data, are not appropriate. That is why I merely report differences in percentages or frequencies, without tests of significance. The smaller Standard Cross-Cultural Sample of 186 societies (Murdock and White, 1969) attempts to circumvent the problem of relatedness of cases by sampling cultures that are supposedly "independent" of each other, but the effect of cultural diffusion can only be reduced, not eliminated.

The choice of boundaries of cultures or societies is also quite problematic. Unlike organisms, societies or cultures do not have skins. Furthermore human cultures range in size from a few hundred people to hundreds of millions. In the HRAF, the smaller groups are thus overrepresented, if one considers that population size is of crucial importance (as it certainly must be in terms of adaptive success). The HRAF is a sample of *societies*, most assuredly not a sample of human *populations*.

The categories of analysis in the HRAF are also open to many questions. They certainly do not reflect the sociobiological thinking underlying this book—both an advantage and a shortcoming. It is an advantage because, whatever biases they have, they were devised independently of the hypotheses tested here, and thus are not suspect of being prosociobiological. It is a shortcoming because the existing categories often bear only an indirect and imperfect relationship to what a sociobiologist would want to know. Consequently real relationships are often weakened or hidden by "noise" in the data. When imperfect and "noisy" data *do* reveal strong associations in the expected direction, however, the presumption is that better data would yield even stronger relationships. For a detailed critique of the "Murdock style" of comparative analysis from a British anthropologist, see Barnes (1971).

When all is said, however, the HRAF still remain the most impressive and easily retrievable source of comparative data on human societies. The tool is very imperfect, and must be used critically and with much circumspection, but it is about as good as it can be, given the unsystematic nature and uneven quality of ethnographic data. The main sin in the use of HRAF data is an exaggerated faith in the validity of the statistical tests of significance to which these data are often *improperly* subjected. Taken as a rough and handy tool of preliminary hypothesis testing, and as a suggestive source of new hypotheses, HRAF is invaluable. The detailed analysis of the specially chosen case, especially the seemingly exceptional case, still remains an essential complement to the quantitative style of cross-cultural comparison, and, in this book, I make extensive use of both methods.

3. Feminists might find this formulation sexist, asking why it should not be put that women exchange men. The ethnographic facts speak against the feminist formulation, however. In all known unilineal descent societies, whether patrilineal or matrilineal, it is quite explicitly males who exchange females rather than vice versa. This is not to say that women are not often consulted; women may even, in some cases, be quite influential behind the scenes; but the official legal transactions are run by men: in patrilineal societies, the bride is given away by her father, brother, grandfather, or collectively by all of her male kinsmen; in matrilineal societies, the mother's brother, the mother's mother's brother or another *male* relative on the mother's side plays that function, either individually or collectively.

4. The clitoris may be excised, or at least nicked, usually at puberty, and girls in such societies as the Kikuyu of Kenya are not considered marriageable until the operation has been performed (with an ordinary iron knife and without the benefit of anesthesia other than squatting in a cold stream just before). Even such a "modern" leader as Jomo Kenyatta, President of Kenya, who earned a Master's degree in anthropology from the University of London, strongly defended clitoridectomy in his thesis, *Facing Mount Kenya* (1964). As for infibulation, it consists of sewing together the lips of the vagina in unmarried girls—practiced among various peoples of the Horn of Africa.

5. There are a few exceptions such as the well-known Nayar (Fox, 1967; Gough, 1959). Less than one percent (eight out of 858) of the societies in the Murdock (1967) sample institutionalize separate residence for husbands and wives, or so-called *duolocality*.

6. The terms "virilocal" and "uxorilocal" are more accurate than "patrilocal" and "matrilocal," because the practice refers not to the father or to the mother, but to the sex of the spouse who stays put. Notwithstanding their inaccuracy, the terms "patrilocal" and "matrilocal" are extensively used in the anthropological literature because of their association with "patrilineal" and "matrilineal." Here, I shall opt for the more precise usage.

7. A "cross-cousin" is either the child of a father's sister, or of a mother's brother. By contrast, a "parallel cousin" is the child of a father's brother or a mother's sister. Under a rule of unilineal descent, cross-cousins *necessarily* belong to different clans, while one-half of the parallel cousins necessarily belong to the same clan as ego. Under matrilineal descent, children of the mother's sister belong to ego's clan; under patrilineal descent, father's brother's children do. The children of either a father's sister or a mother's brother, on the other hand, can never belong to ego's descent group, whether under patriliny or matriliny. For an actual demonstration, see Fox (1967) or Pasternak (1976).

8. There is considerable controversy on *how* harmful inbreeding is in human populations (Cavalli-Sforza and Bodmer, 1971; Lerner, 1968; Shepher, 1979). Long-inbred populations may, in some cases, be quite reproductively successful. Repeated inbreeding can produce homogeneous strains peculiarly well-adapted to their environment. Inbreeding can produce fortuitously favorable genetic combinations, and repeated inbreeding will have the long-term effect of flushing deleterious recessive genes out of a population's gene pool. While inbreeding is an individually risky strategy in a hitherto outbred population, a repeatedly inbred population can produce highly viable and prolific strains, as, in fact, seems to be the case of a number of human groups such as the Mennonites (Darlington, 1960). Among the Yanomamö, Chagnon found cousin marriages to be more fertile than more outbred marriages (Chagnon and Irons, 1979). All these populations, however, are far from maximum inbreeding; practically none of their members are the offspring of parents who share more than one-fourth of their genes by common descent. There is no question that inbreeding between siblings, or between parents and offspring, carries a heavy genetic load. An analysis of American and French populations yielded an estimate that the average individual carries the equivalent of four genes that are lethal in homozygous form (Wilson, 1978). A 1972 study by Eva Seemanova of the offspring of Czechoslovak women confirms the high risk of close inbreeding. These women had, between them, 161 children born out of incestuous unions with brothers, fathers or sons, and 95 children from nonincestuous unions. Of the incestuously conceived children, 9 percent were stillborn or died before the age of one, and 40 percent suffered from serious mental or physical defects (mental retardation, dwarfism, heart deformities, and so on). By contrast, only 5 percent of nonincestuously conceived children of the same group of women died before the age of one; none suffered from serious mental retardation; and only 5 percent had apparent physical defects (Wilson, 1978).

Plates 1 and 2. The mother-infant relationship has many common features in the primate order. Above: baboon mother and infant near Cape Town, South Africa, 1989. Below: Peruvian mother and toddler in Taraco, Puno, Southern Peru, 1973. Single, spaced births, long pregnancy and lactation, and close, protracted mother-offspring bonds characterize the primate order.

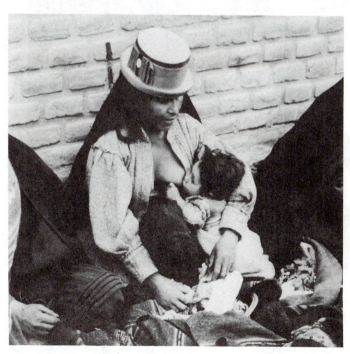

Plate 3. The African family is in transition. Here is the traditional compound of a large virilocal, extended, polygynous family in a Nupe village of West-Central Nigeria, 1968. The dense walled-in cluster of dwellings typically houses the compound head, his two or three wives, his married sons and their wives and children, and his unmarried daughters.

Plate 4. A first transition stage. Three sisters-in-law married to three brothers share a common residence in an urban shanty town (Khayelitsha) near Cape Town, South Africa, 1989. The household consists of three brothers, their mother, their three wives, and their 13 children, all 20 people sharing about 30 square meters of the corrugated iron shack. The family is still virilocal, extended, and prolific, but monogamous.

Plate 5. A small, urban, monogamous, neolocal, nuclear family of university-educated parents in Harare, Zimbabwe, 1989. They married relatively late and are likely to have no more than two or three children whom they will strive to raise to their own high standards of education.

Plate 6. Family transformations in India. An extended, virilocal, monogamous peasant family with high fertility in Tamil Nadu, India.

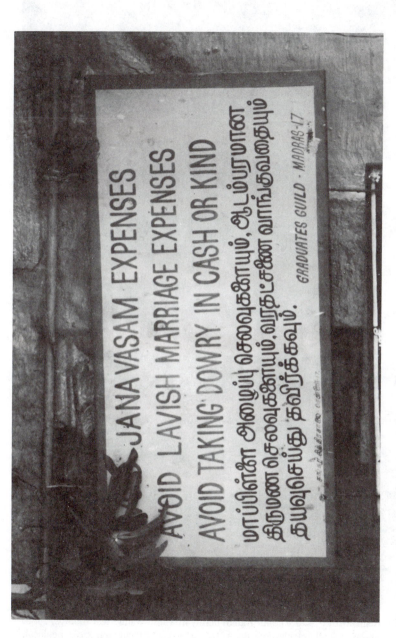

JANA VASAM EXPENSES

AVOID LAVISH MARRIAGE EXPENSES

AVOID TAKING DOWRY IN CASH OR KIND

மாப்பிள்ளா அழைப்பு செலவுக்கோயும், ஆடம்பரமான
திருமண செலவுக்கோயும்,வரதட்சணை வாங்குவதையும்
தவறுகியது தவிர்க்கவும்.

GRADUATES GUILD - MADRAS-17

Plate 7. University-educated, Westernized Indians (in this case, a "Graduates guild" in Madras) frequently advocate family planning, abolition of traditional dowries, avoidance of status-motivated expenses, and freedom of choice of marriage partners. They do not always practice what they preach, however.

Plate 8. A small-town, white collar Indian family in Tamil Nadu, near Madras, 1986. The husband is high school educated and a civil servant. The family is nuclear, neolocal, and monogamous. The parents intend to have no more children than the three daughters shown in the picture.

Plate 9. A disorganized family characteristic of many conquered people in post-slavery societies. The parents, poor agricultural workers of mixed Khoisan-European descent, near Cape Town, South Africa, are unmarried and alcoholics. Their baby died shortly after the picture was taken — 1989.

Plate 10. Another peasant family from a conquered group, Quechua-speakers from Cuzco, Southern Peru (1973), but a stable, successful one. The family is monogamous, neolocal, and nuclear, but quite prolific — seven surviving children.

Plates 11 and 12. Two contrasting lifestyles within the same society. Above, secular Jewish woman struts in obvious sexual display on the Tel Aviv beach, Israel, 1988. Below, Hasidic women and children in the hyper-orthodox quarter of Meir Shearim, Jerusalem, Israel, 1988. Characterized by extreme sexual puritanism and segregation, that culture allows little direct contact between prospective spouses before marriage. They live 45 minutes by car from the beaches of Tel Aviv, but a world apart.

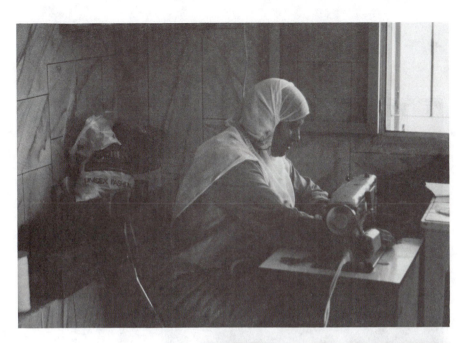

Plates 13 and 14. Gender roles, though biologically predisposed to a considerable extent, show cultural flexibility as well. Two extremes within Israel (1988): an Arab woman sewing at home and a Jewish soldier of the Israel Defense Force.

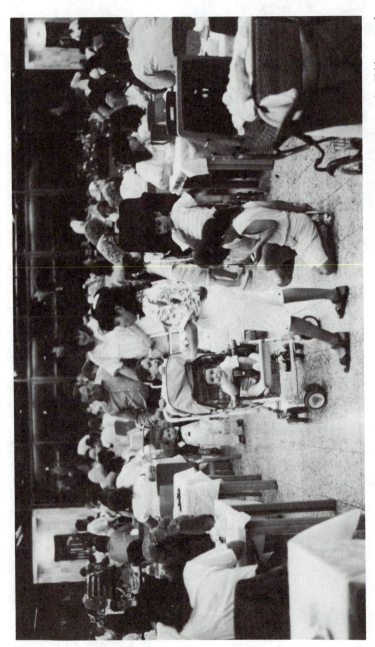

Plate 15. Two large Utopian movements tried to minimize the importance of marriage and kinship, the secular Kibbutzim of Israel, and the religious Hutterites of the Western United States and Canada. In both cases, marriage and the family reasserted themselves as thriving institutions. Above, the communal dining hall of a Galilee Kibbutz, Israel, 1988. Extended, three-generation families sit at "their" tables for dinner.

Plates 16 and 17. Above, a Hutterite family in Washington State, USA, 1987. All property is communal and seating at meals is sex- and age-segregated in the communal dining hall, but living quarters are family based. Below, a Hutterite boy takes younger children for a walk while adults attend a prayer meeting. Repeated endogamous marriages between Hutterites make for a high degree of in-breeding, and thus the community as a whole is practically an extended family.

Plate 18. The family is the focus of rites of passage in nearly all cultures, and rites of passage, in turn, revolve around biological events: birth, puberty, mating, death. A middle-class, small-town marriage in San Jerónimo, Cuzco, Peru, 1973.

Plate 19. An Ixil peasant woman buries her husband, surrounded by her children and in-laws, Nebaj, Guatemala, 1966.

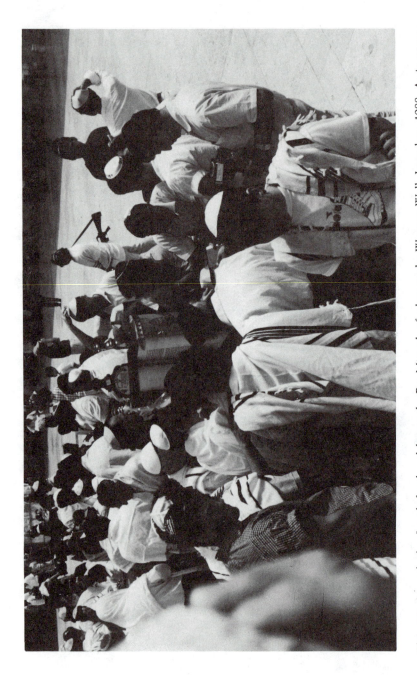

Plate 20. An orthodox Jewish family celebrates the Bar Mitzvah of a boy at the Western Wall, Jerusalem, 1988. As in many traditional family rituals, the sexes are segregated, despite the inevitable biological complementarity of both sexes in creating and maintaining the family.

PREINDUSTRIAL SOCIETIES:
San, Yonomamö, Navajo, Nupe

In the previous two chapters, I have attempted to buttress my arguments from the corpus of ethnographic literature, including the aggregated data compiled from the Human Relations Area File. In the next two chapters, I intend to narrow the empirical focus by examining more closely six societies, four preindustrial and two industrial. By analyzing how specific human groups adapt to, and modify specific environments, I hope to demonstrate that the basic structure of human societies, and especially the structure of kinship and marriage, is constrained by a number of noncultural parameters.

It is true that human family systems vary widely, and, so as not to stack the cards in favor of my argument, I have deliberately chosen widely disparate societies. My case studies are not only far apart geographically (South and West Africa, North and South America and East Asia), but they are as different as possible in terms of technology (from hunting and gathering to industrial), habitat (semidesert, savannah, tropical rain forest and temperate zone), political organization (from classless, stateless groups to giant world powers), population (from a few hundred to hundreds of millions), and, most importantly for our purposes, types of kinship and marriage organization.

Any nonrandom choice of case studies is justifiably suspect, and there is no question that I knew enough about all the societies I chose to have had good reasons for choosing them. All I can do by way of justifying my choice, therefore, is try to convince the reader that *maximum cultural diversity* and adequate information were my main criteria of selection. One of the central themes of this book is that human cultural diversity is in good part the adaptive product of the interaction of the human genotype and a multiplicity of physical, biotic and man-made environmental factors. This is especially true of the basic structural features of human social organization.

The next two chapters are, therefore, designed to illustrate how specific types of kinship and marriage organization are not the gratuitous and fortuitous products of human invention but become fully conprehensible only within the framework of evolutionary theory. Human social organization is, indeed, in good part a cultural creation, but it is an *adaptive,* not a random, creation.

Evolutionary theory is nothing new in anthropology and sociology. The early decades of both disciplines were dominated by it; only later did the social sciences partially turn away from it (Morgan, 1877; Spencer, 1874; Westermarck, 1891). The evolutionary current continued to survive throughout the history of social science thinking, however, and now experiences a distinct revival (Harris, 1975; Lenski and Lenski, 1978; Parsons, 1977; Service, 1971; Steward, 1955, 1977; White, 1959). My main bone of contention here with the mainstream of evolutionary theory in the social sciences is that human evolution, even *recent* human evolution, is not *purely* a process of *cultural* adaptation (although it is always a *partly* cultural process). Human culture is made possible by a special set of mental abilities that our species developed, enabling us to adapt faster and more successfully (at least in the short run) to environmental conditions. It remains constrained, however flexibly, by the kind of biological animal we are.

However strikingly different the societies we will examine are, they are all recognizably human. Their members behave in many ways that would be highly predictable even to complete strangers. They have hit on structural solutions to sets of environmental parameters that are astonishingly similar in their basics to the solutions independently invented by unrelated peoples in similar circumstances elsewhere. Obviously, there is a fundamental reason for these multiple evolutionary convergences on similar solutions. The reason is that we all belong to the same species. Ants and termites, however admirably altruistic, do not invent unilineal descent, lineage exogamy and cross-cousin marriage. Humans do, again and again, when placed in certain constellations of ecological and technological circumstances.

The details of human culture do indeed vary, and many of these cultural variations are but the unpredictable product of flights of human creativity. There is much in human culture that this book does not purport to explain or predict and that is, I suspect, inherently irreducible to *any* theoretical treatment, precisely because it can only be apprehended descriptively and because it constitutes *adaptively gratuitous* cultural variation. I also sympathize with humanists who clamor: *vive la différence.* Indeed, the unexplainable is often the most intrinsically fascinating. There is something to rejoice about in the fact that a Vivaldi concerto, a Van Gogh landscape, a Ming vase, a Benin bronze will never be captured in a grand evolutionary theory and must forever remain approachable only in their own terms. The basics of human social organization, however, are most emphatically *not* elusive to theoretical treatment.

The case studies that follow illustrate that, as human societies become larger, more differentiated, more technologically complex, and more politically centralized, their kinship and marriage system undergo profound adaptive changes, within the broad limits set by the human biogram. Human kinship and marriage systems evolve from the highly flexible models of hunters and gatherers, to the highly structured systems of stateless horticultural and/or pastoralist societies, to the less structured systems of agrarian societies, to the, once again, extremely flexible family institutions of industrial societies. More concretely, hunters and gatherers typically have small local kin groups of open and flexible composition, bilateral descent, alternative rules of residence and a choice of marital partner unfettered by prescriptive rules of endogamy, exogamy or cousin marriage.

Stateless horticulturalists have much more structured kin groups and marriage rules, based typically on unilineal descent groups with definite rules of residence, explicit restrictions of exogamy and, commonly, preferential or prescriptive kin marriage. A more efficient system of production makes for denser populations, allowing larger societies. Principles of kin selection and reciprocity are extended to create more solidary, cohesive groups in response to the selective pressures of intergroup competition. Within the group, male competition for females becomes more intense, too, as surplus production renders polygyny more feasible. That surplus gets invested in reproductive women, the scarce resource *par excellence* for men, and polygyny becomes more prevalent than in hunting and gathering societies.

With the rise of states, both the lineage structure and the elaborate systems of marital exchanges between unilineal kin groups are gradually eroded, as the political functions of these institutions are increasingly pre-empted by a specialized governmental structure based on coercion. Polygyny continues to exist, but it becomes increasingly restricted to the ruling classes who eagerly convert their power and wealth acquired through plunder and taxation into reproductive fitness.

In industrial societies, the family loses not only its political functions, but also many of its economic and educational functions. Not only does the state control and pre-empt more and more areas of life, but the industrial mode of production favors a small, mobile family unit. The latter is thus increasingly reduced to its simplest, nuclear, monogamous, neolocal expression. The evolution of the human family has now come full circle. Advanced industrial societies have recreated, through a long evolutionary path, much the same kind of mobile, seminomadic, nuclear, bilateral family, minimally restricted by collateral relatives, by extended kin obligations and by prescriptive marriage or exogamy rules, as existed in the simplest, smallest societies. The very fact that the contemporary industrial family shares so much with that of hunters and gatherers suggests that there is an irreducible minimum of human mating and reproductive systems without which we would not be fully human. At least attempts to eliminate the family even in that minimum form have so far proven both unsatisfying and unworkable.

Let us now attempt to retrace the crucial moments of that evolutionary journey by means of our case studies, keeping in mind that the societies we will examine are not in a time sequence—thus merely suggestive of an evolutionary process. Ideally, it would be nice if we could follow a human society for a few thousand years. Failing that, we must be satisfied with the synchronic study of different societies representing different stages of evolution. This procedure has been widely decried in the social sciences during the antievolutionist phase of the last 40 or 50 years, but the comparative method still remains one of the best sources of evidence available for the reconstruction of evolutionary sequences, and an indispensable complement to historical, archeological and paleontological data.

THE !KUNG SAN

The !Kung San are one of the subgroups of the people who used to be called "Bushmen" but who, because of the pejorative connotations of the term, are now generally called San. The San number approximately 55,000 people, scattered over vast semidesertic stretches of the Kalahari, mostly in Botswana and Namibia. Their ancestors have lived in Southern Africa for at least 11,000 years—probably much longer. Indeed, they are a much older aboriginal stock in Southern Africa than the Bantu-speaking peoples with whom they share their habitat and San once covered a much wider area than they do today. The San were gradually pushed back into more and more arid and marginal zones, first by invading Bantu groups and, since 1652, by encroaching Europeans. They probably numbered from 150,000 to 300,000 before European contact, but were systematically exterminated by the Boers from the area which is now the Republic of South Africa. They have been extensively studied during the last quarter century, especially the !Kung who remain the least acculturated of the San, and one of the few groups to be still principally hunters and gatherers (Lee and De Vore, 1968, 1976; Thomas, 1959; Marshall, 1959, 1965; Silberbauer, 1965; Silberbauer and Kuper, 1966). My own account is entirely drawn from these sources.

At the turn of the century, perhaps about 60 percent of the surviving San were still primarily hunters and gatherers; today, less than five percent can still be classified as such, and, with the Pygmies of Central Africa, they are virtually the only hunters and gatherers left on the African continent. Together with Eskimos of the Arctic, a few aboriginal Australian bands, and a handful of tiny groups in Asia and possibly in the Amazon Basin, the San constitute the scattered remnants of a mode of subsistence that once covered the planet and to which hominids adapted for millions of years. Contemporary hunters and gatherers account for perhaps one-thousandth of one percent of the world's population and they may vanish entirely within the next generation. There are, of course, many more people who continue to rely on fish and game for a crucial part of their diet but they are also agriculturalists, pastoralists or both.

Perhaps the main reason why the San have been studied as extensively as they have is that they have been seen as "living fossils," as survivors of a way of life that had been the lot of our ancestors for most of our evolutionary history. The !Kung San are prime candidates for the status of living fossils, for they are not only hunters and gatherers, but they also live in a tropical bushland environment close and similar to the presumed craddle of mankind somewhere in the Rift Valley of Eastern Africa. It must be emphasized however, that the San are *not* fossils; they are our living contemporaries who have continued to evolve for precisely as long as the New York stockbroker or the Parisian metro conductor. For many centuries, the San have been in sustained contact with pastoralists and agriculturalists with whom they have waged war, traded and interbred. Their technology has long included a sophisticated use of accurately aimed metal weapons—in no way comparable to that of early hominids.

The vast majority of the San now survive only by becoming virtual serfs of neighboring Bantu and European agriculturalists and pastoralists who have encroached on nearly all of their traditional habitat. To survive at all, the San have had to continue evolving like the rest of us. Thus, the few who did survive as hunters and gatherers are not living ancestors "stopped dead" in their evolutionary tracks, but rather successful adapters to a rapidly changing environment who made the best of a bad bargain. Now, the last hunters and gatherers face the additional problem of surviving the assaults of anthropologists and cameramen who want to record the last throes of our evolution as hunting primates. Even though the !Kung San are not fossils, they have the misfortune of being the next best thing to a living museum showcase. Hence their appearance in these pages as exemplars of the simplest type of human social organization. In speaking about them, I will use the "ethnographic present"; that is, the present tense will refer not to the currently existing situation, but to ethnographic accounts spanning the last quarter century (Lee and De Vore, 1976).

The !Kung live in the Kalahari, a semidesert and savannah straddling the Tropic of Capricorn, at an average altitude of 1100 m. Temperatures fluctuate between noon highs of 35 to 45°C in the summer (October to March) and 25°C in the winter (June and July). Occasional night frost occurs in the winter. Rainfall is restricted to the hot summer months, comes in localized storms and fluctuates widely between 200 and 600 mm a year. There are a few permanent underground rivers, but surface water is limited to widely spaced water pans, some permanent, others temporary. Vegetation ranges from small shrubs to fairly dense savannah. The San name some 500 animal and plant species, of which some 150 plant and 100 animal species are eaten. Vegetable foods are varied, fairly reliable in supply and nutritionally rich. They include some 30 species of roots and bulbs, an equal number of berries and fruits, as well as melons, nuts, leafy greens and gums, and they provide between 50 and 80 percent of the diet by weight, depending on the season. Thirteen species supply the bulk of the vegetable diet. Nearly all vegetable foods are collected by women and children.

Game, especially large game, is less predictable than plants as a food source. Fourteen species of mammals, ranging in size from hares to giraffes, supply the overwhelming bulk of San animal protein—hunted exclusively by men. People also eat other animal foods such as insects, eggs, honey, birds and reptiles, collected by men, women and children. Hunting success is inversely related to size of prey. The main weapon used against large mammals is the poisoned arrow, although the spear is used in the final kill. Prey is also sometimes scavenged from large cats. Men hunt in groups of three or four; a hunting trip may last several days. Ten to 30 km are covered in a day's hunt, and men spend an average of about three days a week hunting. Dogs, the San's only domestic animals, are used in hunting.

About 840 !Kung live in 36 separate bands, 28 of which still relying strictly on hunting and gathering. Band size in one area varies from eight to 57, for an average of 25; in another, from 16 to 61, with a mean of 34. The !Kung exploit an area of 11,000 km² (roughly the size of Connecticut) containing only nine permanent and four semipermanent sources of water. Availability of water is the main ecological limitation of the !Kung. During four or five months a year, they must camp near water pans; thus they cannot make maximum use of many parts of their habitat.

Earlier accounts of !Kung social organization presented it as having at least a mild patrilineal emphasis, although lacking named, structured patrilineages (Marshall, 1965). This was in line with the earlier anthropological view of prototypical hunting and gathering societies being made up of virilocal, territorial, exogamous bands (Steward, 1955). Some hunting and gathering societies do approximate that model, but most of them, including the San, have much more loosely structured groups, much better suited to arid, marginal habitats (Lee and De Vore, 1976). !Kung social organization clearly reflects these ecological constraints. The basic, and indeed the largest effective social unit is the band, averaging 20 to 40 people. Each band camps in a concentrated cluster of small, conical grass huts. Each hut, about 1.8 m in diameter and 1.5 m high, is home to one of the nuclear families of which the band is composed. Huts, built by women, are arranged in a roughly circular space, the center of which serves as a communal area. Each family maintains a fire for cooking and warmth outside its dwelling.

Descent is traced bilaterally. There are no lineages—rather overlapping groups of ego-centered kindreds. That is, there are no mutually exclusive groups of kinsmen that act corporately beyond the nuclear family. The band is not a localized lineage made up of kinsmen of one sex and their in-marrying spouses. Rather, it is a loose collection of bilaterally related kinsmen and spouses. Consistent with bilateral descent, the !Kung have an "Eskimo" type of kin terminology, as do Western societies: all cousins are called by the same term, as are all uncles and aunts, but cousins are differentiated from siblings, and parents from uncles and aunts. Band composition is best described as semistable, as nuclear families can and do move between bands for shorter or longer periods of time. The band is clearly not an exogamous unit. About ten percent of married couples live in the same band as *both* husband's and wife's parents.

Marriage rules are also loose. There is an incest taboo applying to all members of the nuclear family and bilaterally extended to various categories of kin and affines, but there are no clearly defined *groups* that are either prescriptively endogamous or exogamous. To be sure, most San marry other San, but San women also intermarry and interbreed extensively with their Tswana and Herero neighbors. Incest taboos and the small size of bands ensure that most people marry outside their own band, but there is no rule that they should. Physical propinquity, subject to the incest prohibitions, seems to be the main determinant of who marries whom. First marriages are arranged by the parents, often before the girl's puberty. Polygyny is permitted but uncommon. In a sample of 353 !Kung studied by Marshall (1959), 88 men were married to 97 women; nine men were bigamous—some ten percent of the married men. No man had more than two wives.

Second or later marriages are usually contracted by previously married adults and by mutual consent rather than parental arrangement. Polygyny is often sororal but is not limited to this type. Divorce can be initiated by both sexes. It is done by mutual consent or by leaving the spouse—without formality. It is more common among young spouses than later in life. Since there is no bridewealth and little property to contend over, divorce is fairly easy, although, as we will see, a husband acquires rights in his wife through extended bride service with his parents-in-law. Adultery seems fairly infrequent; biochemical blood analysis reveals that only two percent of a sample of San children studied by Henry Harpending have a genotype incompatible with that of their sociological fathers (Trivers, 1972). Widowed or divorced women are free to remarry and generally do so. Co-wives live closely together, sharing the same hut and fire, caring for each other's children (including nursing). Of course, with sororal polygyny, children of ego's co-wives are nephews and nieces, and are much more closely related to each other than regular half-siblings ($3/8$ instead of $1/4$ assuming no relationship between the parents; but as the parents themselves are often kinsmen, the real coefficient of relatedness even more closely approaches $1/2$).

Marriage, or at least first marriage with a young girl, entails for the husband the obligation to perform bride service for his parents-in-law. This service is of indefinite duration, but customarily lasts until three children are born. With prolonged lactation (three to four years) and child spacing (four to five years), this period of bride service typically lasts 12 to 15 years. The service consists mostly of hunting. After the bride service is completed, the man is free to return with his wife and children to the band of his own parents, but he does not always do so. Indeed, he may already live in the same band as both his parents and his in-laws since the band is not exogamous. In a sample of 114 married couples, 22 were virilocal, 24 uxorilocal and 15 neolocal; 12 were living with both sets of parents and 41 couples no longer had any living parents. The !Kung clearly cannot be said to have any prescriptive rule of residence, once the bride service period is completed. Thereafter, nuclear families are free to join practically any band where they can claim kin or affinal ties, a flexibility that allows for easy population adjustments to shifting resource bases.

These flexible residence rules give rise to a multiplicity of types of extended family. The same person often goes through several phases of family life: first as a young child in an uxorilocal extended family; then as an adolescent in a virilocal extended family, or perhaps in a neolocal polygynous family; then as a young spouse in an uxorilocal extended family again; and as a mature and older adult in an extended, virilocal family once more.

There is so little to inherit among the !Kung that the question of rules of inheritance is not very meaningful. Marshall (1965) speaks of a "patrilineal emphasis" in inheritance, but better and more recent evidence suggests a more bilateral pattern (Lee and De Vore, 1976). Much of the little personal property a person has is destroyed at the death of the owner. Rare and valuable objects, such as metal weapons, are preferentially passed on to the eldest son but, in his absence, to a spouse, a daughter, a sibling or some other relative. Marshall also claims that "headmanship" is passed on from father to son, but her account makes it clear that the "headman" heads practically nothing, except perhaps the decision-making in moving and relocating the camp. Again, later researchers are dubious that one can meaningfully talk of a band "headman." There seems to be no authority structure over adults outside the family, and indeed relatively little outside the *nuclear* family. The !Kung are a completely stateless and classless society.

Land, as such, is not owned, although access to valuable, scarce and spacially fixed resources on the land is collectively controlled and defended by the band. The band is clearly the main social unit of resource utilization and sharing, especially for the water pans and the valuable patches of vegetable foods in the area surrounding them. There is a raging and sterile dispute in anthropology whether hunting and gathering societies are territorial, with most cultural determinists taking the position that they are not. The dispute is sterile because territorial behavior is always the product of the interaction of genotype with environment. Different species differ in the propensity to be territorial in the way they defend or mark territory, and in the types and purposes of their territory (mating, breeding, foraging and so on). Furthermore, within the same species, different ecological conditions evoke different behavior depending on reliability, distribution, scarcity, seasonality and defensibility of resources (Emlen and Oring, 1977; Dyson-Hudson and Smith, 1978). Humans are no exception, and the !Kung, being human, also exhibit various forms of territorial defense behavior that are peculiarly well adapted to their environment and, thus, while recognizeably human, also different in some respects from the territorial behavior of human groups living in different habitats.

Like all human groups, it seems, the !Kung defend their family dwellings as "breeding territory." Each family clearly has its defended hut and the hamlet as the whole is a territory collectively defended by the band. Foraging territories are less clearly and sharply marked, but they exist nonetheless. An individual has access to land resources by virtue of his membership in a band. This usufructuary right to land resources is passed on patrilineally in about 40 percent of the cases in a sample of 151 men, and matrilineally for 27 percent of them. In the remainder of the cases, the men belonged to the band of *both* of their parents or of *neither* of them. It might be said, then, that band membership acquired by rights of bilateral kinship, marriage or simply prolonged residence entails rights to share the band's resources.

The latter include, in the first instance, preferential access to a source of water. Water pans are associated with specific bands, but there are insufficient water pans for every band to have its own. The pattern of rainfall thus dictates the pattern of settlement. During the rainy season and the beginning of the dry season, abundant and scattered sources of water favor maximum population dispersal. Late in the dry season, the population is maximally concentrated around the last permanent water pans and several bands often share one—with the consent of the "owning" band. Since rainfall is erratic and unpredictable, the best system is one where different bands grant each other a mutual right of access to whatever sources remain available. (They are not always the same ones from year to year.) So, access to all-important water resources is preferentially vested in "owning" bands but extended to a broader system of !Kung-wide reciprocity in periods of scarcity.

Patches of choice vegetable foods are often many kilometers away from water pans. It thus takes much time and energy expenditure by the women to exploit them, since the camp is generally close to the source of water, especially during the long yearly drought. Being a highly localized, predictable and valuable resource, vegetable patches are jealously guarded by the respective bands that own them. Vegetable food is fairly reliable—indeed it constitutes perhaps two-thirds of the caloric intake in the !Kung diet—but getting it is labor-intensive. Most of the repetitive drudgery of foraging is done by women for their respective immediate families. Vegetable food is not routinely shared at the band level—nor indeed are the smaller but more common catches of animal protein. Basically every woman forages for herself and her immediate family, but with a clear allocation of who can forage where, at least for the better patches. There is enough for everyone, so why compete? Getting the food is mostly a question of work, hence the concern to optimize productivity through territoriality. You do not want to walk 20 km in the hot sun, only to discover that the melon or root patch on which you counted has already been harvested by strangers. Besides, conservationist considerations also dictate a territorial strategy: a family manages more carefully a patch on which it has to rely year after year.

Big game is much less reliable. Antelopes and giraffes migrate over vast areas that greatly exceed the boundaries of band territories. Therefore, the !Kung regard their entire range as a common hunting preserve where anyone can pursue and kill game. The resource is highly valuable—but unpredictable in time and space. A system of ownership based on either territory or individual animals would thus be quite unworkable. Instead, the basic unit of ownership in hunting is the poisoned arrow with which nearly all big game is initially wounded. The owner of the first arrow to wound the animal has a preferential claim on the meat. Big kills are relatively rare, but, when made, create a temporary abundance of a quickly perishable resource for a band of 30 to 40 people. Therefore, the best strategy to supply *some* meat to everyone with some degree of regularity is to share the kills. This is precisely the !Kung solution. The meat is distributed at the band level after a big kill, but it is *unequally* distributed according to a complicated double distribution system based on shares allocated according to who owned the weapons used in the kill, who took part in the hunt, and the kin and affinal ties of the hunters.

In summary, the !Kung are a small-scale society, stateless and classless, composed of groups of size 20 to 40 on the average. The overwhelmingly important bases of their sociality are kin selection and reciprocity. The use of coercion is minimal, being almost entirely restricted to age and sex differentials within family groups and, even there, very gently exercised. The !Kung are clearly an adult and a male-dominated society, like all human societies, but neither children nor women are mistreated. Children, especially young children, are tenderly treated by adults of both sexes; disciplining is very mild. Male domination, while evident from who makes the preponderant decisions in such important matters as hunting, marriages and the location of camps, is also gently maintained. There are no real headmen who can boss others around—at least not outside the circle of extended families. There are no priests, property owners or craftsmen with any special privileges. Authority is limited to kinsmen and spouses. Differences in prestige are based largely on individual merit and performance, such as success as a hunter.

Kin selection and reciprocity operate at three main levels of sociality: (1) within the family, both nuclear and extended, (2) within the band and (3) between bands. The essential features of !Kung social organization, including their kinship system, are to a large extent predictable from basically two sets of conditions: (1) their humanity and (2) the multiplicity of environmental factors that shape their life. The !Kung have a loose, flexible form of social organization that enables them to maintain small but strongly solidary groups of kinsmen and spouses. These groups can both alter their composition in response to environmental changes and, given their level of technology, keep a human biomass close to the carrying capacity of their habitat. They achieve that delicate environmental balancing act by engaging in complex exchanges of women, services and physical resources on the basis of both kin selection and reciprocity. In so doing, they, in effect, greatly reduce the uncertainties of their existence, optimize their survival chances and maximize their inclusive fitness. Infanticide is common but is done to maintain child-spacing, thereby improving the survival chances of older children.

The main limitation of !Kung society is, of course, size. Their technology sets stringent limits on population density in their habitat, putting an upper limit of about 60 on the number of people who can live together. Because of that limitation, the !Kung, the other San and, indeed, all hunters and gatherers left in this world have been playing a losing game to much stronger human competitors. That is probably the source of their much vaunted "peaceful nature" (Thomas, 1959). Against their overwhelmingly more powerful and numerous neighbors, the price of survival is keeping a low profile. Historical evidence points to a much higher level of aggressiveness in their initial contacts with Europeans two or three centuries ago, when they regularly raided Boer cattle and were in turn hunted down by mounted Boer commandos. Their present peacefulness is thus not so much the expression of an angelic nature, as their last-ditch adaptive response on the road to extinction. They have reached their ultimate evolutionary *cul-de-sac*. Superbly adapted to hunting and gathering, they find the alternatives open to them appalling: their women can become concubines of their neighbors, and the men their serfs. Some make the transition, however painfully and reluctantly. Others would rather die or starve.

This account of !Kung society is only a bare sketch. It does not pretend to describe, much less explain, all there is to know about !Kung culture. We have not touched on their unique "click" language, on their sophisticated religious beliefs, on their magnificent jewelry, on the captivating beauty of their music. The poet would say that we have not captured their soul; it is just as well that we have not, because that is about the last thing they possess. Nevertheless, all of the essential features of their social organization are derivable from the fact that they are human animals living in a particular kind of environment to which much of their culture is an incredibly complex adaptation.

THE YANOMAMÖ

Numbering an estimated 10,000 to 15,000 people, the Yanomamö live in the jungles of the Orinoco basin in southern Venezuela and the adjacent areas of Brazil. They have been studied most extensively by Chagnon, from whose extraordinarily detailed ethnographic accounts the present pages are mostly summarized (Chagnon, 1966, 1974, 1977; Chagnon and Irons, 1979), and also by Lizot (1976, 1977). They are one of the few remaining groups in the world whose direct contacts with the Western world have been limited to a few sporadic encounters with anthropologists, missionaries and film-makers, but Western trade goods acquired from neighbors or occasional visitors, notably steel axes and machetes, are much in evidence. Although much more isolated from outside contact than the San, the Yanomamö represent a much more complex society. They live in some 125 to 150 politically independent villages ranging in size from 40 to 250 inhabitants, but with 75 to 80 people on the average. They are agriculturalists as well as hunters, fishermen and gatherers. Their kinship and marriage system is highly complex, leading to a form of social organization which, although still classless and stateless, is far more structured than among the San.

The Yanomamö live in one of the last dense tropical forest habitats left in the world—the upper confines of the Orinoco and its tributaries. They have adapted to it through a simple but effective technology which includes pottery-making; hunting with curare-poisoned arrows; weaving of vegetable fibers for ropes, baskets and hammocks; slash-and-burn agriculture and bark boats for water transport. In recent years, access to machetes and steel axes greatly facilitated the process of forest clearing, the necessary prelude for the cultivation of fields. Some 85 percent of the diet is provided by agriculture, the main food crops being principally plantain bananas and secondarily sweet bananas, manioc, xanthosoma, sweet potatoes and maize. Tobacco, cotton, arrow cane, pigments, avocados, hallucinogens, medicinal herbs and a number of other plants are also grown. Dogs are the only domestic animals, except for an occasional pet monkey or parrot. Men spend a lot of time hunting small mammals (armadillos, monkeys, rodents), a wide variety of birds, as well as more desirable bigger game, such as tapirs, anteaters, deer and wild pigs. Fish are caught by poisoning rivers. Many other species of animals, ranging from insects and their by-products (honey, grubs) to rodents and reptiles, and many wild plants are also collected. Game, however, is unpredictable, and areas close to villages are quickly depleted. The Yanomamö could not subsist without the bulky, starchy foods that are produced by agriculture.

Lizot, who studied Yanomamö groups similar to Chagnon's, estimates that over three-fourths of their diet, in both weight and calories, comes from agriculture, which occupies one third of the total time devoted to food-gathering or food-producing activities. Hunting and fishing take nearly half of the time and produce only about 15 percent of the diet's weight and caloric content, accounting for over three-fourths of the protein intake. Gathering of wild vegetable foods is the least productive activity, since it occupies nearly one-fourth of the Yanomamö's working time, bringing in less than ten percent of the total food bulk, calories and protein consumed (Lizot, 1977, p. 513).

Yanomamö live in circular or oval villages made up of an outer 3-m high palisade for protection, and a single, large, doughnut-shaped, straw-roofed lean-to. The center of it is an open space ranging from a few meters to 100 m in diameter. A large, single-slanted, thatched roof forms the vast dwelling; the high side of the roof is left open on the central plaza, while a low wall, parallel to the outer palisade, meets the low side of the roof. Family groups occupy sections of this great house. The size of these villages, their location, their foundation and their fragmentation into smaller groups are mostly a function of the complex patterns of alliances, warring and feuding—both within villages and between them. Minimum village size for military defensibility is about 40 or about 15 men of fighting age. Villages over the size 100 or 150 often fission due to disputes that frequently arise over marital infidelity. Fission is followed by resettlement of the splitting faction or factions considerable distances away. According to Chagnon (1974), Yanomamö warfare is not clearly related to population density or resource scarcity.

Like all human societies, the Yanomamö ascribe clearly different roles to men and women, and to different age groups. Boys are preferred to girls; the society is clearly male-dominated. Long before puberty, young girls begin to help their mothers in the performance of such female household tasks as infant care, food cooking, water hauling and firewood collection. Girls are given in marriage by their male kinsmen with little consideration of their wishes. Women generally do not participate directly or overtly in lineage political affairs, and are bossed by their husbands. Wives are commonly beaten, burned and wounded and occasionally even killed by irate husbands. A woman's main protection against a cruel husband is her brother but wife-beating is considered a mark of concern for her. Only older women gain a measure of respect and are immune from chronic mistreatment by husbands.

Boys are treated indulgently, but they are raised to be fierce and goaded into being aggressive. They are allowed to play and extend their adolescence much longer than girls. Men do all the hunting and much of the agricultural work, but women accompany their husbands in the fields and help with the planting and weeding. Hunting, warfare and political affairs are the male concerns *par excellence*. Men enjoy more leisure than women, often spending their afternoons talking, chanting and inhaling hallucinogenic drugs.

There is not much division of labor beyond age and sex. Every adult is capable of performing all the tasks expected of his or her sex. However, villages have headmen. The headman is the most politically astute man in the village, but his authority is diplomatically rather than peremptorily exercised, so as not to offend his quickly aroused fellow villagers. The village headman acts as a moderator in intravillage fights and shows leadership and authority in warfare and relations with outsiders, but he is clearly not a boss with clear-cut executive powers except during periods of very intensive warfare. He relies on persuation and skill to sway or influence others, successful by virtue of lineage connections and personal qualities rather than executive office. Sometimes several men contend for the headmanship in the same village and, since there is no clear political office, headmanship can only be measured by actual influence. The Yanomamö, in short, are still a clearly stateless and classless society. Nobody is allowed to order anyone who is not a wife or a junior kinsmen. There is no authority or leadership above the village level. Every village is thus a politically independent entity.

Aggressiveness is a central feature of Yanomamö society and an admired quality of males. There are graded levels of violence ranging from the chest-pounding duel to the war raid. Often fights that begin with chest-pounding escalate into contests using long wooden clubs, the flat side of machetes, the blunt side of axes and spears—all the way up to the full-scale raid. The object of a war raid is to kill one or more of the enemy by surprise and to flee without casualties. Abduction of women is a desirable side benefit and occasionally even the main intent of the raid. A captured woman is often raped by all the men in the raiding party, and then given as a wife to one of them, usually a prominent man. The ultimate form of violence is massacre by treachery, e.g., by inviting the enemy to a feast and then slaughtering him when unarmed. The first causes of hostilities between villages are sorcery, murders, sometimes food theft but most commonly club fights over women where a serious injury or death occurred. As we have seen, the less violent fights, short of killing, that frequently take place within a village are most commonly over women. These sometimes cause a village to fission, and the new villages may then start raiding each other. Once started, raiding between two villages becomes reciprocal and a long-lasting hostile relationship becomes self-perpetuating.

All this behavior only becomes comprehensible within the context of the social structure of Yanomamö society, a structure that is almost entirely defined by ties of kinship and marriage. If Yanomamö aggression and warfare are not a contest for subsistence resources brought about by ecological constraints, what is it? Why do men fight? The answer that Chagnon suggests is that they fight basically over access to women of reproductive age in order to increase their inclusive fitness. It should be noted here that, although Chagnon now interprets his data in the light of kin selection theory, he did not go into the field to support sociobiological theories. Indeed, sociobiology began to infiltrate the social sciences at least a decade after his field work in the mid 1960s. Initially, Chagnon started out armed with elegant Lévi-Straussian models of marriage by exchange—models developed in fact around South American societies quite similar to the Yanomamö. Chagnon initially suspected that actual behavior significantly deviated from these models for demographic reasons. Indeed, he quickly discovered that, while these elegant models were not a figment of Lévi-Strauss' fertile imagination, helping to make sense of much Yanomamö behavior, reality was more complex and fitted the model only very imperfectly.

Let us start with the formal schematized model of Yanomamö social organization, disregarding the complexities of actual behavior. The Yanomamö have a classical system of exogamous patrilineages with prescriptive bilateral, cross-cousin marriage. Descent is traced in the male line and residence is virilocal. A village is generally composed of two groups of patrilineally related males and their spouses. In theory, men may only marry women from patrilineages other than their own. This includes real or classificatory bilateral cross-cousins, i.e., mother's brother's daughters, father's sister's daughters and other female relatives in a structurally equivalent relationship (e.g., a father's father's sister's daughter). Cross-cousins cannot possibly belong to the same lineage as ego; thus, cross-cousin marriage is compatible with lineage exogamy.

Generally, two localized lineages or segments thereof engage in repeated exchanges of women with each other. Men, in effect, swap sisters whom they may not marry with other men who are preferably cross-cousins. These systems of exchange between two exogamous lineages give rise to a classical "dualistic" or "moiety" organization, but among the Yanomamö, the exchange system may be extended and generalized to more than two lineages.

In keeping with this type of kinship and marriage organization, the Yanomamö have an "Iroquois" type of "bifurcate merging" kin terminology. All lineage members in ego's generation call each other "brother" or "sister," that is, all parallel cousins are assimilated terminologically to siblings, while cross-cousins are called by a different term. Thus, the kin terminology stresses the unmarriageability of lineage members and the marriageability of members of other lineages. So males call their male cross-cousin "brother-in-law" and their female cross-cousin "wife," whether a marriage has taken place or not. In effect, all female cross-cousins in other lineages are potential wives and all male cross-cousins are potential brothers-in-law.

Marriages are arranged by the males of the localized patrilineage. Specific girls are given or promised to specific men, often before puberty, although cohabitation generally follows puberty. Women prefer to marry within the same village where they can rely on their brothers for protection against abusive husbands. Since villages statistically tend to be composed of two patrilineages, often subdivided into several segments paired-off through matrimonial exchanges with corresponding segments of the other lineage, many marriages take place within the village and between cross-cousins. The primary function of the patrilineage as a corporate group is the disposal of its female members in marriage and the establishment thereby of matrimonial ties with other corporate patrilineages.

Not all Yanomamö marriages conform to that ideal model of brother-sister exchange between the paired patrilineages of a village. Some marriages take place between members of the same patrilineage, i.e., violate the rule of lineage exogamy; others result from exchanges between villages and from forcible abduction in war raids. Still, the model "works" to the extent of giving Yanomamö society its basic structure. Almost two-thirds (44) of 69 marriages in two villages conformed to the prescribed model. Lineages are male-controlled corporations that swap women for mates. Lineages tend to pair off in localized village groups that form political communities made up of two intermarrying groups. The arrangement looks cozy enough. Yet, the Yanomamö constantly fight with each other, both *within* and *between* villages. Why can't they live happily ever after?

According to Chagnon, they do not compete over food or other environmental resources. Land, water and fuel are all abundant and agriculture can easily sustain the present population. The one scarce resource where men compete is women of reproductive age. Men are thus engaged in a competitive struggle to maximize their reproductive success, and they succeed quite unequally. First, there are more males than females in the population (about 115 males to 100 females in a sample of 840 from seven villages), due to a greater incidence of female infanticide (Chagnon, 1977, p. 74). (Children of both sexes are killed at birth if the mother is already nursing a child and nursing lasts at least three years, but there is a distinct preference for male children because they grow up to be warriors and hunters.) Second, polygyny is strongly desired and fairly frequent. About one-fourth of the married men have two or more wives; hence many men, especially younger men, have none. Adolescent girls are married off at puberty to older men, leaving adolescent and postadolescent males without mates of their own age. Some adolescent boys have homosexual affairs at that age.

Many men over 35 are polygynous; hence, survival to middle age will generally ensure fairly high reproductive success, but warfare makes for a high casualty rate among younger men. Consequently, many men never have children, while some, especially headmen, have many. Among the

central Yanomamö studied by Lizot (1977), 13.2 percent of the marriages were polygynous, but only 1.4 percent of married men had more
than two wives. A sample of 20 headmen studied by Chagnon had 71
wives (3.6 per head) and 172 children (a mean of 8.6) between them,
while 108 other men over 35 years of age had 258 wives (2.4 per man)
and 449 children (4.2 per man) (Chagnon and Irons, 1979). Reproductive success is clearly linked to both age and political influence. Political
influence, in turn, is a function of the size of one's lineage. A lineage, as
we have seen, is first and foremost a corporation, the main function of
which is to obtain wives for its male members in exchange for its own
women. Large lineages are thus in a position to give and to receive more
wives, not only as an absolute basis, but also relatively. Headmen invariably come from the largest lineage in a village and large lineages are often
able, through raiding or influence-wielding, to secure more than their
share of women. Thus, there is a clear advantage to maintaining large,
powerful lineages: they form more effective systems of kin selection.

   This is more easily said than done, however, because there is intense
competition for women *within* the lineage and fights between agnates
frequently erupt over women. Lineage solidarity is constantly un-
dermined by this rivalry which often leads villages to fission. Two principles are thus in conflict: the larger the localized lineage, the better the
chances of getting women, but the more intense the competition over
women, the greater the probability of a split. Larger lineages, on the
average, include more distantly related agnates than smaller ones and
violent disputes are thus more likely to arise.

   Between brothers, a measure of solidarity is maintained. Older
brothers get more than their share of wives, but they mitigate sibling
rivalry by sometimes giving younger brothers sexual access to their
wives, or even by passing on their wives to younger brothers after a few
years, when they acquire new wives. Women, in short, are carefully kept
in the family consistent with the hypothesis that people maximize inclusive fitness. Polygyny, incidentally, is often sororal, thereby increasing
solidarity between co-wives. Co-wives who are sisters contribute to each
other's fitness by sharing child-raising tasks. Between more distantly
related agnates, such as parallel cousins, kin selection is much weaker,
and fights over women frequently erupt, leading the lineage to fission.
Agnates need each other to get wives, but, once they get them, they
compete against each other for access to them. Close agnates cooperate
because kin selection operates strongly between them, but among distant
agnates, kin selection is too weak to overcome contradictory reproductive interests.

   Kin selection, of course, does not stop at the lineage. Indeed,
everyone has many close relatives who are not members of one's lineage.

Such is inevitably the case with a rule of unilineal descent. The system of prescriptive marriage with close kin, especially bilateral cross-cousins, ensures a very special type of social organization. Several generations of marriages between cross-cousins and other close kin outside one's lineage ensure not only that spouses are close kin, but also that they are frequently *closer* kin than many members of one's lineage (Chagnon and Irons, 1979).

Add to this a condition, such as the Yanomamö have, whereby two localized segments of two patrilineages living in the same village consistently pair off by swapping women in preference to matrimonial exchanges with other eligible segments of patrilineages. You then have some solidary villages that are made up of two main patrilineages, which may each be subdivided into symmetrically paired segments. We now have a classical dualistic organization so dear to French structuralist anthropology, even though, among the Yanomamö, this dualistic organization is not clearly mapped on the ground. (That is, the villages are not clearly divided into two residentially distinct segments.)

Two fundamental consequences flow from such a system: (1) Cognates within one's village (who also tend to be mates and in-laws) tend to be more closely related to ego than are agnates in other villages and even in ego's own village. (2) Within villages, subgroups of cognates linked through reciprocal exchange of women tend to be more closely related than many agnates in the same village. The larger the village and the sharper the divisions between these paired segments, the truer this becomes and the higher the probability of conflict and fission is.

To the layman, this may seem like an arcane argument, but it touches on a fundamental aspect of anthropological kinship theory, namely the sterile dispute between "descent" and "alliance" theorists (Fortes, 1953; Fox, 1967; Lévi-Strauss, 1969). Descent theorists (many of them British Africanists) argue that the *social* principle of unilineal descent and its consequent lineage organization take precedence over the system of alliances resulting from reciprocal exchanges of women between exogamous lineages. Alliance theorists (many of them French Americanists) have argued the opposite. The kin selection theory proposed here does not contradict either view; rather it suggests that *alliance and descent are the two sides of the same kin selection coin,* a conclusion also arrived at by Chagnon and, indeed, already implicit in Fortes' notion of "complementary filiation" (Chagnon and Irons, 1979; Fortes, 1959). Kin selection and reciprocity operate in both unilineal organization and matrimonial exchange systems.

Yanomamö behavior strongly supports this interpretation. If lineage solidarity were the paramount principle of social organization, then we would not expect frequent conflicts to erupt between lineage members.

Instead, we would expect the lineage to be the peace group, and conflicts to polarize along lineage lines. Logically, then, villages should be localized sections of lineages. In fact, we find that villages consist of more than one lineage; that conflicts do not polarize along descent lines; and that the lineage is not a peace group. At least for the Yanomamö, unilineal descent is thus clearly not the paramount principle of social organization.

The alliance model does seem to fit the Yanomamö data better, and this is hardly surprising since the model was largely developed around societies similar to the Yanomamö (Lévi-Strauss, 1969). Groups most likely to exchange women also tend not to go to war with each other. The alliance model, however, implies that reciprocity is the main cement of sociality. Applying a simple kin selection model appears to give a more parsimonious explanation of lines of solidarity and cleavage in Yanomamö society. Chagnon documents that closeness of biological relatedness is a better predictor of who sides with whom, who clashes with whom and where villages fission, than either lineage membership or matrimonial alliances alone.

For example, although allies generally do not clash, women can rely on the protection of brothers against abusive treatment by their husband, despite the fact that husband and brother are each other's brother-in-law. It might be objected that the men concerned are also often cross-cousins—therefore less likely to clash. Indeed they are, but not when the choice is between a sister and a cousin. Kin selection theory would predict that a man will side with his sister against his cousin, but with cousin–brother-in-law against his more distant agnates.

Village fission also illustrates the principle of kin selection. When villages split, it is not along lineage lines. An isolated lineage, forming a village by itself, would have to seek all of its women in other villages and would not be a viable reproductive unit. Instead, paired segments of two lineages separate from the rest of their respective lineages, form a new village jointly and henceforth constitute the basic unit of warfare and politics. To be sure, the density of matrimonial ties between lineage segments is a good predictor of where the cleavages might occur, so kin selection theory does not contradict the predictions of alliance theory. Instead it suggests that the predictions of alliance theory work to the extent that, in this particular instance, they overlap with kin selection principles. Lineages in which men regularly swap their sisters with cross-cousins are necessarily highly interrelated.

None of this is to deny that reciprocity is also an important cement of sociality. Reciprocity and kin selection can be, and often are, mutually reinforcing. However, in a system of prescriptive marriage between close kin, one cannot validly assume, as alliance theorists do, that the system relies mostly on reciprocity. Nor can one assume, as descent theorists tend to do, that kinsmen outside the lineage are almost inevitably of less consequence than lineage members. Chagnon's data clearly show that among the Yanomamö, as in countless other human groups, people tend to favor kin over nonkin and close kin over distant kin. This is the simplest principle with the best fit to the data.

THE NAVAJO

The Navajo, a subgroup of the Apache, speaking an Athabaskan language, are the largest indigenous ethnic group in the United States. Their reservation, on the confines of Arizona, New Mexico and Utah, covers about 59,000 km², and they number over 100,000 people. They are perhaps the most extensively studied non-Western group anywhere in the world; some anthropologists have jokingly suggested that the ratio of Navajo to social scientists studying them cannot be very far from one to one. Indeed, the two categories now overlap: there are a number of Navajo anthropologists. From the vast literature on "The People," as the Navajo call themselves, I have relied mostly on Aberle (1961b), Bellah (1952), Leighton and Kluckhohn (1947), Kluckhohn and Leighton (1946), Reichard (1928) and Witherspoon (1975).

The Navajo habitat ranges in elevation from 1200 to 3000 m above sea level, averaging 2000 m. Mean annual rainfall varies from 120 to 600 mm, making Navajo country quite dry: 55 percent is semidesert, 37 percent steppe and 8 percent humid. Rainfall is irregular in both place and time; temperatures fluctuate widely between hot summers and cold winters. Killing frosts vary considerably, making the growing season as short as 90 days or as long as 200 days.

The Navajo arrived in their present location, along with other Apache groups, perhaps 800 to 900 years ago, having been in contact with Europeans since the mid 16th century. Before their arrival in the Southwestern United States, they were hunters and gatherers, but they adopted agriculture from sedentary Pueblo Indians and livestock raising from the Spaniards. By the 18th century, their economy was based on a mixture of agriculture (maize, beans and squash being the main crops, using some rudimentary irrigation) and pastoralism (mostly of sheep, but also of goats, horses, donkeys and some cattle). Overgrazing, erosion and rapid livestock and human population increases since the late 19th century have badly overtaxed Navajo country. Currently many Navajo live off the reservation with wage labor and handicraft production (silversmithing, blanket weaving) for the tourist trade importantly supplementing the Navajo economy.

With their conquest by the United Stated Government in the 1860s, the Navajo were incarcerated between 1864 and 1868; then ruled by the colonial bureaucracy of the Bureau of Indian Affairs; adjunct, first of the United States Cavalry and later of the Department of the Interior. They now enjoy some internal autonomy under an elected Tribal Council established in 1923, but they have been subjected to many restrictions—notably on the amount of livestock allowed under a permit system. The Tribal Council is entirely a creation of the U.S. Government. Prior to their incorporation into the United States, the Navajo were a stateless society with no single central political body. The Navajo sometimes assembled in large numbers for ceremonial purposes—perhaps to organize warfare. These assemblies, which have not been held since 1800, seem to have taken place every two to four years, during the winter, lasting only a few days. There was nothing, however, resembling a central governing body for the nation as a whole.

For a people that has been changing as rapidly as have the Navajo under the impact of a multiplicity of influences, it is difficult to choose an "ethnographic present," but, following Aberle (1961), I have picked roughly 1930 as the date to describe Navajo culture. The Navajo are neither nomadic nor totally sedentary. Rather, the same family may alternate between several widely dispersed but permanent houses, called *hogans*. A hogan is an hexagonal, single-room dwelling made of logs covered by earth, and some 6 to 8 m in diameter. The settlement pattern is dispersed, each family unit living by itself. Many families, especially the ones with large sheep herds, have two or more residences, and move from one to the other to make the best use of available grazing, cropland, water and firewood. In such a marginal environment with so many niches created by differences in altitude and with so many erratic changes created by irregular and patchy rainfall, human settlement is subject to numerous ecological constraints that must permit easy relocation of small groups. Hence, the dispersed and flexible settlement pattern.

There is a clear, but not a rigid, sexual division of labor. Women keep house, cook, take care of children, gather food from the fields, weave baskets and make pottery. Men do most of the agricultural work, build houses and corrals, look after horses, cattle, wagons and leather goods, cut wood and haul water. Children of both sexes gather firewood and tend sheep flocks, as do older people. Silversmithing is done mostly by men, as is leather work. There is some artisanal specialization beyond age and sex: ceremonial practitioners and herbalists and, in addition, a number of part-time specialists fostered by the tourist trade or contact with the outside: silversmiths, blacksmiths, masons, carpenters and so on.

In the past, "slaves" or non-Navajo war captives, lived among the Navajo but they often intermarried with the Navajo and their children were free. Among the Navajo proper, there are great differences in livestock ownership and wealth between individuals and family groups, but no crystallized class differences. The Navajo are still a classless society, although much more economically differentiated than either the San or the Yanomamö. One of the important advantages of wealth for men was the acquisition of additional wives through payment of a bridewealth of as many as a dozen horses. Not all marriages involved bridewealth, and, as the Navajo are a matrilineal society, bridewealth did not confer any paternal rights—only sexual rights over the woman.

Both ownership and inheritance rules are complex, flexible and inconsistent, as a result of Western acculturation. Certain resources are held communally by all Navajo, especially water, timber and patches of salt bush (used by livestock). Farm and pasture land belong to a family for as long as it is actually used, but it cannot be sold or alienated. Animals are individually owned and earmarked (ownership of livestock begins in childhood). The produce of livestock (wool, milk, meat) is, however, shared by families. Fruit trees are owned by either individuals or family units. Strictly personal property, disposable at will, is largely limited to clothing, jewelry, saddles and ceremonial equipment. Traditionally, property was inherited matrilineally, but there is a gradual shift to bilateral inheritance and the resulting uncertainty provokes a great many disputes.

The Navajo have matrilineal descent. They are divided into 46 exogamous matriclans, ranging in size from 1 to 3600, for a mean of 750, usually named after localities. Clans are not localized, however, even though certain clans tend to be concentrated in certain areas. Most areas have members of ten to 20 clans living intermingled. Conversely, more than half of the Navajo clans live in ten or more areas. Exogamy is practiced not only with the mother's matriclan, but also with the father's matriclan. Clans are not ranked in relation to each other; they lack authoritative functions and hold no property.

Groups of two to five or six clans tend to be linked and to be thought of as distantly related. These clan groups are supposed to be exogamous, although not nearly as rigidly as one's own clan. Clan groups are not named and they tend to be of approximately equal size, being made up either of a couple of large clans or more smaller ones. Clan groups constitute units of mutual aid and hospitality that extend reciprocity beyond the confines of the clan. Broadly, one expects help principally from people who are *not* marriageable. Geographical dispersal of clans ensures that one can find hospitality and help in most areas of Navajoland.

For most purposes, the main unit of daily interaction is the "local clan element," that is, the members of a given clan living in a certain area and close relatives of these members also living nearby. These local clan elements are the largest meaningful units of collective responsibility and joint action for purposes of holding curing ceremonies, settling disputes, assuming responsibility for debts, as well as daily mutual aid. They are, in fact, loosely organized neighborhood associations of kinsmen.

It will be noted that even though the Navajo are emphatically matrilineal, bilateral kin ties are by no means insignificant. The father's matriclan is subject to the same exogamy rules as the mother's. Close kin belonging to different clans do cooperate. Some property is passed bilaterally or patrilineally. The father is an important figure in the household. According to Reichard (1928), "The children have about the same attitude toward the father as our [white American] children have—except that they do not consider him the family bank!"

The basic unit of residence is the family, living in a isolated homestead. The preferred rule of residence is uxorilocal, so that the standard extended family group is composed of a woman, her husband, her unmarried sons and her daughters with their husbands and children. Many family groups do not conform to this ideal, however. Between one-third and two-thirds of families, depending on the area, are nuclear, that is, follow neolocal residence. Of the extended families, between 60 and 80 percent are uxorilocal. A survey of 3700 families showed 53 percent nuclear families, 32 percent uxorilocal extended families, 5 percent virilocal and 10 percent mixed.

Polygny, now legally forbidden by the Tribal Council, was traditionally practiced, accounting for about ten percent of all marriages. There is a preference for sets of brothers to marry sets of sisters, but there is no evidence of preferential cross-cousin marriage in historical times. Sororal polygyny is preferred and both the sororate and the levirate are practiced. There is also a preference for stepdaughter marriage: a man may be married simultaneously to a woman and her daughter by a previous marriage.

These preferential practices create networks of intermarriages between pairs of local clan elements, but not as close as would be found under a system of cross-cousin marriage. Such loosely paired local clan elements form in effect fairly ill-defined local communities that tend to be endogamous, although not strictly so. Traditionally, these local communities may have been better defined and may have practiced cross-cousin marriage. They also constituted political groupings of perhaps 60 to 200 under a consensually chosen ritual leader. Interestingly, the leadership, though subject to community approval, tended to be passed on from father to son, *not* from mother's brothers to sister's son as might be expected in a matrilineal society. War leaders tended to be self-selected, probably from among community leaders, but until the creation of the

Tribal Council, there was no permanent Navajo state or government. The leadership pattern was, however, somewhat more structured than among the San or the Yanomamö.

Contemporary Navajo communities range in size from 50 to 1200 individuals. They are no longer clearly dualistic in social organization, and include members of several clans, from three to 28, although patterns of preferential marriage result in some pairing-off between clans. Since clans vary in size from a few to several thousand members, their representation in local communities also varies widely. Many of the larger communities are made up of two to six larger clans that collectively account for more than half of the population, and a number of smaller clans. The numerically preponderant clans in a given community almost invariably do *not* belong to the same clan group, and thus are free to intermarry. Thus all the restrictions of clan exogamy are maximally compatible with the high rate of community endogamy.

Marriage among the Navajo takes many forms, from a ceremonial one with bridewealth arranged by the parents, to an informal one. Marriages between two previously unmarried persons tend to be more formal; they are usually initiated by the groom's parents. However, when a girl enters a polygynous household where her sister is the first wife, no ceremonies take place. Bridewealth is not required for a woman's second marriage. Virginity at marriage is not considered essential for a woman, but sometimes the bridewealth is returned if the girl is not a virgin. In ceremonial marriages, the wedding party is held at the bride's home and it is the bride's kinsmen who bear the expenses thereof. Normally, the young couple is expected to establish uxorilocal residence, especially after a first marriage. There is no set amount for the bridewealth. In many cases, it is quite low, but rich families expect a higher bridewealth, so there is some tendency for richer families to intermarry. The value of the bridewealth is often cancelled by the cost of the wedding party.

As in many matrilineal societies, divorce is quite common, especially for younger adults. The main reasons for divorce are adultery of either partner, incompatibility, refusal of sexual relations, laziness or sterility. A divorce results from either partner leaving the other. The children stay with the mother; a father is not responsible for support of children after divorce. After divorce, both parties are equally free to remarry and often do so without ceremony or bridewealth payment. Paradoxically, a ceremonial first marriage allows both partners to remarry more freely after divorce. Leighton and Kluckhohn (1947, p. 83) estimate that "only about one woman out of three and one man out of four reaches old age with the same spouse."

A number of children are born out of wedlock, although illegitimacy carries a stigma and bastards are called by derogatory terms. Unmarried mothers sometimes practice abortion or infanticide, but these practices are regarded even more unfavorably than illegitimacy. Besides children born of premarital unions, a number of children are also the result of adulterous unions. Often the line between a proper marriage and a casual cohabitation is not clearly drawn. Aberle (1961b, p. 129) reports that a man who has sleeping partners in four communities may be said to have four "wives." From the looseness of marital ties, it may be concluded that the probability of paternity in Navajo society is relatively low, as we should expect in a matrilineal society. It should also be noted that men make little concerted attempt to control the sexuality of women as is generally the case in patrilineal societies.

In terms of kin terminology, the Navajo have a "bifurcate merging" Iroquois system. Parallel cousins are distinguished from cross-cousins; members of the clan from other relatives; and matrilateral from patrilateral kin. Whenever possible, affines are called by consanguineal kin terms. Navajo culture prescribes different formal relationships between individuals according to sex, age, generation and specific consanguineal or affinal relationship. Relations between affines are often tense, uneasy and, as we have seen, fragile, since they are often broken by divorce. There is a strong avoidance of contact between mother-in-law and son-in-law to express respect.

Traditionally, the mother's brother was the main authority figure in the household. He had jural authority over his sister's children; was the main disciplinarian; and passed on his property to his uterine nephews. Today, it is clear that the father shares many of these responsibilities with the mother's brother, and that the roles of mother's brother and father are, in fact, not sharply distinct. This may be partially the result of acculturation to a dominant society that has bilateral descent, but conflict and overlap between these two roles is common in many other matrilineal societies as well. The importance of the father's kinsmen is reflected among other things by the exogamy rule applied to the father's clan as well as the mother's clan. Even the father's father's clan is avoided for purposes of marriage. Bilaterality of kin ties is also expressed in joking relations between grandparents and grandchildren. Joking, including sexual bantering, is permitted with all grandparents, although it is somewhat freer and more unrestrained with paternal grandparents. A similar pattern of reciprocal and bilateral joking exists between parents and children—and between nephews and nieces, and uncles and aunts.

The Navajo are clearly a male-dominated society, although women own property, including livestock, in their own right, and have considerable economic influence and sexual freedom. In both the public and the private family spheres, however, men are politically dominant. The ultimate jural authority was traditionally vested in the mother's brother, but the husband is often the *de facto* head of household, although the marital bond is relatively fragile. The mother's brother typically resides far away from his sister and nephews, with his wife and children, and, thus, his actual day-to-day influence is thereby reduced. In the localized clan element, it is the senior male who functions as head of that localized matrilineage.

In conclusion, the Navajo have, like the San, but unlike the Yanomamö, a flexible settlement pattern in which local groups can form, reform and move in response to unpredictable changes in the distribution of environmental resources. Like both the San and the Yanomamö, they are still a stateless and classless society, although the degree of wealth and status differences, artisanal specialization and leadership crystallization is considerably greater. The main structure of Navajo society, as for the San and Yanomamö, is still constituted by the double network of kin and affinal ties, based on a mixture of kin selection and reciprocity.

Despite a clearly matrilineal organization and a preference for uxorilocality, kin selection operates bilaterally. While it may be argued that Navajo society is moving toward bilaterality as a consequence of acculturation to the larger white American society, there is plenty of evidence from other matrilineal societies that kin selection is not restricted to kinsmen belonging to one's clan or lineage. This is also true of patrilineal societies as we have seen with the Yanomamö.

The striking difference between a strongly patrilineal society like the Yanomamö and a matrilineal one like the Navajo, however, is not in the relative dominance of men and women. It is true that Navajo women are better off, relative to men, than Yanomamö women, and are economically and sexually more independent, but both societies are clearly male dominated. There are many patrilineal societies, for instance in West Africa, where the position of women is at least as good as among the Navajo. The main difference lies in the stability of marriage and the salience of affinal ties. Among the patrilineal Yanomamö, adultery occurs, but marriage is relatively stable; women are jealously kept within the control of the patrilineage; and men come to blows with each other over women, often within the patrilineage. Among the Navajo, marital ties are brittle and men make little effort to retain control over the reproductive power of women. Consequently, affinal ties are distant and ambivalent, and consaguineal ties, including lineage and clan ties, take precedence over affinal ties.

To be sure, some attempt is made to consolidate affinal ties through the sororate, levirate, sororal polygyny and stepdaughter marriage. Multiple marriage ties are often formed between two clan groups, whose members thus establish multiple consanguineal as well as affinal ties. However, extensions of rules of exogamy to the clan group, and to the father's clan, and the absence of rules of preferential cross-cousin marriage impede the systematic inbreeding characteristic of classical preferential marriage systems. Possibly, the Navajo did at one time have such a system of preferential cross-cousin marriage and a more cohesive network of affinal ties, but there is no hard evidence that this was the case.

Marriage instability, premarital and adulterous pregnancies and a high incidence of loose extramarital unions, all make for a relatively low probability of paternity—a condition common in matrilineal societies. A man cares individually whether a child is his or not, but there is no corporate group of men policing paternity and keeping women's reproductive capacity within the male group. Since the offspring are members of their mother's lineage, the matrilineage is not, as is the patrilineage, a corporation of men claiming the reproductive power of women for its own perpetuation. The matrilineage is merely a solidary group of kinsmen related through females.

Throughout this account, I have so far refrained from referring to Witherspoon (1975) who has written the most recent and extensive monograph on Navajo kinship and marriage. His monograph is particularly interesting for my purposes because Witherspoon's central thesis is that kinship and marriage have everything to do with culture and nothing to do with biology. He approvingly quotes Schneider (1965) and attacks Fortes (1959) and Firth (1936) for daring to suggest that human social organization reflects in some respects the biological facts of copulation, parturition and nurturance. He explicitly states the antithesis of sociobiology (1975, p. 13):

> There is, however, no necessary relationship between reproduction and solidarity. Not only the actual processes but the nature as well of reproduction are culturally explained. . . . If the reproductive processes in a given culture have any meaning in terms of human solidarity, it is because the reproductive processes in that culture have been imbued by the culture with meaning related to human solidarity. In such a case the reproductive processes would serve as symbols of kinship. If a culture did not imbue any of the reproductive processes with meaning in terms of solidarity, then such a culture would have no kinship system.

Witherspoon's entire monograph is a remarkable demonstration of the absurdity of his thesis, for two facts become strikingly obvious upon reading it: (1) that the Navajo *cultural* view of kinship and marriage shows constant awareness of biology, and (?) that any attempts by Witherspoon to twist Navajo ethnography to support his thesis leads him to contradict most other authors, or, even worse, to subject the flimsiest of evidence to the most far-fetched interpretation and the most convoluted reasoning. Being a competent and honest ethnographer, however, he gives a mass of evidence to show that the Navajo are, in fact, pretty good amateur sociobiologists.

Witherspoon sets out to "prove," *inter alia,* that the father–child relationship among the Navajo is at least as much one of affinity as of consanguinity (1975, pp. 29–36, 45–46). To buttress this argument, he lamely asserts that, "Some Navajo say it is good to marry into one's father's clan" (p. 31), which flatly contradicts the overwhelming bulk of the reported facts. Marriages into the father's clan are not only extremely rare, but they are regarded as only slightly less incestuous than marriage into one's own matriclan. Indeed, there is even a strong tendency to avoid the matriclan of both *grandfathers,* showing considerable bilaterality in the Navajo conception of kinship, as Witherspoon is forced to admit (pp. 43–44, 121).

The best refutation of Witherspoon's thesis is contained in his own account of the way the Navajo view kinship and marriage:

> . . . kinsmen are those who sustain each other's life by helping one another, protecting one another, and by the group sharing of food and other items of subsistence. When this kind of solidarity exists kinship exists; when it does not exist, there is no kinship. . . . (p. 22)

> Through their distinctiveness, males and females are related to each other as complementary equals. Specifically, this means relations of exchange and reciprocity. In Navajo society a woman bestows sexual favors on a man in exchange for something of economic value. (p. 24)

> In Navajo culture, kinship is distinct from, but juxtaposed to, affinity. Kinship solidarity is framed and focused in the concepts of sharing and giving. Nonkinship solidarity is framed in systems of exchange and reciprocity. One of the major forms of nonkinship solidarity is that of marriage and affinal relations derived from marriage. Whereas kinsmen must not copulate, the primary symbol of affinal solidarity is found in sexual intercourse. (p. 23)

> . . . the primary bond of kinship in Navajo culture exists between mother and child. The primary affinal bond exists between husband and wife. Other kinship and affinal ties are secondary or more distant because they are linked by one or more intermediary persons or categories. (p. 27)

> There are many ethnographic data which suggest a relation of filiation between father and child in Navajo culture and society. (p. 32)

> Navajo culture also defines a child as a descendant of its father. (p. 42)

> Children are considered to be descendants of their father's clan. . . . A Navajo also considers all those of his maternal grandfather's matrilineal clan to be his maternal grandfathers. . . . Likewise a Navajo considers all those of his paternal grandfather's matrilineal clan to be his paternal grandfathers. (p. 44)

> In summary, we can say that the Navajo descent system is bilateral, formulating unilineal, inclusive categories on the mother's side and non-lineal exclusive categories on the father's side. (p. 48)

All this boils down to a formulation of Navajo kinship and marriage that is much more compatible with a sociobiological formulation than with Witherspoon's cultural determinist position. Navajo culture explicitly defines kinship in terms of biological relatedness and links biological relatedness with the expectation of altruistic behavior. It stresses the mother—child bond as primary and correspondingly deemphasizes (but does not ignore) the more uncertain father—child bond. Marriage is explicitly defined by mating and affinal ties are based on reciprocity and exchange. In short, Navajo culture, like countless other human cultures, openly recognizes the biological bases of mating and reproduction; a-vowedly organizes the native model of Navajo society around these biological facts; and unequivocally states that kin selection and reciprocal ties of affinity are the main cement of sociality. Witherspoon's competing explanation of Navajo culture is to explain culture in terms of itself, which is no explanation at all.

THE NUPE

With the Nupe of Nigeria, we clearly leave the realm of "simple" or so-called "primitive" societies and we enter that of complex preindustrial societies. To be sure, the British anthropologist, S. F. Nadel, did indulge in a bit of hyperbole in titling his classic study of the Nupe, *A Black Byzantium* (1942); Bida, the Nupe capital, "stands" to Constantinople as, say, Luxembourg does to Paris. All the same, the Nupe are a highly complex, stratified society, with a large degree of craft specialization and several centuries of political centralization in a highly hierarchical feudal state.

The most extensive study of the Nupe was conducted by Nadel (1940, 1942, 1954) in the 1930s, and since the present account is based largely on his, supplemented by Forde (1955) and Temple (1922), the ethnographic present refers to that time. Numbering 326,000, according to the 1931 census, the Nupe live at the confluence of the Niger and Kaduna rivers, in west-central Nigeria—north of the Yoruba and south of the Hausa. They occupy a flat, low-land tropical savannah, ranging in altitude from 50 to 250 m above sea level. An abundant rainfall of some 1600 mm a year falls mostly from June to September. The rest of the year is much drier. The vegetation is intermediate in density between the lush tropical rain forest to the south and the sparser savannah to the north. A network of rivers criss-cross Nupe country, flooding some of it during the rainy season and providing natural irrigation. Daytime temperatures fluctuate mostly between 30 and 35°C, and humidity between 60 and 90 percent. A wide range of endemic diseases includes sleeping sickness, bilharzia, malaria, dysentery, yaws and venereal diseases.

Soil is relatively fertile, and a complex agricultural technology allows population densities as high as 120 to 150 inhabitants per km² in some districts, but more commonly in the 30 to 100 range. Agriculture is regulated by a lunar calendar; makes use of natural flooding for irrigation; follows a complex system of manuring, fallow and crop rotation; and relies on a multiplicity of crops. Millet, sorghum, yam and rice are the main staples, but peanuts, cotton, cassava, maize, sweet potatoes, okra, melon, red pepper, sugar cane, beans and mangoes are also cultivated. The hoe is the main implement; the absence of the plow and draft animals makes the Nupe tropical horiculturalists rather than an advanced agrarian society, even though their social organization is more characteristic of the latter.

The Nupe keep a variety of domestic animals, but livestock ownership does not play a major role in the economy or diet. Cattle and horse breeding is limited by sleeping sickness. Poultry is ubiquitous, and sheep and goats are kept, but not pigs. Donkeys are used as beasts of burden and the few horses are largely prestige symbols for the aristocracy. Large game has been virtually wiped out and hunting is more a sport than an economic activity, but fishing is fairly important in some districts.

The sexual division of labor is rigid. Women take no significant part in any primary productive activity, such as hunting, fishing or agriculture. The main female tasks are child-raising, housekeeping and the preparation and serving of food. An important female role that gives the women access to cash and a large measure of financial independence, however, is retail trade. It is the woman who is responsible for the sale of surplus food and, consequently, Nupe markets, as indeed markets in much of West Africa, are dominated by female traders. The men do all the agriculture work, hunting and fishing.

Beyond the division of labor by sex, the Nupe have a wide range of specialized crafts—many organized in guilds. Most of these specialized artisans are found in the towns. They include blacksmiths, brass- and silversmiths, carpenters, builders, butchers, tailors, leather workers, various kinds of weavers (cloth, hat, mats, baskets), dyers and glass-workers. Most of these crafts are engaged in by men, but women do some types of weaving, some dyeing and pottery. In addition to skilled craftsmen producing goods, there are many people engaged in service occupations: barbers, doctors, scholars, court historians, judges, musicians, teachers, religious leaders, diviners, merchants of various kinds and semiprofessional prostitutes who often are kola-nut sellers as well. A complex system of government also makes for scores of specialized political offices, to many of which titles of nobility are attached.

Nupe government, to which Nadel devotes much of his attention, resembles in many ways that of other Islamized societies of West Africa and, indeed, bears many similarities with medieval Europe. Nupe tradition puts the origin of the kingdom in the mid 15th century and the penetration of Islam with the conversion of the king around 1770. Half a century after the Nupe royal family became Muslim, it was conquered by the Fulani, who established a new dynasty whose descendants became vassals of the Emir of Gwandu. The Nupe kingdom thus lost part of its sovereignty and became incorporated into the vast feudal empire established by the great Fulani conqueror, Usman dan Fodio. Such it remained until the whole of Northern Nigeria was, in turn, conquered by the British, who, in the first years of the 20th century, reduced the Nupe, along with their Fulani overlords, to the status of a colonial people.

The British did, however, install a system of "indirect rule," whereby the Islamic faith was left undisturbed and the ruling Muslim aristocracy was kept in place, although, of course, stripped of ultimate power. The political system to be described is that which was established since the Fulani conquest and kept in place by the British colonial administration. In 1960, Nigeria became independent from Britain and these traditional institutions of precolonial kingdoms, while not totally abolished, are now empty shells. We will, however, describe the system as Nadel found it in the 1930s.

The capital of the kingdom is Bida, a town of some 25,000—the largest in Nupe country. Its population consists mostly of titled noblemen (who are also political office holders), their kinsmen, retainers, clients and servants, as well as traders, teachers, prostitutes, soldiers and craftsmen and their families. From Bida, the rest of the emirate is ruled; taxes are collected; justice administered; and so on. The countryside, inhabited overwhelmingly by peasants, is divided into districts administered by vassals of the king called *Etsu* by the Nupe, or Emir, according to his Muslim title.

There is no need to go into the details about this extremely complex feudal system based on a multiplicity of patron–client ties between higher-ranking and lower-ranking noblemen—and between noblemen, commoners and slaves. Such a tie between vassal and suzerain or between patron and client is based upon a personal relationship of loyalty, obedience and service on the part of the social inferior, and of protection and favor on the part of the social superior. Chains of clientage relations operate on all levels of Nupe society from the highest to the lowest, perhaps going through half-a-dozen or more persons. A high-ranking nobleman who is a vassal of the king, is the patron of lesser noblemen who, in turn, have commoners and slaves as their clients and retainers.

Some of these positions of power are territorially defined fiefs, while others are functionally specific offices (such as Chief Justice or head of the King's bodyguard); some of the holders of these positions are appointed by the king; others are hereditary or semihereditary. At the bottom of this political hierarchy are village communities taxed by their feudal overlords, although enjoying some measure of autonomy under a local chief (sometimes hereditary, sometimes appointed) assisted and advised by a council of elders.

Naturally, such a complex pyramid of patron–client ties rests on far-reaching inequalities of power, wealth and status. In fact, nearly all political relations are defined as unequal. The inequality that pervades Nupe society (and, indeed, any politically centralized society) is reflected not only in the individual relations of patron to client, but also territorially. There is a clear distinction between the capital city and local peasant villages. Bida, the capital, is a bustling center of commerce, government, education and official Muslim religion, characterized by a cosmopolitan life-style offering a range of luxury goods and services that are not available elsewhere. Prostitution and professional music and dancing, for instance, are largely limited to Bida. Most of the aristocrats live there—the principal consumers of jewelry, brass- and silverware, leather goods, fine embroidered clothes and other luxury items produced by specialized craftsmen in the capital.

By contrast, the local village is a much poorer, less differentiated society where practically everyone is a peasant, except an occasional blacksmith and priest. The town–country contrast is not simply one of wealth; it is also one of life-style, culture or subculture. The culture of the aristocracy at Bida is much more Islamized than in the countryside where the pre-Islamic substratum of Nupe culture remains much more unchanged. This, as we will see presently, is reflected in kinship organization and marriage.

Inequalities inherent in the political system are also mirrored in a complex class stratification reminiscent of the "estates" of medieval Europe. At the apex is the royal clan, made up of three Fulani patrilineages, descended from the Fulani conqueror. The head of each of these three royal patrilineages takes his turn as king at the death of his predecessor (kingship is never inherited from father to son). Although the Fulani royal clan intermarried extensively with the Nupe, adopting Nupe language and culture, it still considers itself distinct from the rest of the population. Below the Fulani royal nobility are various classes of Nupe noblemen—some hereditary, others commoners or even slaves or descendants of slaves elevated to aristocratic status by royal favor. The nobility are entitled to wear a blue turban and a sword and must be addressed deferentially by their social inferiors.

Ranking lower than the nobility is what might be called the urban, professional, petty bourgeois class, made up of untitled commoners living in the capital, characterized by above average wealth and education. This class includes Muslim teachers and religious leaders, merchants, craftsmen and people in "modern" occupations, such as clerks in the British colonial administration. The largest group in the Nupe population are, of course, the run-of-the-mill peasants who form the broad basis of the social pyramid.

Slavery, before it was officially abolished by the British, was common. Slaves were either captured or bought and they were the property of their master who had absolute power over them. Female slaves often became a wife or concubine of their owner, bearing free children. Favorite male slaves of leading noblemen could rise to important political or military positions; indeed, certain titles in the lesser nobility are still reserved for slaves or descendants of slaves. While slavery is now officially abolished, patron–client ties are not, and slave ancestry still carries the burden of low social status.

So far, I have drawn a sketch of the Nupe that, although very brief, probably gives the reader a fairly good picture of what kind of society they represent. The interesting thing is that I have done so without any reference to either kinship or marriage, except for a brief mention that the royal family was patrilineal. If the reader goes back to my account of the San, Yanomamö and Navajo, he will find that he can gain no such overall picture of the structure of these simpler societies *without* reference to kinship and marriage. With the Nupe, clearly, we have a very different level of social organization. Sociality is no longer based overwhelmingly on kin selection and reciprocity, although these two forces continue to operate. In addition, we now have a *coercively* organized society, the structure of which is not comprehensible without extensive reference to *political relations* between superior and inferior.

Indeed, such is the thrust of Nadel's monograph, *A Black Byzantium* (1942). Of 420 pages of fine print, only five pages are devoted to kinship and a dozen of scattered references to marriage. Nadel (1942, p. 33) concludes his short kinship chapter: "Let me say in conclusion that kinship structure in Nupe is not that dominant, all-enveloping structure which we know from many primitive societies. Although it bears upon religious life, education, and the organization of production, it is greatly overshadowed as a determinant of social behavior by the factors of political organization and, in economic life, by economic interests proper. Indeed only because of its lesser significance in social life could we omit the detailed description of Nupe kinship from the sociological analysis with which this book is concerned."

Since this book is about the family, however, let us try to retrieve from Nadel's sketchy account the basics of the Nupe system of kinship and marriage. The Nupe are clearly a patrilineal, virilocal society at all class levels. The basic residential unit is the extended, polygynous, virilocal family, made up of a man, his wife or wives, his unmarried daughters, his sons with their wives and children and possibly his younger brothers with their wives and children. Such an extended kin group lives inside a walled compound, internally subdivided into smaller units. The head of the extended family lives in a house by himself; so does each of his wives with their young children. Each wife comes to visit him in rotation at night. Another section of the family compound houses the unmarried sons, a third the unmarried daughters, and one or more others yet younger brothers or married sons of the head with their wives and children. These localized segments of patrilineages form groups of about eight to 60 people covering three or four generations, living in three or four to a dozen or more round mud-walled straw-roofed, single-room houses, some 6 to 8 m in diameter.

The Nupe call such a localized kin group *emi* or "house," or sometimes *katamba,* after the name of the entrance hall to the compound. The physical size of these virilocal compounds varies according to location and social status. In rural villages where space is less valuable, the compounds tend to be larger than in Bida, and persons of wealth and rank have bigger compounds than peasants because they have more wives, children and retainers. Households of high-ranking noblemen of the royal family occupy entire wards of Bida and contain hundreds of people. The localization of patrilineages extends beyond the *emi* to the *efu,* which are village wards made up of adjacent and related *emi.* Lack of space in Bida makes for greater dispersion of patrilineages than in the rural areas, with the exception of the large households of prominent aristocrats.

At the level of the local community, several lineages typically share a given village, although some villages are associated with a single founding ancestor. This mythical kinship exercises little if any influence on concrete kinship claims and obligations—or on the political structure. It merely identifies the village with its founder in a loose way. Nupe villages are compact assemblages of walled family compounds, typically numbering several hundred people. Some of the larger district towns exceed a thousand in population. Residence is, of course, completely sedentary.

Lines of authority in the patrilineage are clearly determined by seniority, being passed from father to son, and from older brother to younger brother until the entire generation of male siblings is exhausted. Most rights and obligations are passed on patrilineally (such as support in old age or help in gathering bridewealth) and so is inheritance of land, the most important form of property in this fully agricultural society. However, other relatives are by no means ignored. The mother plays an important role as a source of help. For example, women pass on their personal property to their daughters, and men to their sons. Moreover, material help from the mother and her patrilineal kinsmen is regarded as the ultimate safeguard in case patrilineal support proves inadequate. This is especially important because successful woman traders are often economically better off than their husbands and can confer many advantages on their children (as distinguished, for example, from the children of co-wives). As in all unilineal descent societies, we see that kin selection operates bilaterally, despite a clear patrilineal emphasis in the transmission of authority and land property. The bilateral extension of kin selection is confirmed by Forde (1955) who writes: "The Nupe term *dengi* connotes kinship in the widest sense to include all recognized cognates, but the effective *dengi* of an individual consists mainly of his agnates. . . . Maternal kin ties, on the other hand, are rarely traced or effective beyond one or two generations. . . . At the same time kin ties traced through the mother may afford opportunities for advancement."

Kin terminology is bifurcate merging of the Iroquois type. All members of ego's generation in the lineage group are called "brother" or "sister"; all members of ego's children's generation "son" or "daughter"; all members of ego's parents' generation "father" or "mother." There is a further seniority distinction made within generation (between senior and junior brother, between father and "little father," and so on). This reflects succession of authority by descending order of seniority of siblings.

Kinship plays a key role in the organization of labor, both in farming and in crafts. A clear distinction is made between individual work, the proceeds of which are strictly personal, and collective family work. Even fields and granaries are categorized as either personal or familial. Every male, from the age of 8 or 10, is allocated some personal land, which is worked after the collective work is done. Collective work is done in parties made up of men living together in a section of a family compound, typically two to four men, although in the past these work parties seem to have been much larger, perhaps ten to 15. The typical work group consists of brothers or half-brothers under the leadership of a father, father's brother or older brother. The family head supervises the work but does not take part directly, so that the leader of the work party is generally the agnate next in seniority.

All produce of collective work is given to the family head who acts as manager of the family enterprise; feeds, clothes and houses his junior kinsmen; pays the taxes; provides their bridewealth; and allocates resources according to his perception of their needs. Of course, these localized patrilineages fission, as they cannot grow indefinitely. Traditionally, a man could leave the compound of his father or senior brother after he had more than two wives and several children, typically in middle age. Nadel notes, however, that extended families show an increasing tendency to break up at the death of the head. That is, brothers are less likely to remain together after the death of their father than was the case in the past, and work groups are becoming smaller, although still much bigger than they would be with a nuclear family system.

Despite the clear patrilineal character of Nupe society, the patrilineages lack generational depth. Their efficacy as cooperating groups of kinsmen is largely limited to the members of extended families who actually live close to one another. There are no clans, nor even corporate patrilineages beyond these localized segments. The only exception is in the royal family where genealogical consciousness is greater and where the three related lineages that alternate in the kingship may be said to constitute together a royal clan organized for political action, namely, for the exercise of coercion over the rest of the society. The other lineages are not only generationally shallow in terms of effective solidarity (going back only three or four generations), but they are not organized for political action.

For those familiar with classical African segmentary lineage systems in stateless societies like the Nuer, for instance, the contrast is striking. In these stateless societies, the solidary lineage structure is frequently activated for kinsmen whose common ancestry goes as far back as eight, ten or even 12 generations. Indeed, that lineage structure, if we are to believe anthropologists, like Evans-Pritchard (1940) and other "descent" theorists, is practically synonymous with the political organization and charter of these societies.

Very possibly, the Nupe too had such a "deep" lineage structure before they became a state. With the creation of a state, many of the political functions of lineages are usurped by the ruling class. Perhaps the most fundamental shift from a hitherto stateless society organized on the basis of unilineal descent to a state is that authority, which was formerly limited to kinsmen according to a principle of seniority, is now claimed over nonkin by virtue of social superiority. Even then, the ruling class often finds it convenient to continue invoking kin selection principles to foster its internal class solidarity, as Nadel says Nupe aristocrats do. The recent weakening of lineage ties among commoners that Nadel noted and that the Nupe are aware of and bemoan also supports this interpretation.

A further confirmation of the thesis that Nupe lineage and marriage structure was profoundly affected and weakened by the emergence of a centralized state is provided by the marriage system. There are, in fact, two marriage systems; one for commoners and another for the nobility. Like nearly all African societies, the Nupe are keenly polygynous, but polygyny in a stratified society assumes a different character from what it

Schema 2. Structural Synopsis of Four Societies

Ecological Factors	!Kung San	Yanomamö	Navajo	Nupe
Location	Namibia–Botswana	Venezuela–Brazil	United States	Nigeria
Habitat	Savannah and semidesert	Tropical rain forest	Semidesert	Savannah
Mode of Production	Hunting and gathering	Horticulture, hunting and fishing	Horticulture and livestock	Advanced horticulture and some livestock
Settlement Pattern	Seminomadic camps	Sedentary villages	Semisedentary dispersed homesteads	Sedentary villages and towns
Size of Local Community Group	20–40	40–250	50–1200 (dispersed)	200–25,000
Urbanization	No	No	No	Yes
Openness of Community Groups	Open	Fairly closed	Open	Closed
Population Density per km²	.01	.02	2.0	30–150
Total Population (Approximate)	1000	10,000	100,000	325,000

represents in a classless society. In the latter, polygyny is largely a function of age and to some extent of individual wealth and prestige. But, in a stratified society like the Nupe, it is overwhelmingly a class privilege. Monogamy is the reluctant fate of many peasants, while the powerful and the wealthy are highly polygynous. Power and wealth, in short, are converted into biological fitness. The more powerful a man is, the more reproductive access he has to women. Even peasants manage to be polygynous in middle age or old age, but they rarely have more than two wives. Nobles, on the other hand, rarely have *fewer* than the four official wives allowed by Islam and quite often they have many concubines in addition. Former kings had between 100 and 200 wives and concubines. Also, aging wives past childbearing age are divorced and replaced with more nubile ones. Nupe noblemen, Nadel tells us, expect, and get, the pick of their female subjects.

The extent to which the Nupe nobility convert their power into fitness goes well beyond the mere accumulation of wives by seduction and bridewealth payment. They have, in fact, fostered a double marriage system which works entirely to their advantage. The traditional, that is, pre-Islamic system of marriage is based on lineage exogamy and relatively high bridewealth payment in cash and gifts, but without preferential cross-cousin marriage. Such systems of "generalized exchange" as Lévi-Strauss (1969) calls them, are quite common in Africa, and for Nupe peasants, this marriage system continues in effect.

Nupe aristocrats frequently take commoners as wives and concubines according to the traditional mode, but they have adopted an additional and highly convenient marriage system for themselves. We have seen that conformity to Muslim customs is highly correlated with rank: the higher a person's social status, the more orthodox and the more Islamized he is. Muslims favor parallel-cousin marriage between the children of brothers. Such marriages violate traditional rules of lineage exogamy, but are widely practiced among the Muslim nobility, whose lineages, therefore, are not exogamous and are highly inbred. Aristocrats benefit in two ways from parallel-cousin marriage, as Nadel tells us: first, they reinforce the solidarity of noble lineages through inbreeding and, second, they save themselves bridewealth payments. Since the bride stays in the lineage, bridewealth is not required. In addition to marrying endogamously noblewomen as high-status wives, aristocrats are also free to marry exogamously and with bridewealth payments as many commoners as they can afford. Before the abolition of slavery, slave women could be captured or bought, and taken as concubines as well. For commoners and slave women, of course, these hypergamous unions to aristocrats offered avenues of upward nobility, if not for themselves, at least for their children. For noblemen, it is difficult to conceive of a better way to maximize fitness.

But the fitness benefits of social privilege for the aristocracy do not stop there. Nadel tells us that adultery is common, but not divorce. He then qualifies these statements and shows again how class-stratified the Nupe breeding system is. Traditionally, women were supposed to be virgins at marriage, and remain faithful to their husbands, as is characteristic of patrilineal societies. For example, Temple (1922) writes, "Until a man has married a virgin with due ceremony, he is accounted a nobody." This is still the case in aristocratic families where women are closely controlled and kept in *purdah* (seclusion). This is also still the norm in the rural areas where few nobles live. But in Bida, immorality and semiprofessional prostitution are rampant. Many married market women pick up some extra money by having sex with men who can afford them; their husbands are powerless to stop this. They are even reluctant to divorce their unfaithful wives because they might have to forfeit part or all of the bridewealth, and they lack the funds to acquire another wife. In short, they cannot afford a divorce!

For aristocrats, on the other hand, divorce is easy and frequent. It is initiated mostly by men, who, to conform to the Islamic limitation on four official wives, renew their stock for maximum nubility. One former king discovered what must be the ultimate fitness formula: he married off his superannuated divorcées to his vassals and peasants for a lower-than-customary bridewealth. The recipients, as Nadel puts it, "were either glad to find a 'cheap' wife or else afraid to refuse so exalted a gift" (1942, p. 152).

To summarize, the Nupe illustrate how the development of a state, and the class distinctions that arise therefrom, affect the whole structure of a society—especially the marriage and kinship system. Kin selection and reciprocity continue to operate; however, coercion plays an increasingly important role, not only in the political system proper, but in reproductive fitness through hypergamy. One sees a weakening of both the lineage structure and the system of matrimonial exchanges so characteristic of stateless agricultural societies. Many of the political functions inherent in the lineage organization and the marriage exchange system now devolve to the state and are manipulated for the benefit of the ruling class. This process of functional devolution of kinship and marriage is even more striking in industrial societies, which will be discussed in the next chapter.

SUPPLEMENTARY READINGS

Additional readings for this chapter are readily available since each of the four societies was extensively described. For the San, Thomas (1959) provides a layman's introduction, to be followed by Lee and De Vore (1976). Chagnon's two lively paperbacks on the Yanomamö (1974, 1977) make especially engrossing reading because of the extensive insights they give

INDUSTRIAL SOCIETIES:
The United States and Japan

By now, it should be obvious to most readers that industrial societies have extremely unusual systems of kinship and marriage—systems that have had to adapt extremely fast to radically altered ecological and technological conditions. Industrial societies, meaning mostly North America, Europe, Australia and Japan, and incipiently, some of the more successful Latin American, African and Asian countries, such as Mexico, Brazil, Argentina, South Korea, Taiwan and South Africa, are different from one another in a number of ways, as we shall see when examining the contrasting cases of Japan and the United States. Nevertheless, countries in the process of industrialization undergo broadly similar transformations in their family systems; these convergent changes are relatively independent of the specific culture these societies had in the first place and are overwhelmingly adaptive modifications to the system of production. "System of production" is merely a short-hand phrase to describe a multiplicity of interactions between ecological, technological and organizational factors.

What are some of these changes in the family systems of industrial or industrialized societies?

1. Relative to other bases of social organizations, the family becomes both less important and less permanent. Industrial societies have numerous other ways of organizing people: political parties, schools,

professional groups, trade unions, business and state bureaucracies, voluntary associations—to name only a few of the more important ones. Despite all these, the family remains important, but only as one of several major types of social organizations, no longer as the all-important one that it is in simpler societies.

2. A number of functions traditionally assumed by kin groups have been taken over, at least in part, by more specialized agencies. This is especially true of two central functions. The first is education of the young beyond the first five or six years of childhood and typically for well over a decade of formal schooling. It is often forgotten how restricted to industrial or industrializing societies mass public education is, beyond a few weeks or months of initiation schools or religious training. Recently, a number of Third World countries have attempted to emulate industrial countries in this respect, but with limited success. The second is the system of production that is almost completely divorced from family units. The family is still an important unit of economic consumption, of course, but no longer a significant unit of production. Here, too, it is easy to forget how recent this phenomenon is. Even in complex agrarian societies, the family is still the basic unit of production, except in a few large-scale enterprises such as mining, shipping and plantation agriculture. The first phase of industrialization in countries like England, France and Japan was still characterized by a lot of cottage industry and family firms. Only in more advanced industrial countries is the divorce between family and economic production almost complete. The phenomenon is barely a century old in a few countries; much less in a few more; still largely unknown in most.

Another way of formulating these changes is to say that industrial societies represent an advanced stage of a process of functional and structural differentiation in which other more specialized organizations and groupings have developed side-by-side with the family, assuming some of the latter's functions and claiming more of people's energies and attention. In spite of all these onslaughts, and indeed, in some cases of deliberate attempts to phase the family out (as in the 1920s in the Soviet Union), the family is still alive and well in industrial societies. But it is, in many respects, a diminished family, both in absolute and relative importance, and a streamlined family reduced to its simplest, smallest and most flexible expression.

The most glaringly obvious limitation to family organization in a society where the system of production is outside the home and where market conditions, changing technology, changing skills, shifts in regional development and a multitude of other conditions require constant relocation, is *size*. To survive with such conditions, the family in industrial societies has to be small, at least as a residence unit, if not necessarily as a network of cooperating kinsmen. Among the industrial societies, Japan probably has gone furthest in trying to cushion the impact of industrialization on the family and in substituting a quasi-familistic system of industrial paternalism with life-long employment in a single firm, but even the Japanese family is moving in the same general direction as that of other industrial societies. These are three main ways in which a family can be made smaller, more movable, more flexible and more responsive to outside constraints. The industrial family adopted *all* of them:

1. It adopted neolocality as the main rule of residence, thereby shedding all or most of the relatives outside the nuclear family.
2. It eliminated polygamy, *de facto,* and increasingly, *de jure,* as well. Countries, polygamous until recently, are shifting to compulsory or at least preferential monogamy as they begin or hope to enter the industrial era. Examples are Turkey after World War I and China after the Communist take-over. Would-be dissidents, such as the Mormons in the United States, were quickly brought back under the monogamous fold. Interestingly, Japan, the first non-Western country to industrialize, was one of the few monogamous societies long before the Meiji Restoration. (There was a lot of dalliance with mistresses in the nobility, but there was no polygyny and little institutionalized concubinage in traditional Japan.)
3. It reduced its fertility to levels approaching zero population growth—even somewhat below in some countries (Table 1).

Paradoxically, the industrial family looks somewhat like the family in some of the simplest hunting and gathering societies. The latter, we saw, also have to be very mobile to follow their natural resources: game, water and so on. A loose system of bilateral descent and neolocal residence with shifting combinations of nuclear families is a flexible system suitable to both the simplest and the most complex of societies, the reasons being basically the same: to make the best of available resources, given the level of technology, or, in other words, to maximize individual benefits.

DECLINE IN FERTILITY

Industrial societies present a puzzling problem to sociobiology. Why has the level of fertility declined steeply in industrial societies and, especially, why do the most urbanized and affluent classes in these societies who can most afford children have, on the average, the fewest? Does not this behavior contradict the postulate of fitness maximization that underlies natural selection theory?

Table 1. Economic Development and Demographic Characteristics, Selected Countries, 1973–1977 [a]

| Country | Development Indices | | | | Demographic Indices | | |
	Per Capita Income in 1977 U.S. Dollars	Percent Population Urban	1973 per Capita Paper Consumption in kg	Percent Literate	Annual Percent Population Increase	Life Expectancy at Birth (Years)	Crude Birth Rates per 1,000	Crude Death Rates per 1,000
Industrial Countries								
United States	7,060	74	46.2	99	0.6	72	14.7	8.9
West Germany	6,610	88	19.7	99	−0.2	71	9.7	12.1
France	5,760	70	11.4	97	0.4	72	15.2	10.4
Japan	4,460	72	19.9	98	1.1	74	18.6	6.5
Great Britain	3,840	78	28.5	99	0.1	72	12.4	11.9
Semideveloped Countries								
South Africa	1,320	48	7.7	46	2.5	52	42.9	14.4
Brazil	1,010	59	2.6	67	2.8	61	37.1	8.8
Turkey	860	43	1.7	55	2.7	57	39.6	12.5
Albania	600	34	—	70	2.5	67	33.3	8.1
North Korea	430	43	0.1	90	2.6	61	35.7	9.4
Poor Countries								
Bolivia	320	34	0.9	38	2.6	47	43.7	18.0
Egypt	310	45	1.3	40	2.3	52	35.5	19.7
Nigeria	310	18	0.3	25	2.7	41	49.3	23.6
India	150	21	0.3	29	2.1	50	34.6	16.9
Bangladesh	110	9	0.2	25	2.7	47	49.5	20.5

[a] Sources: Population Reference Bureau (1977); UNESCO (1975); United Nations (1976).

Let us look at the situation more closely. First, only a few societies have achieved low birth rates (under 20 per 1000), using both abortion and reliable contraceptives; they have only done so in most cases for one or two generations (Table 1). Many other human societies have resorted to population control measures, especially when ecological conditions required them. For example, some hunters and gatherers have practiced infanticide, especially female infanticide. Voluntary abortion, *coitus interruptus,* extravaginal intercourse, celibacy and condoms are among other means of population control used by a number of preindustrial societies for several centuries or even millenia. There is little evidence, however, that all of the practices combined made a dent in human demography until perhaps a century ago. That is, many of these practices were perfectly sensible adaptations to adverse ecological conditions, merely preventing the birth or survival of offspring who would have been unviable in any case, either because of genetic defects or because of adverse environmental conditions.

Conscious decisions to control population increase under these circumstances make perfectly good sense in terms of inclusive fitness. It is better to cut your losses before parental investment is heavy: contraception is better than abortion; early abortion is better than late abortion, abortion is better than infanticide. In fact, the immediate aftermath of birth is generally the latest stage at which preindustrial societies deliberately attempt to limit population. Better to have a few viable offspring than many unviable ones. Humans are extreme K strategists, as we saw earlier. Therefore, it is very sensible for an intelligent K strategist who has to make a heavy parental investment to curtail his reproduction in anticipation of adverse conditions that may jeopardize his fitness. For most of human history, the death of some (mostly neonates) contributed to the survival of others. For instance, humans are poorly adapted to lactate for more than one infant at a time. Therefore, it is not surprising to see that many societies practice such things as twin infanticide or a "postpartum sex taboo" to facilitate birth spacing and thus extended lactation. Weaning before the infant is two years old is often a sentence of death in preindustrial societies.

Can the argument that reduced fertility is a fitness maximization strategy be extended to industrial societies? On the face of it, the answer is negative. If desperately poor, "overpopulated" countries like India, Pakistan and Egypt can keep alive their exploding populations, then surely affluent industrial countries could reproduce much faster than they do. Not only do people in industrial societies deliberately reduce their fertility; they even expend considerable resources to keep unviable offspring (like victims of Trisomy 21 or "mongolism") alive. Why?

The phenomenon of deliberate fertility reduction on a mass scale by those who can best afford to reproduce may be too recent to provide the necessary data for a definitive answer. Contrary to what is sometimes supposed, the rich countries did not become rich because they limited their populations; they curtailed their population growth largely *after* they had become more prosperous and were already well on the road to industrialization. This is clearly shown by the statistics in Table 1. All the wealthy industrialized countries have low birth rates, while the semideveloped countries on the road to industrialization typically still have birth rates that are not appreciably lower than those of the poorest countries. The well-known phenomenon of "demographic transition" took place. As preindustrial societies industrialized, they went through three phases: a period of relatively stable population with high rates of both fertility and mortality; a phase of rapid population increase during which the death rate decreased rapidly but the birth rate remained high; finally, a phase of slow growth with relatively low birth and death rates. A look at Table 1 will show that a number of semideveloped countries have low death rates in the same range as the industrial countries, combined with still high birth rates. Today, however, even the poorest countries have sufficiently lowered their death rates through the control of epidemics to ensure a population explosion.

This sequence of events, still being replicated in countries on the threshold of industrialization, clearly suggests that the deliberate curtailment of fertility only becomes an attractive prospect to economically secure populations with some degree of assurance that the children they produce will survive. Usually this proposition is put in the reverse form: people in "underdeveloped" countries "overreproduce" in the expectation of high mortality. In fact, however, if there has been a conscious change in reproductive behavior in response to changed environmental conditions, it clearly must have taken place in industrial countries—not in countries where the changes have not yet taken place. It is the reproductive behavior of industrial societies that is deviant, begging for an explanation.

There is also evidence that, at least in the earlier phases of industrialization, it was the urban population that overwhelmingly contributed to a lowered birth rate. Even in preindustrial societies, cities were demographically aberrant places that largely grew by migration from the countryside more than by natural increase. Preindustrial or early industrial cities were unhealthy; high population density fostered epidemics; men frequently outnumbered women for economic reasons; and the women were relatively infertile because of disease, prostitution, alcoholism and other causes. Traditionally, then, the city was a demographic parasite feeding on its hinterland.

However, until industrialization was well under way, the demographic effect of cities was relatively small. Few preindustrial societies had more than 10 (or at most, 20) percent of their population living in towns. In highly industrialized societies, on the other hand, with 80 to 90 percent of the population urban, it is the reproductive behavior of city dwellers that largely determines the demography of the entire country. Here we have a first level of the answer to our question: industrial societies have lower fertility rates, partly because they are highly urbanized. Cities, it seems, are no places to raise the young. Why?

There are four possible explanations. First, it may be argued that cities are such a highly unnatural environment for our species that they may well lead us into biological extinction. The primatologist Desmond Morris (1969) has most eloquently and wittily developed that thesis, comparing urban existence to life in zoos of our own making. According to this thesis, our behavior under conditions so widely at variance with the environment for which we are biologically adapted, leads to all kinds of aberrations, of which reduction in fertility is one. We fail to reproduce as much as we otherwise would, perhaps for similar reasons that some other animals fail to breed in zoos. The thesis is amusing to play with, but highly speculative and difficult to validate or invalidate.

Second, there are those who argue that we restrict our reproduction for the good of the species. Wynne-Edwards (1962) suggested that other animals do likewise, but few biologists accept his group selection arguments. Now, since we are a self-conscious animal able to conceive of and forecast Malthusian catastrophes, we have, at least theoretically, the ability to forestall the gloomy scenario of a run-away population explosion. There may be a few highly ethical individuals who actually refrain from reproducing out of such loftily altruistic motives, but they would be selected against, and the likelihood that they are numerous enough to make a perceptible dent in the birth rate is extremely low. More conceivably, governments dictatorial enough to impose draconian restrictions on reproduction may arise in the future, but none has succeeded yet, or is likely to at present, as Indira Gandhi recently learned when her son's zeal for compulsory sterilization lost her the Indian prime-ministership. If anything, most governments so far have encouraged reproduction through tax rebates, family allowances, free medical and educational services and the like. At present, the voluntary nonparent in industrial societies is being doubly penalized: not only does he reduce his fitness, he is also expected to make a quasi-parental contribution through taxes to the fitness of his reproductive compatriots. The second hypothesis, then, is most clearly at variance with the facts. If we fail to reproduce as much as we could, it is not for reasons of altruism. The overwhelming majority (95 percent by most estimates) still want to have children (though not so many) and their decision to reproduce or not seldom has anything to do with concern for famine in Bangladesh or in the Sahel.

This leaves a third hypothesis: that we deliberately restrict our fertility for good and individually selfish reasons. This argument, in turn, can take two variant forms. The first is that we continue, despite appearances, to maximize our fitness by pursuing to its logical conclusion our extreme K selectionist strategy. Most people continue to want children but not "too many"; "too many" is defined by parental capacity to make children fit into an industrial environment. Better to have only two children who are university graduates with good jobs, a secure income and a good home to raise four highly viable grandchildren in, than eight badly educated, underfed children who are likely to become juvenile delinquents, to be shot by the police or locked up under conditions of compulsory celibacy in the state penitentiary, so that, in the end, they may end up producing few or no grandchildren. We know that the cost of raising a child in an industrial society at a level of health and education that will secure him or her a good, steady, middle-class job is staggering and ever escalating. Most parents are aware of this and very few can afford to carry more than two or three of these "capital-intensive" offspring through college. Therefore, they deliberately choose not to try the impossible.

This form of the "selfish" explanation of limited fertility in kin selection terms has, I believe, some explanatory power. A number of people behave in just that way for just these reasons. But it is not a complete explanation, for it fails to account for a puzzling fact about industrial societies. In preindustrial societies, there is a clear positive correlation between reproductive success and social status. Because of polygyny, this is even truer of men than of women. The high and mighty have more than their share of children and grandchildren. In industrial societies, however, the reverse tends to be true: parents who can least afford children tend to have most. Clearly, factors other than kin selection are at work.

This leads us to the second and, in my view, complementary, variant of the "selfish" explanation of restricted fertility—namely, that people in affluent societies come to value increasingly things that are made possible through advanced technology and a high material standard of living but from which "excessive" reproduction detracts.* This factor becomes increasingly important with increasing affluence, affecting most strongly the highly urbanized, the highly educated, the highly competitive and success-oriented—in short, the upper strata of industrial societies. However, the more affluent society becomes, the more the effect of reduced fertility percolates down the class structure.

Let us, for purposes of illustration, take the contemporary United States. Having six children on a farm in Kansas is some economic burden to be sure, but does not drastically alter one's life, especially if the mother stays at home. Trying to raise six children in New York City is quite a different proposition. Family space, for one thing, is reduced from the 160-acre farm to the 1200-square-feet apartment. The cost of living is so high that the incentive for the wife to earn wages increases proportionately, and, of course, if she works outside, she can't very well be pregnant and raise infant children all the time. For most urban families, having two children or having six children is the difference between a comfortable middle-class standing, often sustained by a double income, or what most Americans have come to consider intolerable poverty. Not unexpectedly, many people opt for fewer children.

The very rich, it might be argued, are spared that dilemma. They can sustain many children in luxury. Some, of course, do just that, and still manage to get their offspring into the White House and the Senate. Many, however, prefer to restrict their reproduction so as to be freer to pursue artistic, academic or literary careers; to play roulette in Monte Carlo; to dedicate themselves to transcendental meditation or to do whatever else strikes their fancy. This is, of course, doubly true of women who find it much more difficult than men to combine reproduction with extrafamilial pursuits. It is, therefore, women rather than men who are probably responsible for most of the recent change in reproductive behavior in industrial societies.

Why, then, do the poor, especially the urban underclasses, continue to have relatively high levels of fertility? Such behavior is often attributed to ignorance, stupidity, moral profligacy or a combination of these. I would like to suggest that for the underclass of industrial societies moderately high fertility is in fact a paying strategy because it maximizes biological fitness without jeopardizing much else. The "welfare mother" does not have to be concerned about giving up her career as a pianist, ballerina or interior decorator. The unemployed ghetto youth does not face the choice of early marriage or admission to Princeton University,

---

*Harris (1977) gives an extreme variant of this hypothesis, and in its extreme form his argument breaks down. Harris explains reproductive behavior in terms of parental calculations of economic costs and benefits. Parents have children, he states, to the extent that there is something in it for them, in terms of economic returns on their investment. In peasant societies it pays to have children to help on the farm; in industrial societies children are an almost pure drain on family resources. Harris concedes that there are some "intangibles, such as the joys of watching children grow up" (1977, p. 188), but he comes close to disregarding these biological factors. The problem with his interpretation of fertility is that, in sheer economic terms, children are a considerable burden in all societies. Even in agrarian societies, adults would do economically better by banding together rather than by having children who, if they are lucky enough to survive, may start pulling their weight ten years down the road. Harris' "explanation" renders all reproductive behavior problematic, except in terms of his "intangibles," surely not a very satisfactory theory. This is not to deny that economic cost−benefit considerations *do* consciously enter parental decisions to invest in offspring, but reproduction is almost always a bad *economic* bargain for parents. Consequently, there must be more in it for them, and that "more" is, of course, fitness.

nor is his sweetheart worried about being accepted in a Vassar sorority. The janitor of the tenement house does not face the problem of postponing fatherhood to take that long-planned Caribbean vacation with his wife. On the other hand, underclass parents have the assurance that the "transfer payments" of the welfare state will keep their children alive, above the level of starvation. To be sure, their fitness may be reduced by such hazards as drugs, encounters with the police, time in jail and a higher probability of being the victim of a murder, rape, robbery or assault, but still enough of them can be expected to survive and pass on their genes. So, why *not* have children?

Of course, not all lower-class parents behave or think that way. Some opt for lower fertility with the hope of upward mobility into the middle class; a few succeed. But so long as the rewards for lower fertility seem few and remote, high fertility is a rational strategy for the poor in welfare states, or, indeed, for the masses of the Third World. There is evidence that a country's birth rate only begins to decline after it has reached a standard of living sufficiently high to give a large percentage of the population a realistic hope of improving their standard of living by curtailing reproduction. A deliberate choice of lowered reproduction, insofar as it entails a fitness reduction, must have compensating benefits; the latter, however, are still largely limited to the economically secure classes of industrial societies. For the underclass of industrial societies, as well as the masses of the nonindustrial Third World, these benefits are still unattainable. The impoverished are, in the true, literal sense, proletarians. They make the best of a bad political and economic bargain and that, for them, means to continue to play the old fitness game.

In summary, three main conditions have, in combination, transformed human reproductive behavior in industrial societies: (1) the creation of an unprecedented economic surplus, made possible largely through tapping vast quantities of nonrenewable fossil fuels; (2) the distribution of some of that surplus to a broad middle class that has come to include the majority of the population, living securely above the subsistence level; and, (3) a reliable technology of contraception that is not only cheap but that minimally interferes with the proximate mechanisms of sexuality, while maximally interfering with reproduction.

Let us take up the three points in sequence. Economic surplus began to be produced in substantial quantities in agrarian societies, but it was appropriated by a small proportion of the population, typically under ten percent. For the peasants of agrarian societies, the choice was drudgery with children or drudgery without children. They wisely chose the former, thereby continuing to play the old fitness game. For the wealthy and powerful of agrarian societies, their high standard of living was not threatened by successful reproduction, since their wealth came from exploiting the peasants. They could, therefore, have their cake and eat it too: appropriate surplus production and maximize their fitness through polygyny. Understandably they did both, to the limit of their ability to screw the peasants, in both senses of that graphic, if earthy, idiom.

The industrial mode of production, after a half-century or so of unspeakable horrors in its early phases, made surplus accumulation possible on such a staggering scale that even the rapaciousness of capitalists could not prevent the gradual percolation of economic benefits down to wider and wider strata of the population. By the 20th century, a few privileged societies had grown enormously wealthy, in part by exploiting the rest of the world as a colonial empire. In these industrial societies a growing middle class was increasingly secure in enjoying the fruits of prosperity, while, at the same time, the peasantry and proletariat dwindled in size or even disappeared almost entirely in their classical form. More and more people could enjoy the benefits of better medicine and hygiene; better clothing, diet and shelter; more leisure, education and social services; cleaner, easier and shorter work; and hitherto unthinkable material luxuries. In the space of a couple of generations, there was a sudden and unprecedented increment in things *worth living for.*

Why then is not this material and technological bonanza converted into reproduction? The answer, of course, is that much of it is and has been. The population of industrial countries exploded during the early phases of their development, and the few technical and medical benefits that reach the poor countries today are immediately converted into more successful reproduction as we know from Third World demography. Only recently, and in few countries, is the population stabilizing, and that, as we have seen, happened mostly *after,* not before, the achievement of a high standard of living.

My contention is that it took modern contraception to halt the population explosion that industrialization made possible—in short, to escape the Malthusian trap. This statement is not as obvious as it sounds because *deliberate* population control has characterized human societies for thousands of years, largely through infanticide, especially female infanticide, but also through abortion, abstinence, *coitus interruptus,* masturbation, postpartum sex taboos and so on.

Population control in advanced industrial societies, however, is different from what it was in earlier eras in at least two major respects:

1. Many of the earlier attempts to control population growth enhanced rather than reduced individual fitness. Infants were killed when they were judged to be unviable (e.g., when malformed or in the case of multiple births) or when they jeopardized the fitness of their mothers or of older siblings less likely to die before reproductive age. Much

infanticide and abortion was thus a fitness-enhancing way of cutting your losses at the least costly time, and in the comparatively rare cases when prolonged lactation had failed sufficiently to space births.

2. Earlier methods of population control were energetically costly (infanticide), dangerous (induced abortion) and emotionally and/or physically painful, or at least stressful (infanticide, abortion, continence, *coitus interruptus*). Even the methods of the early industrial age (condoms, douches, diaphragms, sponges) were constraining and messy; therefore, none too reliable.

Modern contraception is still far short of perfect. The perfect contraception is often described as the one that would have no physiological side-effects and that one could "forget about." Instant, reversible, cheap, do-it-yourself vasectomy or tubal ligation is the elusive ideal. Even then, however, it would still require a conscious act, so one could not completely "forget about it." Why does so much contraception fail, even with our remarkably efficient modern methods? Why is not induced abortion completely obsolete?

Apparently many contraception attempts fail either because of our intolerance of even relatively minor interferences with our sexual behavior (e.g., putting on and wearing a condom or diaphragm), or because of our obscure subconscious desire to make it fail or at least to "take chances." On the face of it, such self-defeating behavior is irrational and calls for an explanation. Contraception is a conscious way of "fooling Mother Nature" and, as we have seen, this can only be done at some cost. As Dawkins (1976) brilliantly states, the ultimate unit of natural selection is the gene rather than the individual organism. The different alleles of the same gene compete with each other for representation in the next generation, and the individual organisms in which they are carried at any given time are, in a deep evolutionary sense, mere "survival machines" for genes, a gene's way of replicating itself.

The evolutionary development of human consciousness, including intimation of one's own mortality, was a momentous event in the history of our species. It implies, of course, a measure of free will and, therefore, some measure of ability to fool the very mechanisms that were selected for in the evolution of our species. This entails, at the limit, the conscious ability to escape the biological imperative of reproduction itself, i.e., deliberate contraception, not for fitness-enhancing purposes—that is biologically unproblematic—but for the purpose of subordinating reproduction to other more valued goals.

We know that we must die and, therefore, that this unique assemblage of genes that never was before, never will be again after our death. We have been programmed to love ourselves, directly, and indirectly in our children and relatives, because that is how our constituent genes were selected in the first place. Genes that had this effect in their carriers were selected for. But human consciousness now turns that self-love against the genes. We use the proximate mechanisms of genetic selection, including sexual behavior, not only as means to the end of gene reproduction, but as ends in themselves. We proclaim, in effect, that we love the entire assemblage of genes we call "me" better than our genes taken separately, and that therefore we are going, in some circumstances, to gratify that "me," even at the expense of reproducing our genes. Our genes may be theoretically eternal, but we know that we are highly ephemeral; therefore, we want to make the best of our short lifespan, especially now that we have a good deal to live for.

For all our self-consciousness, we continue to have a powerful urge to reproduce and much contraception is merely an attempt to pick the most convenient time to do so. That is, much contraception intends to postpone—not to prevent reproduction. Other indications of our continued fitness drive are the more-than-chance failures and the irrational chance-taking that accompany much use of contraception, even among experienced, knowledgeable people, and the countless reports of diminished pleasure and lowered "spontaneity" with even the most sophisticated forms of contraception. We would like to forget about it, but, of course, we cannot quite do so. We are embarrassed to ask; we dislike being reminded; having to "mess around" with it badly disrupts the flow of erotic encounters. In short, we like to copulate with *abandon*. Our genes still see to it that we do.

It remains to be seen what balance will be struck between the biologically evolved impulse to maximize fitness and the consciously developed impulse to maximize other forms of self-realization. The spectre of planetary ecocatastrophe makes us hope for a continuous extension of deliberate population control and, therefore, for the intelligent application of sociobiology to defeat our biological programs.

Let us now take a closer look at two highly industrial societies with very different cultural traditions, the United States and Japan. To what extent do their marriage and kinship systems differ and to what extent do they converge on a similar solution to similar ecological and technological conditions?

THE UNITED STATES

The visitor from a "normal" human society—that is, from the kind of society we invidiously refer to as "primitive," would, of course, be struck by a number of very strange things in America, not least of which would be our mating and reproductive arrangements. First, he would find not one, but a multiplicity of marriage and kinship systems. If he travelled extensively enough, he would in the remote corners of Alaska, the Southwest, the Northwest and a few other isolated pockets find the remnants of aboriginal peoples with a wide variety of kinship systems but who, nevertheless, might appear to him more "normal" that the great mass of Americans. He would, among some of them, recognize some basic features of social organization that would be at least vaguely similar to those of his own society. If he came, let us say, from a polygynous, matrilineal society, there would be many things among Navajo that would be familiar to him. But our visitor would quickly come to the conclusion that these peoples, however sensible and normal they may appear to be, seem to fare very poorly in the United States—much more poorly at any rate than the exotic newcomers who conquered them. So, clearly, "normalcy" does not seem to work very well in America.

Such a view would perhaps be further confirmed by a visit to Utah. There our visitor, say from an African pastoralist society, would find an interesting white tribe with a fascinating oral tradition strangely similar in some respects to his own. Once, he would learn, these "Mormons" or "Latter Day Saints" behaved as sensibly as his people do: prominent, well-established men had several wives and many children, as befitted their status. A few of the more traditional of these tribesmen are, in fact, still polygynists, but they are relentlessly persecuted by fanatical monogamists around them. In the Mormons' early history, so ferocious was the persecution by the monogamists, in fact, that they were forced to move thousands of miles into an inhospitable desert of salt flats that no one else wanted. Still, when the monogamists later caught up with them and surrounded them, the Mormons were forced to renounce polygyny as a condition of acceptance into the larger society. Yet, the monogamous families who rule America accept as their sacred text and the compilation of their history, tradition, laws and ethics a book which openly approves of polygyny.

Our visitor would encounter other kinds of family systems. He would find, for instance, that many brown-skinned people who speak Spanish and came from South of the Rio Grande want to have many children and like to live in larger extended families like most sensible people do. They pretend to agree with the dominant "Anglos" that monogamy is a good thing, but they secretly prefer polygyny as witnessed by their popular witticism: "*Yo soy soltero, la casada es mi mujer*" ("I am a bachelor; my wife is the married one"). Once again, normalcy does not seem to do these people much good in America, for most of them are much poorer than other Americans and are considered inferior.

Other immigrant groups, like the Chinese and the Japanese who had virolocal extended families and, in the Chinese case, practiced polygyny, also seem to have been forced to conform increasingly to the monogamous, neolocal, nuclear family characteristic of the Anglos. They certainly had to give up polygyny; their lineage and clan organization became weaker; economic and political circumstances disrupted their larger families, and, to be successful, they too had to conform to the dominant Anglo mold. They too were persecuted and despised by the dominant group, though less so now than was once the case, perhaps because by now their family structure is much like that of the Anglos. They make do with one wife and few children, and they do not take their ancestors and relatives as seriously as they once did.

Yet another strange family system that our visitor would find in America is the "matrifocal family." This he would find mostly among people who are called "black" (even though many of them are not), and whose ancestors, a little over a century ago, were slaves of the Anglos (Frazier, 1948; Moynihan, 1965). Slavery would not strike him as odd, although the American brand of it if he would find more than averagely nasty. Apparently, slave families were disrupted; husbands and wives were separated by sale, as were mothers and children. Even today, many women among blacks do not have a resident husband, maintaining the primary responsibility for raising their children.

Some of the Anglo social scientists argue that it was not so much the heritage of slavery that disrupted the black family and created the "matrifocal" type of organization, but rather the nature of proletarian urban life and the "welfare" system in America (Fogel and Engerman, 1974; Gutman, 1976). Some have argued, for example, that fathers are encouraged to disappear because otherwise the women are not eligible for welfare payments. This revisionist view of the black family is supported by the sharp rise in rates of matrifocal families, illegitimacy, teen-age pregnancies, children on welfare and other symptoms of the outcaste status of the black urban underclass in recent years. If these things were the heritage of slavery, conditions might be expected to improve as the experience of slavery recedes into an increasingly distant past. In fact, the opposite is true: conditions have worsened drastically since the famous "Moynihan Report" (1965). In 1965, 26 percent of black children were born illegitimate; in 1976, illegitimacy passed the 50 percent mark. In 1965, 71 percent of black children were living with both parents; by 1977, under half (47 percent) did so. In 1961, 14 percent of black children were on "welfare", compared to 38 percent in 1977.

Whatever the reason for the matrifocal family, our visitor would conclude that this is not a successful form in America either. It is found disproportionately among blacks, who are another pariah group in the society; and the more economically and socially successful blacks usually have stable, monogamous, nuclear families with few children, much like their white middle-class counterparts. Home ownership statistics clearly show that husband—wife families fare much better economically than families with a female head. In 1970, well over two-thirds (71.1 percent) of the former owned the home they occupied, compared to just less than half (49.5 percent) of the latter (U.S. Bureau of the Census, 1973).

All these types of American family systems, although they persist, are regarded by most members of the dominant, white, Anglo group as somehow deviant, pathological or at least "traditional" (a euphemism for "backward" in America). Our visitor would be told that there is a "superior" type of family to which most "good" people conform. The ideal system, he would be told, goes something like this.

Sex is great fun, but because it is such fun, it is also sinful. God simply did not mean people to have such a ball. That is why He instituted the sacrament of marriage, which is a solemn undertaking by a man and a woman to love each other until death and to raise their children properly. In exchange for their prosaic obligations, they get an official license to have as much fun together as they are capable of achieving. Indeed, to make sure that nobody misses out on anything, there are many "how-to" manuals, complete with detailed instructions and explicit pictures to help one achieve that pinnacle of marital bliss: the synchronic orgasm. Should you still fail to achieve it, there are a multitude of "marriage counselors," "sex therapists," "transcendental meditators" and sundry quacks and would-be professionals who will gladly relieve you of some of your paycheck to bring you to orgasm at just the right pace. Americans only too gladly support these parasites of marital bliss, for good sex is held to be, if not the only value in marriage, certainly the *sine qua non* of a "successful" union.

Marriage is mostly the private business of individuals involved. Dependent children are conceded to have an interest in their parents' marriage, and the state sanctions the union and enforces family law, but relatives and in-laws are expected to stay out of it. In practice, of course, relatives and in-laws *do* interfere to some extent, but they seldom, if ever, arrange marriages or even manage to hold them together. To minimize "outside" interference with marriage, couples are supposed to establish neolocal residence, if not immediately upon marrying, as quickly as possible thereafter. The imperatives of the all-important job—the key to supporting a family of one's own—will make it unlikely that either spouse will live close to many relatives. Each nuclear family is basically on its own, for better and for worse. In practice, relatives sometimes help one another and many parents continue to support their adult children, but the norm is one of independence of the nuclear family, of neolocality and of primacy of the husband—wife and parent—child bonds, at the expense of all others.

Descent is bilateral, but kin obligations are so diluted by physical distance and by the emphasis on the nuclear family that there are relatively few well-defined larger kin groupings. This varies somewhat from group to group: extended kin ties are more prevalent in some traditional upper-class circles, among recent immigrants and in some of the smaller and more endogamous religious groups. All the same, kin selection operates only weakly beyond the nuclear family.

Marriage, being so highly personalized and sexualized, is subject to only few restrictions and loose ones at that. There is an incest taboo on full and half-siblings, parents, children, grandparents, grandchildren, nephews, nieces, uncles and aunts—that is, on all relatives related by $\frac{1}{4}$ or more. Beyond that, marriage between cousins is not encouraged and various religious denominations or political jurisdictions impose a few more restrictions on some more distant relatives and in-laws, but hardly anyone takes these very seriously, nor is there consensus about these rules. Indeed, most people are not even aware that they exist. Since there is no well-defined kin group beyond the nuclear family, there is no clear rule of exogamy, other than that which necessarily follows from the incest prohibitions. As for the rules of endogamy, they are mostly preferential rather than prescriptive. Until the aftermath of World War II, a number of states forbade interracial marriage between whites and blacks, but the Supreme Court declared these statutes to be unconstitutional. Statistically, most people continue to marry within their "racial" group, although interracial marriages are becoming somewhat more common. There is also a preference for marrying within religious groups, ethnic groups and class groups, but little stigma attaches to the substantial member of people who overlook these mild preferences.

In short, any person above the legal age (which varies from state to state—generally one or two years lower for girls than for boys) can marry any person of the opposite sex who is not a close relative. While the American population is still far from panmictic, only "racial" boundaries still constitute significant barriers to marriage and interbreeding; even these are not absolute as a look at the "black" population quickly reveals. In the absence of clear rules of exogamy and of significant endogamous restrictions, marriage in the United States serves almost no function as a mechanism of reciprocity between groups. Not uncommonly, even the close kinsmen of the bride and of the groom meet at the wedding and on rare occasions thereafter. They are not expected to have extensive relationships with one another. Occasionally, weddings even take place in the absence of all relatives and the "two sides" may never meet at all. In the great majority of cases, such relationship as is established between the kinsmen of the two spouses is an incidental outcome of the spouses' decision to marry, rather than a necessary prelude to the marriage.

It is interesting to note how closely the dominant Anglo-American system of marriage and kinship, described in detail by Schneider (1968), follows the biological paradigm of this book. Marriage legitimates sexual relations for the purpose of reproduction. There is a sexual division of labor, with the main burden of child-rearing falling on women, but with fathers expected to make a substantial material contribution. While monogamous in theory, American society tolerates and expects more promiscuous behavior on the part of males. Socially and economically successful males have access to more, and younger, women. Descent is traced equally in all lines and closeness of kin (in such matters as law of inheritance) corresponds closely to degree of biological relatedness (Farber, 1973).

Schneider would have us believe that the biological reality of mating and reproduction is *independent* of any society's normative rules about kinship and marriage (1968, p. 6). The convergence, in the case of the American system, he suggests, is accidental. He goes so far as to say that Americans take a very biological view of kinship and marriage because they have developed that special cultural product: biological science (pp. 114–115). This ultimate cultural *reductio ad absurdum* is also taken by Sahlins (1976). To him, sociobiology (in particular) and science (in general) are merely cultural artifacts, particular ways of looking at ourselves and our environment among a potential infinity of such "scientific" systems. We think that biology is important, not because it *is,* but because we have been made to believe it is important by an elite that uses science as a prop for the status quo. Sociobiology, Sahlins contends, is a form of capitalist ideology, rather than a scientific theory about the real world.

Quite conceivably sociobiology could be *both* scientific theory and political ideology. There is no recipe to prevent science from being used and abused in defense of interests. However, the notion that American kinship and marriage rules are derived from the cultural system of Western folk science disregards the fact that the former antedate the latter. Both our kinship system and our scientific apparatus are culturally specific ways of tracking a real world external to these cultural products. Every human society has such a cultural system for tracking the realities of its environment. Some of these systems are more accurate than others, but *none* is arbitrary and independent of external realities.

THE CONTEMPORARY AMERICAN NUCLEAR FAMILY

Husband and wife are largely on their own, geographically, economically and emotionally. For both partners, marriage marks a departure from what sociologists call their "family of orientation" (that is, the nuclear family in which they were raised) and the creation of a new "family of procreation." In case of crisis, people often fall back on relatives, especially parents in the case of women, but there is no institutionalized extended family which, as a matter of expected daily routine, can be relied upon for assistance. Extended family ties are largely limited to casual visiting if kinsmen live nearby; if, as is often the case, they do not, these contacts are typically limited to the telephone, correspondence and formal gatherings for rites of passage—mostly funerals and weddings. After marriage, regular contact is normally kept with parents, but more sporadically with siblings, although even these occasions may be a year or more apart if distances are great. Grandparents are rather shadowy figures for many Americans. Roughly three-fourths of American undergraduates whom I ask to give the first and last name of all four of their grandparents flunk the test. (Few, for example, know their grandmothers' maiden names.) First cousins are often, but not always, known by name; more distant relatives are barely known to exist and typically ignored.

Substantial numbers of American households include *some* relatives other than parents, spouses and children, and can thus be termed "extended families," but there is no single category of relative who is routinely expected to share residence with the mated couple and its offspring. In 1970, 4.9 percent of the people who lived in family units, and 4.4 percent of all children under 18, lived in extended families— roughly one out of 20 (U.S. Bureau of the Census, 1973). Such "extended" families as exist in America are not comparable to those in societies where one particular residence rule normally throws together specified classes of relatives and in-laws. In America, "extended" families are generally considered undesirable. The arrangement is often defined as temporary and a matter of convenience or economy, rather than a valued tradition. Even aged parents are often considered intruders in their children's "family of procreation." Contact between grandparents and grandchildren is generally mediated by the parents and is at their sufferance, especially if the grandparents are either physically enfeebled or financially strained.

The nuclear family, then, is practically the only viable kin group left in American society. Indeed, as far as the dominant white population of the United States is concerned, the nuclear family is not a new development. In 1790, the mean family size was 5.7 members and in 1975, it was 2.9; nearly all of that decline is attributable not to a shift from extended to nuclear family, but rather to a reduction of fertility (William J. Goode, 1963; Winch, 1977). In 1970, roughly four American households out of five (80.4 percent) were families, and, of these, roughly 19 out of 20 were nuclear families (U.S. Bureau of the Census, 1973). The nuclear family thus remains very important—more important, in fact, than in many simpler societies where the extended family is the focus of kinship organization.

The key reason, of course, why the nuclear family retains its importance in industrial societies is that, so far, no satisfactory substitute has been found to raise children, especially during the first five or six years. Demographic statistics show this clearly. In 1970, 83.1 percent of all American children under 18 lived with both of their parents, a remarkably high figure considering the relatively high divorce rate in contemporary American society. Another 13.4 percent of all children under 18 lived with one parent. That left only 3.5 percent living with neither parent, and, of them, two-thirds lived with other relatives, mostly grandparents. Only 1.2 percent of all Americans under 18 did *not* live with kinsmen (Table 2). For children under 6, the figure was even lower: 0.8 percent (U.S. Bureau of the Census, 1973). American statistics also show the asymmetry of parental investment for women and men. Of the children under 18 living with only one parent in 1970, six times as many lived with their mothers as with their fathers. For children under 6, the disproportion was over seven times as many. As for children living with one parent *and* grandparents, maternal grandparents were over ten times more likely to live with their grandchildren than paternal grandparents (U.S. Bureau of the Census, 1973).

One might think that the recent divorce epidemic is changing this picture. Indeed, by 1976, the percentage of children under 18 living with both parents had declined to 80.0 percent (from 83.1 percent in 1970), but the percentage living with *at least* one parent marginally increased from 96.5 percent in 1970 to 97.0 percent in 1976 (Winch, 1977). In fact, American children were slightly *more* likely to live with *some* kinsmen in 1976 than in 1970: 99.3 percent versus 98.8 percent (Table 2). Most interesting of all is the trend toward an increasing asymmetry of parental investment that accompanied the divorce epidemic. In 1970, six times as many children under 18 lived with their mothers as with their

Table 2. Percentage of American Children Under 18 Years of Age Living with One, Both or No Parents, by Race, 1970 and 1976 [a]

Living Arrangement	1970			1976		
	Total	White	Black	Total	White	Black
Total	100.0	100.0	100.0	100.0	100.0	100.0
In Families	98.8	99.0	98.0	99.3	99.4	99.0
with Two Parents	83.1	87.2	57.6	80.0	85.1	49.6
with Mother Only	11.5	8.5	30.2	15.8	11.8	40.1
with Father Only	1.9	1.8	2.9	1.2	1.2	1.5
with Other Kin	2.3	1.5	7.3	2.3	1.3	7.8
Not in Families	1.2	1.0	2.0	0.7	0.6	1.0

[a] Sources: U.S. Bureau of the Census (1973, 1977a).

fathers; by 1976, the disproportion was 13 to one. Decreasing pair-bond stability thus seems to result in increasing the parental burden on women.

This hypothesis is further confirmed when one breaks down these figures by race (Table 2). Note that 99 percent of both white and black children live with relatives. Kin selection thus seems an equally potent force for both whites and blacks—as indeed our theory would predict. Among blacks, however, just less than half of the children under 18 (49.6 percent) lived with both parents in 1976, compared to 85.1 percent of white children. A staggering 40.1 percent of black children lived with their mother as sole parent, compared to 11.8 percent of white children, a difference which, considering the heavy burden of economic disadvantage imposed on families headed by women, goes a long way in accounting for white—black differences in access to scarce resources.

The racial differential in asymmetrical parental investment is actually *understated* by the above statistics, because the ratio of female- to male-headed single-parent families is much higher among blacks than among whites. White children under 18 living with a single parent are about ten times as likely to live with their mother as with their father, but black children are about 27 times as likely to belong to a "matrifocal" family. In the last few years, the burden of parental investment has fallen increasingly on women of both racial groups as we have just seen, and black men have long abandoned child care to their mates at a greater rate than white men, but the burden of single female parenthood has increased faster in recent years for black women than for white women. Between 1970 and 1976, the percentage of white children living in two-parent families declined only slightly (from 87.2 to 85.1 percent), whereas for blacks the decrease was much steeper (from 57.5 to 49.6 percent).

These statistics clearly show that, the less stable the pair-bond becomes, the more asymmetrically parental investment falls on the mother; this is doubly true in groups long characterized by fragile pair-bonds. These statistics have to be tempered by two sets of facts, however. Paternal investment does not always stop at separation (though it typically is greatly reduced), and some of the "slack" in paternal investment is taken up by stepfathers. Sociobiological theory would nevertheless lead one to expect that both absentee fathers and stepfathers are poor substitutes for currently pair-bonded parents. This expectation is overwhelmingly supported by available data on such things as default rates on child-support payments by divorced fathers, rates of paternal abandonment by both married and unmarried fathers, and the like.

Economically, the nuclear family has lost almost all of its functions as a unit of production in the economy, but it remains an essential unit of consumption for a wide range of products from houses and cars, to appliances, clothing and food. Schools have partially taken over some of the training functions of the family, especially after age six, but most American children still get the bulk of their early socialization in nuclear family groups; the ones who do not are often severely handicapped.

The nuclear family continues to be a key socializing agency for children, besides schools and peer groups; it confers and transfers knowledge, skills, traditions, tastes, prejudices, wealth, prestige (and, conversely, poverty and stigma). It makes for much of the continuity in the transmission of culture and subcultures and for much of the enduring inequalities in education, power and income, as shown by the very limited success to combat these inequalities through formal schooling (Coleman et al., 1966; Jencks, 1972). Much as many ideologies have wished the family away, it is still with us and shows every sign of remaining with us for the foreseeable future.

THE CRISIS IN THE AMERICAN FAMILY

At the same time, there is no question that the American family is under severe and perhaps increasing strain. Nor is there any question where the main locus of that strain is: it is in the pair-bond, or in what is now fashionably termed the "redefinition of sex roles." The evolutionary purpose of the pair-bond, as we have seen, is reproduction and the raising of fit offspring. Eliminate or reduce that function, and the pair-bond is necessarily affected. This is precisely what is now taking place, as shown by three statistical trends:

1. The birth rate had declined from 32.3 per 1,000 in 1900, a rate comparable to that of India today, to 27.7 in 1920, and 19.4 in 1940. The postwar "baby boom" pushed the birth rate into the low to mid twenties again for about 20 years (1945 to 1964), but since then it has stayed well below 20 and was down to 14.7 in 1975 (Table 2).
2. The divorce rate had been rising from 1.6 per 1,000 in 1920, to 2.0 in 1940, to 2.2 in 1960. Then came a sharp jump to 3.5 in 1970, 3.7 in 1971, 4.1 in 1972, 4.4 in 1973, and 4.6 in 1974 (Table 2). This divorce epidemic was accompanied by a rise in the marriage rate (from 8.5 per 1,000 in 1960, to 10.5 in 1974), as some three-fourths of these divorces led to remarriage, but the rate of increase of divorces is much faster than that of marriages. Some divorced people do not remarry or do not remarry as fast as they used to.
3. In the last few years, there has been a sharp increase in the number of unmarried persons living together. Between 1970 and 1976, the number of households made up of two unrelated persons of opposite

sex almost exactly doubled (U.S. Bureau of the Census, 1977b). Despite this rapid recent increase, however, these households still only constitute one percent of all households.

A reliable technology of contraception and of safe, early abortion is changing the whole evolutionary game. Mating is now safely divorced from its reproductive consequences and can therefore become purely recreational. The pallid, odorless, colorless, flavorless condom of yesteryear has given way to the contoured, textured, lubricated, delicately hued condom triumphantly advertised on the pages of our mass-circulation magazines. Mating, divorced from its reproductive consequences, also means, of course, that the asymmetry of these consequences for men and women disappears or at least is greatly reduced and that, therefore, sex roles may be expected to change, as they show many signs of doing.

We may indeed be witnessing the beginnings of one of the greatest and profoundest revolutions in human behavior. Furthermore, since the technology of contraception affects the life of women far more drastically than that of men, it can be expected that female behavior is going to change more and faster than male behavior. Those women who prefer childlessness, either temporarily or permanently, are, in effect, assuming a relationship to the system of reproduction that is far more similar to the male one than was the case before. Put differently, the sex asymmetry characteristic of our species' system of reproduction is being reduced through voluntarily lowered fertility. Since it is women who can most directly control this lowering of fertility, having the greatest interest in doing so, they are the ones whose behavior is subject to the greatest change; that change can be expected to be in the masculine direction, since a nonreproductive woman is most apt to perform most male roles in society.

By this prognosis I do not mean to imply that an androgynous society is just around the corner. Indeed, the changes are likely to be far more gradual than many enthusiastic feminists would hope, because there will be much conscious opposition to change. Nevertheless, the potential for change is there, and the conditions for the control of reproduction are such that both our culture and our genetic make-up may adapt to these technological innovations. For the first time in human history our man-made technology may become one of the selective pressures affecting our genetic evolution. Culture is coming full circle: from being predominantly an outgrowth of biological evolution, it is now becoming one of the causative agents of it.

The industrial family has been pronounced in crisis for some time and modern contraception is not the sole reason for the crisis. The industrial nuclear family system puts an enormous burden on the pair-bond. The married couple in contemporary America consists, in a very real sense, of two persons against the world. There is little effective outside support. The success or failure of the family, unsupported by outside pressures and interests with a stake to keep it going, hinges on whether the spouses can bear to stay together. Not surprisingly in a species where the formation and maintenance of a pair-bond is a complex and by no means automatic or irreversible process, many American couples—perhaps about one in three currently—do not stay together. Divorce rates are steadily climbing in the United States as in many other industrial societies.

However, this high divorce rate must be put in proper cross-cultural perspective. Industrial societies are not alone in having high divorce rates. Divorce, as we have seen, is also frequent and relatively unproblematic in many matrilineal societies where male investment in offspring has been partially shifted from father to mother's brother. In industrial societies, however, divorce seems to be linked with low and decreasing fertility. Divorce is more likely when no dependent children are involved—either before they are born or after they have grown up. In between, many couples stay together "for the sake of the children," as they often consciously express their biological fitness game.

Of all the couples who got divorced in the United States in 1975, 43.0 percent had no dependent children of their own under 18, while 25.5 percent had only one own child. Only 12.6 percent had more than two own children, compared to 15.7 percent of all husband-and-wife families. (U.S. Bureau of the Census, 1977b; U.S. Department of H.E.W., 1977c) The difference in number of dependent children between married and divorced couples does not seem great, but it is greatly understated by the fact that divorced people are much younger on the average than married people and, therefore, are much less likely to have children over 18 years of age. Since the statistics only include children under 18, they understate the number of *offspring* of married people much more than of divorced people.

If children are involved in a divorce, the fewer the better for all concerned. Few or no children leave both marriage partners, but especially the woman, more unencumbered to enter a new pair-bond with a minimum of conflicting claims on their parental investment. As for children of divorced parents, they may have to compete for resources with half-siblings, or, worse yet, with unrelated step-children of one or both of their parents. For dependent children, a divorce is almost invariably a bad bargain.

It is little wonder that lowered fertility promotes divorce. But in an industrial society where low fertility has become the norm, the relationship between divorce and fertility can easily become one of reciprocal causation. Low fertility facilitates divorce, but the anticipation of divorce can easily induce couples to postpone reproduction. Not having children, especially for women, is the safest way of keeping one's options open, not only in terms of changing mates, should a better partner come along, but also in terms of career, education, income earning, leisure-time activities and so on.

The third trend, namely, the increase in the number of couples who live together without being married, is not as significant as it is sometimes made out to be. A stable pair-bond does not require marriage; marriage is merely the cultural institutionalization of the pair-bond. It is safe to assume that most of the people who "live together" are in fact pair-bonded and live much the same way as do their married contemporaries. There are obvious tax advantages in not marrying if both partners work, and, in the absence of children, it would be financially foolish for such people to marry. The other two trends, however, are significant and interrelated.

Without denying the impact of modern contraception technology on sex roles and family structure, there are also conservative forces that will slow down the pace of change. *First,* we are programmed to want children, and although some of us put other values higher, some 95 percent of us *postpone* and *limit* reproduction, without foregoing it. Or, we may think when we are young that we do not want children because we want to travel or to pursue a career, or whatever, but we change our minds later.

Second, we are biologically predisposed to form pair-bonds, and, although probably increasing proportions of young people are increasingly experimental in their sexual relationships, only very few are highly promiscuous for very long. The overwhelming majority settle for stable, "satisfying," "meaningful" relationships, that is, for a pair-bond, after a more-or-less brief period of sexual exploration. Whether the pair-bond takes the form of marriage or "living together" matters little, because the two are functionally homologous and, indeed, are increasingly viewed as such. Very possibly, living together will become the norm for childless couples, marriage becoming even more explicitly a partnership agreement to raise children than was the case hitherto. However, this change would not be very drastic. It would simply indicate that more and more people would become aware of the pointlessness of marriage outside reproduction.

Third, for those who want children (still some 95 percent), there is as yet no good substitute for the family as a place to raise them. Nor is there a prospect of any being devised in the foreseeable future at a cost most of us could afford. *Quality* substitutes, such as the kibbutz or the British "public" boarding school, may be educationally adequate, but they are horrendously expensive, rather emotionally unsatisfying to both parents and children, and inefficient at least for the years of early childhood. Industrial societies give us *alternatives* to parenting, especially for women, and they make parenting something less than a full-time occupation, especially for women. But, if we decide to be parents, the conventional family is still by far the most suitable arrangement.

Fourth, the biology of sex roles is still with us. It is perfectly true that in industrial societies most jobs can be performed equally well by men and women, and there can be no practical or ideological objection (at least as far as I am concerned) to giving both women and men equal access to all positions. But that still leaves one basic job at which women are much better than men—having children. Having and raising children is a big and complex job that still puts greater limits on women than on men, as to other things a person can do. Some men are "good with children," while some women are "bad mothers." By and large, however, women are better motivated to take continuous care of children than men, and the job is such that it takes a highly motivated person to handle it well.

In a number of preindustrial societies, upper-class women have delegated much of their mothering to hired female menials (servants, slaves, wet nurses, governesses), but that solution is no longer within the reach of even the very wealthy of industrial societies. The *"au pair* girl" is hardly a satisfactory nanny because she is unlikely to stay more than a few months; besides, she may run off with the husband. Hardly anyone in a modern industrial society is willing to be the kind of life-long family retainer that the traditional nanny was. Even upper-class women now have to take care of their own children if they want the job to be well done. That, in turn, means either competing with men on less then equal terms when it comes to a professional career, politics, business or some other predominantly male pursuits, or foregoing (at least, postponing) reproduction. Neither the National Organization of Women nor the Equal Rights Amendment will change the biological bedrock of asymmetrical parental investment.

Fifth—perhaps the most controversial point—there are biologically predisposed temperamental differences between men and women that correlate with the sexual division of labor. The best known among these is the linkage between the male hormone testosterone and such behavioral traits as a dominance drive and an active sexual drive. I am not suggesting that men are born to dominate and women to be submissive slaves. The relationships are complex. Both men and women have testosterone, and hormonal balance varies from time to time within individuals—and between individuals of the same sex. It is also known that environmental factors, such as success and high status, can affect hormonal level; there is thus probably a feedback mechanism and a reciprocal causation between hormones and behavior. Some women are more dominance-driven than some men; women can be masculinized through artificial hormone treatment and men can be feminized through castration. When all the appropriate qualifications are made, however, the fact remains that males, not only in our species but in many other mammals as well, tend to be on the average more aggressive and more dominance-oriented than females, and that these behavioral proclivities are linked to testosterone levels (Money, 1965; Hamburg and Lunde, 1966).

The impact of all this for sexual roles, including erotic relationships, is that it supports the conventional wisdom in these matters. Men *are* predisposed to take the active, aggressive role in sexual relationships; they *can be* threatened to the point of sexual dysfunction when women attempt to assume the dominant role; there *is* a clear association between sexuality and dominance, with men predisposed to take the dominant role. These complex relationships are currently under investigation by a group of Israeli social scientists who have suggested a linkage between female dominance in sexual relationships and male sexual inadequacy (Shepher et al., 1977). There is much more than "soft" clinical data about the "castrating" female to support these conclusions. Among many primates, for instance, dominance and submission displays (such as mounting and "presenting") take a quasi-sexual form. The dominant animal irrespective of sex assumes the male sexual posture, and the subordinate animal the female posture, again regardless of sex (Maclean, 1965). This is so much the case that dominance and submission displays often take the superficial appearance of homosexual behavior. Male primates who exert dominance tend to mate and reproduce much more. Politics (in the broadest sense of the struggle for dominance) is thus primarily a male game, the end of which is ultimately reproduction (Tiger and Fox, 1971). Sexual politics, indeed, though not quite as Kate Millett (1970) would like!

Ideological passions unfortunately contaminate our way of looking at data and interpreting them. I am not suggesting that male dominance is good, but merely that it *is*. Nor do I deny that individual women *can* be dominant over individual men. On the average, however, males are dominant and the more dominant have, throughout our past evolutionary history, been the more reproductively successful. Dominance displays in men have been selected as sexual "turn ons" for most women and, conversely, female dominance is a sexual "turn off" for most men. Whether we like this or not, this continues to be the case today and to affect sexual relationships. Women can try to assert their dominance, but it is often at the cost of disrupting existing pair-bonds. Not surprisingly, many women never try.

THE JAPANESE FAMILY

We have just taken a look at what is happening to the American system of marriage and kinship under the impact of the multitude of technological and environmental changes that have accompanied industrialization. The United States, however, is only one society among many. Perhaps the changes taking place here are not the product of industrialization as such, but of the unique features of American culture. Let us look at another industrial society, and one which, until a little over a century ago, developed in almost complete independence of the West. Because human evolution is the product of such a complex blend of genetic, environmental and cultural factors, we can expect both convergences and divergences between Japan and the United States as they industrialized.

Japan, with roughly half the population of the United States, is both geographically more compact and much more densely settled—and culturally more homogeneous. There are, to be sure, non-Japanese indigenes on the Island of Hokkaido, the Ainu. Japan has long been in contact with its continental neighbors, mostly China and Korea, adopting much of its culture from China. Since the late 15th century, Japan also has come into contact with Europe, but until the Meiji Restoration of 1868, it largely shunned outside contacts and tried to restrict it to commerce in a few ports. After the Meiji Restoration, Japan "opened up" to the West, adopted its technology, industrialized and joined the Western powers in their imperialistic quest for colonies. These changes resulted in the immigration of foreigners, mostly Koreans, who form the largest alien minority in Japan today. Defeat in World War II brought a wave of American influence evident in such disparate things as the popularity of hamburgers, baseball and rock music, but, still, Japan remains distinctly Japanese and remarkably homogeneous for a country of over 100 million people. In 1950, for instance, only 1.7 percent of the Japanese population had come from outside Japan, compared to 10.3 percent of the population of the United States (Taeuber, 1958). In 1930, only 0.3 percent of the Tokyo population was foreign.

The cultural homogeneity and continuity of Japan make it easier to talk of "the traditional family" than was the case in the United States, a recent amalgam of multiple immigrant groups superimposed on a wide scatter of aboriginal cultures. In Japan, we are talking of one overwhelmingly dominant culture that has been in place for thousands of years with relatively peripheral outside contacts and only moderate immigration. We are also talking of a country with only a little over a century of "modernity" (if by modernity we mean industrialization), the onset of which was clearly marked by the political event of the Meiji Restoration.

During the two-and-a-half centuries of the Tokugawa Shogunate which preceded the Meiji Restoration, and even long before that, Japan was a feudal society, rigidly stratified into estates. At the top were the nobility, subdivided into the feudal lords proper, *daimyo,* and their professional warrior retainers, *samurai.* Then came the peasants, who made up 80 percent of the population; they were free and owned their land, but they were heavily taxed. The urban classes of artisans and merchants, although they often were wealthier than the peasants, were held in even lower social esteem because they were outside the rural feudal order (Fukutake, 1972). Finally, at the bottom of this rigid hierarchy, came a variety of despised pariah groups holding occupations that were considered defiling. These groups were strictly endogamous, and their descendants, known as *eta* or *burakumin,* are still despised today and considered unmarriageable by other Japanese (De Vos and Wagatsuma, 1967). After the Meiji Restoration, class distinctions became somewhat less rigid, but Japan remains to this day a highly stratified and status-conscious society.

The traditional Japanese rural family is the so-called "stem" family, a group made up of a married couple, their unmarried children and one of their married sons (usually the oldest, sometimes the youngest) with his wife and unmarried children. Such a kin group, typically consisting of three generations of patrilineally related males and their spouses, was an economic unit exploiting, in the case of the peasant family, a small farm. To avoid subdividing the land into uneconomically small units, inheritance was generally by primogeniture; the eldest son inherited the bulk of the estate and took over the family farm. In some districts, inheritance was by ultimogeniture (the youngest son inherited), but the Civil Code instituted universal primogeniture in the 19th century (Fukutake, 1972).

Younger sons with no place on the land went off to the town to become artisans, laborers or merchants, and to establish new family units. Thus the rule of primogeniture had a double effect: it encouraged urban migration and created from the outset a difference between urban and rural families. Rural families were ideally extended families, albeit in the minimum form of the stem family: only the son who inherited the property normally stayed with his parents after marriage. Urban families were frequently nuclear, though the urban migrant could, of course, eventually reconstitute a stem family when his eldest son came of marriage age. The traditional rule of residence was thus virilocal for the eldest son and neolocal for younger sons. In addition, there was also an uxorilocal alternative. A family that did not have a son could adopt a son-in-law *(muko-yoshi)* who would then come and reside with his wife and her parents and could become his father-in-law's heir.

The rule of descent was patrilineal. The basic kin group was the *ie,* a patrilineage held to exist independently of its individual members, through the continuity of descent from father to son. The oldest man in the *ie* was its head and thus also the head of the localized stem family. Family property was passed on through him. On his death, his oldest son would "succeed to the house."

 Marriages were arranged between the two *ie* concerned through a go-between and with a view to matching two families of approximately the same status. However, a bride from a family of slightly lower status was acceptable, considered more pliable and manageable as a spouse and daughter-in-law. That is, there was a preference for class isogamy—or slight hypergamy. There was also a tendency toward village endogamy until the late 19th century, but much less so since (Fukutake, 1972). The in-marrying bride owed obedience not only to her husband but to her parents-in-law and, if she proved unsuitable, her father-in-law could bring about a divorce. All social classes were monogamous, although dalliance with courtesans was practiced among the nobility. Daughters were given away with a dowry and, hence, it was an economic burden on a family to have too many of them. Sons were preferred over daughters, and the eldest son, as the future leader of the *ie* had the highest status. Younger sons were valued as possible heirs, should the oldest son die, but otherwise they were expected to become independent and fend for themselves with only a small share of the heirtance.

In what ways did the Japanese family change during the last century, and to what extent can these changes be interpreted as adaptations to industrial conditions? Like other industrial societies, Japan underwent a drastic lowering of both its death and birth rates. (Taeuber, 1958; Fukutake, 1974). Death rates went down from 25.4 per 1,000 in 1920 (a rate comparable to the poorest countries of the world today) to 10.9 in 1950, to 6.5 in 1975 (Table 3). The latter rate is one of the lowest in the world. A similar downward trend is evident in birth rates, although the last big drop was relatively late: it only came with the beginnings of the postwar economic recovery in the early 1950s. From a birth rate of 36.1 per 1,000 in 1920 (comparable to the Indian birth rate today), there was a gradual decline to 28.1 per 1,000 in 1950, interrupted, however, by a postwar baby boom (34.3 per 1,000 in 1947), similar but on a bigger scale than the one experienced in the United States. Then, there was a sharp drop to 19.3 in 1955. Since then, the birth rate stabilized at this low level; in 1975, it was 18.6, barely lower than 20 years earlier (Table 3). In both birth and death rates, Japan evolved much like the United

States did, but the Japanese decline in both came later than in America. For the last couple of decades, the Japanese and American rates are fairly comparable. Both countries have slowly increasing populations with low birth and death rates (Tables 1 and 3).

This double trend toward fewer children and greater longevity inevitably increases the average age of the Japanese population, again a trend characteristic of all industrial and industrializing societies in the last century. These broad demographic trends do indeed confirm that Japan behaves much as other societies have under the impact of industrialization. But, let us look beyond gross vital statistics to the structure of the Japanese family. How has it changed from the traditional model sketched earlier?

In many respects, the Japanese family has evolved in recent decades toward something similar to the Western nuclear family, partly the result of internal changes in response to industrial conditions, and partly the result of external American influence during the postwar occupation and "democratization." Some of these changes were already taking place before World War II, when Japan was already extensively industrialized, but the rate of change accelerated after the war. The direct American contribution to these changes was the "democratization" program imposed by the United States Armed Forces, which introduced a number of legal reforms in the postwar constitution. Equality of the sexes was proclaimed. Marriage by mutual consent of the spouses was established. Inheritance laws were changed, giving rights to the widow and providing for equal division of property among all children—male and female (Fukutake, 1974). In short, the family was legally transformed from a patrilineal *ie* with a head of household and primogeniture in the transmission of property and authority, to a nuclear, conjugal family with equality of rights between spouses and among children.

The patrilineage and the extended family were not abolished, but the new civil code strongly reinforced the trend toward neolocality and nuclear families in the urban areas, undermining the authority and property structure of the *ie*. While Japan cannot be described as a bilateral descent society, its patrilineality, at present, can best be described as weak and shallow.

Let us look at some of these trends in greater detail. As late as 1955, 96.1 percent of all Japanese households were "kinship households," that is, either nuclear families (59.6 percent) or extended virilocal families (36.5 percent). Although well over half of the families were already nuclear, there was no term in the Japanese language for "nuclear family" until the 1960s (Fukutake, 1974). Many of these nuclear families in time became stem families with the addition of a third generation. Between 1955 and 1970, however, extended families declined from well over a third (36.5 percent) to barely over a fourth (25.5 percent) of all households. In the same period, nuclear families increased from 59.6 to 63.4 percent, while single-member households more than tripled, from 3.4 to 10.8 percent. In 1970, almost nine-tenths (88.9 percent) of all Japanese households consisted of family units, while in the United States only four households out of five (80.3 percent) were family groups. Still, the difference between the two societies is not so much in the proportion of the households which are families, as in the proportion of families that are extended ones. Whereas a fourth of Japanese families are still extended ones, less than one American child out of 20 (4.4 percent) lived with relatives other than parents and siblings (U.S. Bureau of Census, 1973).

Obviously, the combination of lower natality, and a shift from extended families to nuclear and single-member households results in a substantial decline in the size of the Japanese household, but, here again, this change was rather late in coming. Before the war, the Japanese household had an average of five members, (4.98 in 1930); this was still the case in 1955 (4.97 members). Then came the rapid decrease: 4.54 in 1960; 4.05 in 1965; 3.69 in 1970. By comparison, the average U.S. household declined from 4.8 in 1900 to 3.2 in 1970. The Japanese household began to decline in size half-a-century later than the United States and it is still considerably larger, but that difference is rapidly decreasing, from 1.1 persons mean difference in household size in 1960, down to 0.5 persons in 1970 (Table 3).

Accompanying these legal and demographic changes, there have also been important changes in attitudes. Fukutake (1974) reports a postwar decline in *"ie* consciousness," in concern over the family status, in the

Table 3. A Comparative Summary of United States and Japanese Demographic and Family Statistics (1900–1975)[a]

Statistic	1900		1920		1940		1960		1970		1975	
	U.S.	Japan	U.S.	Japan	U.S.	Japan	U.S.	Japan	U.S.	Japan	U.S.	Japan
Life Expectancy at Birth	47.3	—	54.1	42.6	62.9	—	69.7	—	70.8	—	72.0	74.0
Crude Birth Rate	32.3	—	27.7	36.1	19.4	29.4	23.6	17.4	18.3	18.6	14.7	18.6
Crude Death Rate	17.2	—	13.0	25.4	10.8	16.4	9.5	—	9.4	7.0	8.9	6.5
Mean Size of Household	4.8	—	4.3	4.9	3.8	5.0	3.4	4.5	3.2	3.7	2.9	—
Marriage Rate per 1000	—	8.2	12.0	9.0	12.1	9.2	8.5	9.3	10.7	10.0	10.5	9.2
Divorce Rate per 1000	—	1.4	1.6	0.9	2.0	0.7	2.2	0.7	3.5	0.9	4.6	1.0

[a] Sources: United Nations (1976); U.S. Bureau of the Census (1961, 1974); Taeuber (1958).

authority of the patriarchal head of household, in male dominance and in rigidity of sex roles. As an index of the rising status of women, he cites the decreasing difference in age of marriage between men and women. Men now marry around 27, as they did before the war, but, whereas their wives were then on the average four years their juniors, the age disparity has been reduced to 2.7 years.

The general picture that emerges from our comparison of Japan and the United States is one of increasing convergence on a small nuclear family with low fertility, as Table 3 shows. While some of the changes reviewed above were undoubtedly accelerated by the American occupation, they probably would have taken place without it; they certainly were not reversed when the United States withdrew as an occupying force. Indeed, they continued unabated. The "American model" was clearly not incompatible with industrial conditions.

Nevertheless, this picture of rapid change must not be overdrawn. Prewar traditions linger. The *ie* system is greatly weakened but not altogether destroyed. In the rural areas, there are still many traditional stem families, and, even in cities, the more conservative, older people still view the stem family as an ideal. Legal provisions for equal inheritance of property are being evaded in favor of the oldest son. Women have more rights than before, but they are still far from equality with men, or even from the position of their American "sisters."

Certainly, many of the changes are resisted and deplored by many people. This is especially true of the decline in filial obligations to elderly parents, a sacred traditional duty of the Japanese son (Fukutake, 1974). The problem is made doubly acute by the ever-rising life expectancy, now about 70 for men and 75 for women.

To Americans, the Japanese still seem to be strongly familistic and, indeed, the contemporary Japanese family still remains substantially stabler and stronger than its American counterpart. This is most obvious in the divorce statistics. Not only is divorce in Japan less than one-fourth as common in the United States, but it does not seem to be rising substantially in recent decades. In fact, the long-range trend in divorce rates has been downward, from 2.5 to 3.0 per 1,000 in the 19th century, down to 0.7 to 1.0 per 1,000 in recent decades (Table 3). The high traditional rate of divorce in Japan had very different causes from the contemporary divorce epidemic in the United States. It reflected mostly the power of dissatisfied parents-in-law to reject their sons' wives if they did not fit in as submissive daughters-in-law. Contemporary divorce, in Japan as in America, reflects more marital incompatibility of the spouses, but it is neither frequent nor rapidly rising. Both marriage and divorce rates remain relatively constant.

Japan also differs from the United States in that the transformations in its family and kinship structure came at a much later phase of its industrialization process. Japan was highly industrialized long before World War II, but it retained what, to Western eyes, seem to be highly traditional structures much longer than did the United States, or even Western Europe. Part of the answer is that Japan, compared to other industrial countries, was (and still is) a much more culturally homogeneous, not to say monolithic, society with a low rate of foreign immigration. But that is not the whole answer. Until recent decades, and still to an appreciable degree today, much Japanese industry and business consisted of small family firms. Business organization was, thus, not incompatible with the retention of a stable, patriarchal, extended family structure.

Even large Japanese industry differs strikingly from its Western counterparts in the extent to which it is paternalistic and has a stable labor force. While the Japanese family has become smaller and less all-encompassing than it was before the war, large Japanese industry has developed on a giant scale an extraordinarily successful familistic model of industrial organization. The pseudo-family of the modern industrial giant, with its cradle-to-the-grave security system, its stable labor force, its company towns, its organized leisure, its loyalty rituals and all the paraphernalia of capitalistic paternalism has become the new extended family of Japan. The real kin ties have indeed been weakened, but the principles and the ideology of kin organization have been extended to business and industrial organizations to a degree unmatched in any other industrial country. If "the business of America is business," it seems that the business of Japan remains the family. Even General MacArthur could not change that. The American model was imported and forcefully advocated, but the Japanese created an industrial society that remains in important respects significantly different from its Western analogues.

ARE INDUSTRIAL SOCIETIES BECOMING EXTINCT?

The most fundamental question posed by modern industrial societies is the apparent spread of voluntary limitation of fertility. The urban milieu has never been a fertile one, but until the 20th century this was easily explainable by the fact that cities were cesspools whose population was regularly decimated by endemic and epidemic diseases. In recent decades, however, these conditions no longer prevail, at least not in the more affluent, industrial countries. People now have the option of raising more children with a greater probability of success than ever before. Artificial lactation even makes possible a reduction of the successful breeding time down to the gestation period. Historically, women could only successfully bear children every three or four years, and suffered infant mortality rates of up to 50 percent. Now, they have the option of having children every year, and infant mortality has dropped to 5 percent or less.

At the same time, we have developed a technology that enables us to separate reliably recreational sex from reproductive sex, and an increasing number of people deliberately choose *not* to maximize their fitness.

If we adopt Dawkins' (1976) conception of the individual organism as an expendable and mortal survival machine for potentially immortal genes, then perhaps one of the greatest revolutions in human, indeed, in evolutionary history is taking place. There is much evidence that deliberate curtailment of reproduction is motivated by hedonism rather than by altruism. That is, people seldom postpone or forego reproduction because they are concerned about the consequences of the human population explosion. Rather, they do so because they would rather spend their time and money on other things—*largely on themselves.* They continue, in short, to behave selfishly, as they have been biologically selected to do. But their selfishness no longer serves the interests of their constituent genes. Increasingly, resources that were traditionally converted into reproduction are now deliberately being diverted to *other* selfish aims. Or better, the selfishness of the individual organism is overriding the selfishness of the gene.

This development is undoubtedly linked with the growth of *self-consciousness* in our species. With it, come intimations of our mortality and our poignant attempts to evade, postpone or deny our biological demise as conscious organisms. Hedonism, asceticism, mysticism are but different attempts to revolt against our biological destiny, or rise above it. Increasing numbers of self-conscious humans have probably felt like telling their genes to go to hell for thousands of years, but, until recently, celibacy was the only effective means to avoid playing the genes' game, and sex was far too sweet a thing to be lightly abandoned. Effective contraception now enables us to have our cake and eat it too. The cost of hedonism is rapidly diminishing. We are successfully overriding our genetic imperatives by turning selfishness to our interests as self-conscious organisms, even at the expense of our constituent genes.

Of course, we may not be able to do so for very long, before we disappear as a species. However, to the ultimate hedonist, only his own lifespan is of any consequence. Perhaps we are seeing the rise of the first, truly emancipated, ruthlessly selfish "me generation." Insofar as sociobiology provides us with a more realistic model of human behavior, it will contribute to the process of growing self-consciousness and, for better or worse, to our emancipation from our reproductive imperative.

SUPPLEMENTARY READINGS

Sources on the American family are numerous. Indeed, most sociology textbooks on the family and marriage deal with little else. None is written within the framework advanced here, but Carter and Glick (1976), Gary R. Lee (1977), Reiss (1976) and Winch (1977) are among the better recent examples of the genre. On the black American family, E. Franklin Frazier (1948), Gutman (1976) and Moynihan (1965) are among the basic sources. For Japan, Befu (1963), Dore (1965), Fukutake (1972, 1974) and Vogel (1971) are among the best sources in English. As a data mine, the U.S. Census is hard to beat; many of the ideas contained in this chapter could be further investigated by census analysis. For an anthropological view of the American kinship system see Schneider (1968) and Schneider and Smith (1973).

EXTENSIONS OF THE FAMILY

Early in this book, I argued that human societies were basically held together by three mechanisms that evolved successively: kin selection, which we share with countless other social organisms is the oldest and most basic; then came reciprocity, the most elementary form of which appeared with sexual reproduction, but enormously elaborated on by humans; and finally came coercion and, more specifically, the kind of collective, organized, premeditated intraspecific parasitism that humans excel at. If kinship is indeed the most basic, universal, successful and ancient basis of sociality in all social organisms, and if kin selection continues to be powerfully operative in even the most complex human societies, we can expect that the idiom of kinship will be extended to forms of social organization larger than the family. We can also expect that the principles of kinship will be invoked to buttress and to legitimate the other two bases of sociality, most especially coercion. Both of these phenomena are indeed extremely widespread, even in the most differentiated societies.

We have already seen how all human societies institutionalize the sexual pair-bond in the form of a socially sanctioned marriage, and how nearly all preindustrial societies expand the ties of reciprocity inherent in the sexual pair-bond from the spouses to their extended kin groups. This reaches its most elaborate form in the more complex of stateless societies where indeed the fundamental elements of the social structure are derivable from the network of consanguineal and affinal ties between individuals,—and between exogamous kin groups. Many of these societies are, in fact, principally held together by the reciprocal obligations of kinship and marriage, both at the individual and at the group level.

As many of these societies have only a few hundred or a few thousand members, and are largely endogamous at the "tribal" level, they are composed of people most of whom are either kin or affines. The ultimate conclusion of this blending of the principles of reciprocity and kin selection into a single coherent social structure is, as we have seen, the combination of unilineal descent, exogamy and preferential cross-cousin marriage.

Chapter 4 dealt extensively with the modes of extension of kinship to reciprocity; there is no need to return to them here. The development of more and more elaborate, extensive and effective systems of coercion over the last few thousand years of the history of stratified, state-organized societies presented a whole new set of problems, however. It was now necessary to obtain, if not the enthusiastic collaboration, at least the sullen compliance of people in their own exploitation. Ultimately, all systems based on coercion must be prepared to resort to violence and make the threat of violence credible enough to be effective. But naked coercion backed up by the continuous exercise of violence is not an efficient way of exploiting people. If one can deceive people into believing that they are being parasitized for their own good, the cost of the coercive apparatus can be reduced and the exploitation can become all the more efficient.

IDEOLOGY

This is where ideology comes in. Ideology is basically a system of mystifications designed to hide parasitic relationships. As such, ideology was born with the state. Stateless societies have systems of religious, ethical, philosophical, scientific and cosmological ideas, but they do not have ideologies as we have just defined them. All states, on the other hand, have official ideologies. The latter in turn, sometimes (though not always) call forth counterideologies which, if their proponents are successful, can become the legitimating ideology of the new ruling class. Basically, three principles can be invoked to legitimate coercion:

1. The simplest is, of course, the principle that might is right—that is, that power needs no justification. It simply is. This is so simple an idea that it hardly qualifies as an ideology. It involves no deception, merely

describing a state of affairs without seeking an appeal to a higher moral principle.

2. The most ubiquitous principle by which power has been legitimated in preindustrial societies has been through some brand of "paternalism"—that is, by invoking the mechanism of kin selection and creating the fiction of kin relatedness where none exists. We will presently examine many examples of paternalism.

3. Since the 18th and 19th centuries, European ideas of liberalism and socialism have increasingly spread to industrial and industrializing societies. These ideologies have in fact substituted reciprocity for kin selection as the justification of coercion. We are now told that we must obey orders and pay taxes, not because the king is our father and he has our welfare at heart, but because the president of the republic is our democratically elected representative and therefore acts in our interests. The reciprocity principle is invoked equally in the ideologies of capitalist and socialist countries, but both become ever more effectively coercive. In agrarian societies, tyranny was tempered by inefficiency; in industrial societies, modern technologies of violence, transportation, communication and information storage and retrieval make genuine totalitarianism a creeping daily reality.

Ideologies, then, are basically attempts (often meeting with only very partial success) to disguise coercion for purposes of intraspecific parasitism as being either kin selection or reciprocity. Ideologies endeavor to make people believe that unequal exploitative relationships are mutually beneficial either because they are, in some sense, analogous to authority relations within a family where every member maximizes his own fitness by contributing to that of the other members or, if that fiction loses any credibility, because the calculus of reciprocal interest underlines the interactions. Paternalism admits the existence of inequality, indeed, it takes it for granted; but it justifies authority and power through the fiction of kinship. "Democratic" ideologies, whether liberal or socialist, abandon the fiction of kinship, but create that of equality. Familism or paternalism is incompatible with an ideology of equality since power inequalities are glaringly obvious in all human families.

The transition from small, culturally homogeneous, agrarian nation-states to large, heterogeneous, bureaucratic, industrial, multinational states makes paternalism increasingly obsolete as an ideology. It is one thing for a traditional Chinese peasant to accept the fiction that the emperor is, in some remote, mystical sense, his father; it is quite another for the Jewish university professor, the Chicano migrant laborer or the black unemployed youth to believe the same about the President of the United States. The supreme feat of the ruling classes of industrial societies, socialist or capitalist, has been to make at least some people believe some of the time that they live in "democratic" countries—that is, that fundamentally parasitic relationships are symbiotic and based on choice and reciprocity rather than power and coercion.

PSEUDO-KINSHIP:
THE INDIVIDUAL LEVEL

Before we examine in greater detail some of these uses of pseudo-kinship to justify exploitation at the group level of stratified societies, however, let us see how the idiom of kinship is manipulated to suit circumstances at the individual level and in unstratified, stateless societies. Even in these relatively undifferentiated societies, the principle of kin selection is frequently extended in two basic ways: either it is "exaggerated" in the sense that a real but distant kin relationship is treated as a close one, or the behavior patterns (verbal and nonverbal) normally restricted to kinsmen are wittingly or unwittingly extended to certain types of kin-unrelated individuals. The most widespread case is that of putative paternity: in practically all human societies, some husbands behave parentally toward children other than their own. Probability of paternity varies from society to society and is one of the most interesting and least studied aspects of human social organization (Alexander, 1978; Greene, 1978; van den Berghe and Barash, 1977).

Frequently a closer relationship is pretended than actually exists as when a person adopts the child of a deceased sibling. The pretense is often trivial, involving little more than a term of address. For example, in many societies that have "classificatory" kin terms, ego calls "brother" or "sister" all the members of his lineage in his own generation, "mother" and "father" all lineage members in his parents' generation, and "son" and "daughter" all the members in the same generation as his children. Real kinship is "exaggerated," at least verbally, although often this verbal behavior in the use of kin terms can become the basis of cooperative behavior if the circumstances warrant it.

A great many societies also extend the fiction, and sometimes the privileges, of membership in the kin groups to various non-kin. Many lineages formally adopt the in-marrying spouses of their members (husbands in the case of matrilineages, wives in the case of patrilineages). Often this is done systematically for every in-marrying spouse; sometimes, this is a selective process. For instance, in patrilineal Japan, a family without a son would adopt a son-in-law to continue the *ie*. (The grandchildren, in this case, would again be real kinsmen, so Japanese son-in-law adoption was really a convenient way to bend the rules of unilineal descent to maximize inclusive fitness.) In a number of African societies, war captives would gradually be adopted in the lineages of their captors. Indeed, in the case of women being captured by patrilineal societies, this posed no problem at all, since they would generally become wives of their male captors and, therefore, bear children who would in any case become lineage members.

Not commonly, the adoption of nonkin as "honorary" kin involves elaborate rituals and these rituals sometimes consciously attempt to mimic a biological relationship. Such, for instance, is the exchange of blood found in some cultures. Such ceremonials are usually referred to in the anthropological literature as ritual kinship. An extremely elaborate and widespread instance thereof concerns the ties of godparenthood established on the rites of passage of the Catholic Church (baptism, confirmation, marriage). These are especially developed in Spain and Hispanic America where they are called *compadrazgo* (Foster, 1953; Colby and van den Berghe, 1961; van den Berghe and van den Berghe, 1966). At all the main rites of passage consecrated by a sacrament of the Church, the biological parents of the person affected choose one or more godparents who assume religious and secular obligations toward both the individual affected and his biological parents.

A set of quasi-kin terms *(compadre, comadre, ahijado, padrino, madrina)* applies to these relationships, and the behavioral consequences of these ties can be quite considerable, although seldom as great as those of real kinship. In some Catholic countries, such as France, an actual kinsman is often chosen as godparent, but in Latin America the usual choice falls on a nonkin with whom one already has ties of reciprocity or dependence. *Compadrazgo* is thus used to reinforce a friendship or acquaintance between social equals, or to improve to one advantage a relation of inequality. For instance, *peones* on an *hacienda* would often choose the owner as godfather of their children in an attempt to mitigate an exploitative relationship and to transform it into one of benevolent paternalism.

Even in the smallest and least differentiated human societies, then, the calculus of kin selection is not a rigid mechanical one. Rather, kinship is an *idiom* that is culturally manipulated and elaborated upon to suit the circumstances. Variations on the theme of biological kinship are played to create or reinforce reciprocity. The idiom of kinship can and often is a hyperbole—or even a complete myth. One cannot, however, jump to the conclusion, as do many anthropologists, that human kinship is therefore a purely cultural phenomenon (Sahlins, 1976). In every human society, real biological kinship also matters a great deal. Culture elaborates on biology; it is not divorced from it.

PSEUDO-KINSHIP:
THE COLLECTIVE LEVEL

Real kinship, as we have seen, operates both at the level of individual relationships between ego and his kinsmen, and at the level of relations between groups: nuclear and extended families, lineages and clans. The largest human group that usually defines itself as constituting, in some sense, a superfamily of related people is what anthropologists call the "tribe" or "ethnic group." Such a group generally corresponds to an inbreeding population, whether there is an explicit prescriptive rule of endogamy or merely a preference for it. Until the last few thousand years, such ethnic groups were relatively small and inbred, being largely made up of people who could trace common kinship. Indeed, even today, a number of ethnic communities still have that character: for example, many of the remaining "primitive" groups that live on the social fringe of larger societies, as well as endogamous castes or "racial" groups that are otherwise economically and politically incorporated into large, complex societies.

To the extent that ethnic groups are small and endogamous, they do indeed constitute real kin groups. Kin selection is probably the basis for the universality of ethnocentrism in human societies, and the ease with which ethnic sentiments and prejudices can be mobilized for collective action. In recent centuries, however, ethnic groups have tended to become larger, to merge into ever bigger states, and to interbreed through migration. Though most ethnic groups continue to define their essence in terms of common descent, the idiom of extended kinship describes less and less of a biological reality. Ethnicity is increasingly becoming pseudo-kinship. It is one thing for two Ashantis or Yorubas from the same town to regard each other as "brothers"; quite another for two black Americans from Harlem. The latter are likely to have ancestry in several different parts of both Africa and Europe, with perhaps a dash of American Indian blood as well, and are probably only slightly more related to each other than any two Europeans, Asians or Africans picked at random. Their "brotherhood" is a biological fiction, and reflects rather the *cultural* reality of a long history of racial discrimination.

Whether ethnicity reflects a real or a putative blood relationship, however, is often of little consequence. In the context of modern, multiethnic societies, ethnic consciousness is much more the outcome of political and economic relations between ethnic groups than of common kinship. Modern ethnic relations are to be understood primarily in terms of the history of migration, conquest, slavery, discrimination, occupational specialization, land tenure and other socially created factors affecting competition for, and distribution of, scarce resources between ethnic groups. Nevertheless, the fact that the idiom of ethnicity is an extension of the idiom of kinship (real or putative), makes ethnic relations fundamentally different from class relations. Ethnic ties, "racial" ties, caste ties are all ascriptive ties that run in families. Even when many members of one ethnic group are not kin, as is now typically the case, it is still true, given endogamy, that most kin and affines are members of one's ethnic group. That is why, even in highly industrialized societies, the idiom of ethnicity is still basically an idiom of extended kinship. It is kin selection writ large, even when it has largely become a fiction (Francis, 1976; Keyes, 1976; van den Berghe, 1978b).

At this point it is interesting to consider the phenomena of race and racism. All or nearly all human groups define themselves as superior to other groups. But their claims to superiority are generally based on cultural rather than any biologically inherited attributes. This culturally based feeling of superiority is called ethnocentrism and it may take a variety of forms: a claim to greater morality, to speaking a more refined language, to having a monopoly of the true faith, to dressing in better clothes, to waging better wars, to excelling in sports or in the arts. By comparison with the multitude of ethnocentric groups that claim cultural superiority, only a few are racist, in the sense of attributing their superiority mainly to better genes. Racism is not a Western, capitalist monopoly, as has sometimes been claimed. Japan and the Watuzi of Rwanda and Burundi in central Africa are examples of non-Western racist societies (Hayashida, 1976; Maquet, 1961). Nevertheless, most of the world's societies showed little if any racism until they came into contact with the West or became incorporated in European colonial empires.

If my argument that the boundaries between endogamous human groups have kinlike properties and are conceived as extensions of kin groups is correct, then does it not stand to reason that highly visible and inherited phenotypes like skin color, hair texture, facial features and the like, would be used as the main markers of group membership? The answer is that this could be expected only in situations where such phenotypes do a reliable job of discriminating between in-group members and outsiders. Under most historical circumstances, cultural attributes, though not genetically inherited, have been far better criteria of group membership, and therefore also of kinship, than physical attributes. Until the last few centuries, small ethnic groups needed to differentiate themselves mostly from their immediate neighbors, who would typically look very much like themselves. Phenotypes would typically show greater variability within groups than between groups. The discriminatory power of skin color, eye color, hair texture, height or any such readily apparent phenotype to differentiate between the population of neighboring villages or towns in most parts of the world is not significantly higher than chance. On the other hand, minute differences of dialect, of tatooing, of dress style, of etiquette are instantaneously and readily apparent to the attuned eye or ear.

This theory explains not only why racism failed to appear in many societies. It also accounts for how it spread like wildfire when it did, namely with the colonial expansion of Europe, especially in the slave societies of the Western Hemisphere, and in the European-dominated frontier societies like South Africa and Australia. To a greater extent than ever before in human history, large numbers of strikingly different-looking people travelled long distances across large phenotypic gradients and found themselves in sudden and sustained contact—in a situation of gross political domination and economic exploitation. All of a sudden, highly visible phenotypic characteristics became excellent predictors of group membership; not surprisingly they were used as such, and since the relationship between groups was highly unequal, the phenotypical distinctions became highly invidious.

As interbreeding began to attenuate phenotypical group boundaries, racism started receding, as for instance in the 19th century in Latin America, although ethnocentrism often continued unabated. Societies like South Africa and the United States where racism remains at a high level, are societies where high rates of racial endogamy persist and, therefore, where phenotypic group boundaries remain relatively reliable.

Once more, we see how complex the interpenetration of culture and biology is. Since kin selection has proven such an effective cement of sociality in human societies, it has been repeatedly extended to these larger groups of real or putative kinsmen we call "tribes," "nations" or "ethnic groups." The recipe of exhibiting solidarity on the basis of shared genes was evolutionarily successful, so it was culturally used, extended, manipulated and elaborated on. But—and here the plot thickens—it turned out that, in most cases, biologically inherited phenotypes were far poorer markers of ethnic group membership, and hence, of kinship, than cultural characteristics. Therefore, cultural markers typically became the main criteria of membership in a group defined by common biological descent. The paradox is only apparent. Humans, being the intelligent and flexible animals they are, will adopt anything that works. They will become racists in situations where physical traits are predictors of in-group membership; where ethnocentrism works better, as is more commonly the case, they will be ethnocentric. All this cultural variability is, however, an elaboration on the theme of kin selection.

PATERNALISM

Another prominent example of how culture elaborates on the idiom of kinship is paternalism, perhaps the most widespread and successful rationalization for tyranny and exploitation in human history. The cultural invention of paternalism is so simple that it has been invented over and over again. The detailed forms of paternalism vary, but the basic ideology is strikingly similar in a wide range of stratified societies. Fundamentally, paternalism is the use of the familistic idiom of kin selection in nonkin relationships for the purpose of justifying coercion and disguising parasitism. It is *the* ideology of complex agrarian societies, although its germs can be found in simpler states, and it continues to linger on in industrial societies. Let us examine a few instances of paternalism in a range of Western and non-Western societies.

A number of traditional African states foreshadow the paternalism of more complex agrarian states. Most African states, at least the simpler ones of central, eastern and south-eastern Africa, while clearly centralized politically, have not yet developed sharp differences between social classes with distinct life-styles and levels of economic consumption. Such, for example, are the kingdoms of the Zulu, the Swazi, the Shambala and many others (Fortes and Evans-Pritchard, 1940; Kuper, 1947; Murdock, 1959; Winans, 1962). In these kingdoms, the members of one of the clans claim superior status over the rest of the population, usually by invoking a principle of collective seniority, such as that the clan ancestor was the senior of a set of brothers, or was invited by the other clans to rule over them because of his wisdom, or some such legitimizing myth.

The king is chosen from the royal clan, but often by a council of commoners rather than by any rigid rule of primogeniture. He is often described in the literature as being "divine" (Murdock, 1959), not so much in the sense that he is literally believed to be a god, but in the sense that he symbolically incarnates the society as a whole, and is looked upon as the father and nominal owner of everybody and everything. In practice, he is often very far from holding absolute power, being restrained by an unwritten constitution, by a complex system of checks and balances, and by the collective and individual power of the heads of the other clans and lineages. The king typically has a much bigger harem than anyone else; in fact, he often deliberately seeks wives among all the other clans and thereby establishes affinal and kin ties with many of his subjects. Such matrimonial politics can be exercised quite effectively in a polygynous society. Besides consolidating his power through affinal and kin ties, the king also maximizes his reproductive fitness. In fact, extensive polygyny is probably the main fringe benefit of kingship in these societies, because there is little surplus accumulation of material goods. The king leads much the same life-style as his subjects, but he heads a much bigger family and has many more children.

In such relatively simple states, the king plays a double game. On the one hand, he uses his political position to become the head of a mammoth-size family of his own. On the other hand, in the process of acquiring wives, he becomes everybody's in-law and his children collectively become almost everyone's kinsmen. In the process, he becomes at once the head of his own superfamily and the superhead of an extended family that incorporates his whole kingdom. The latter role is usually symbolized in ritual that makes him the living image of the society, a "collective representation" in the Durkheimian sense (Durkheim, 1915). Elementary kingdoms are still in a very real sense vast extended families held together by the central figure of the king.

The picture I just drew is highly schematic and a number of African monarchies deviated from this broad pattern. Some were markedly despotic, like the kingdom of Dahomey; some were much more complex than the model just sketched, like the Ethiopian and Western Sudanic kingdoms (Nadel, 1942; Smith, 1960); some originated in conquest and were ethnically stratified into quasi-castes like the Watuzi kingdoms (Maquet, 1961). However, a number of African kingdoms seem to have arisen from a basically familistic model, in which the royal clan asserted some kind of collective seniority over the other clans, and in which the king became both the symbolic father of the entire society, as well as an actual father of hundreds of his subjects. The very first tangible benefit of political power seems to have been reproductive fitness, long before material wealth was converted into tombs, temples and palaces. For all his hundreds of wives, the African king often dwelled in a mud and thatch hut just a little bit bigger than those of other lineage heads. He ate the same food, and apart from a few regalia such as leopard skin, he wore the same clothes. He was basically a *primus inter pares* among lineage heads, a superfather.

If we want to see paternalism erected into the official ideology of the state and elaborated as a total code of daily conduct, we can do no better than go to the Far East. The Confucian ethic that became the moral basis of the world's largest, longest-lasting and most impressive agrarian society was a prototypical ideology of paternalism. Not only did the model endure over two millenia of political continuity in China, but it was successfully exported to Korea and Japan as well, and important aspects of it have survived industrialization in Japan and Communist revolution in China. Not a bad record as a blueprint for despotism!

Confucianism is essentially one-sided kin selection. It emphasizes filial piety as the ultimate virtue, though of course, it also stresses parental responsibility. The state is seen as the highest extension of the family and the emperor as the father of all his subjects. For additional legitimacy, the Chinese and Japanese emperors also claimed divine ancestry, a claim by no means unique to them.

Most religions are based on a paternalistic model of God—man relationships. "Our Father who art in heaven" is far from a uniquely Christian creation. The supreme godhead is generally conceived of as the creator of all things, and of man in particular, and is thus seen as the supreme parental figure. From this paternalistic (or occasionally maternalistic) conception of the God—man relationship, it is only a short step for those in power to claim to be the representatives of God on earth, or indeed even incarnations of the godhead. The trick was repeatedly performed by most of the world's priests and kings. Such was the case in China, Japan, Ancient Egypt, Imperial Rome, the Christian European monarchies up to the 18th century, the Inca Empire, numerous traditional African monarchies, the Islamic kingdoms, the Hindu and Buddhist states of South Asia—indeed practically everywhere one encounters a well-established monarchical tradition.

Confucianism merely excelled in explicity elaborating paternalism into a code of conduct, ethics, administration and law, regulating the minutiae of daily life in vast bureaucratic states. China, in particular, bureaucratized and rationalized paternalism on a scale hitherto undreamt of. Even after the Communist take-over, China retained a distinctly paternalistic flavor, with Mao as the supreme father figure and the Little Red Book as a collection of neo-Confucian analects. As for Japan, the American occupation was partially successful in dethroning the Emperor from his fatherly and divine pedestal, but the paternalistic model of hierarchical relations thrives in industry, banking and commerce (Dore, 1965).

The career of paternalism as the dominant legitimizing ideology of despotism in the Judeo-Christo-Islamic tradition is no less distinguished. The Christian monarchies of Europe were based on the divine right of kings to rule as the secular representatives of God on earth. The Catholic clergy claimed the same prerogatives in the religious sphere, though sometimes the boundaries between the secular and the religious became fuzzy and conflicts of interest arose. As the God—man relationship in Christianity is openly paternalistic, so are the relations between king and subject and between priest and layman, which are seen as delegated from the godhead. Not only is God "Our Father," but so is by extension every priest and secular ruler. So deeply entrenched was this model of despotism that it survived the Bolshevik Revolution. Stalin (with Hitler easily the most bloodthirsty despot of the 20th century) became a worthy successor to the Czars as father of eternal Russia.

Islam differs somewhat from Christianity in that it officially does not have a clergy and consequently makes even less of a distinction between the secular and the religious. The traditional Muslim ruler is a representative of God, in both secular and religious capacities, and the Islamic faith is also based on a paternalistic model of hierarchical relationships. The same is, of course, true of Judaism as well, which shares with Islam a theoretical absence of a clergy combined with a total fusion of the secular and the religious within a paternalistic conception of the God−man relationship. The father is the authority figure, and, commonly, anyone in authority, such as the rabbi, acquires fatherly properties.

When the European countries expanded their rule overseas, it was a foregone conclusion that they would export paternalism with them. Indeed, the European theory and practice of paternalism achieved its greatest and most explicit elaboration where the legitimacy of European rule was most tenuous, namely, as a system of colonial exploitation and of plantation slavery. Not all the colonial powers were equally racist; some, especially France, Portugal and Spain, based their claim to superiority on language, religion and "civilization," while others tended to stress biological superiority. All, however, developed an almost identical brand of paternalism in their colonies. It was the civilizing mission of Europe to uplift the natives, who were seen as irresponsible, uneducated, backward, grown-up children incapable of ruling themselves. The natives were, therefore, fortunate to be ruled by their superior mentors whose duty it was to assume that "white man's burden." With proper guidance, the natives would slowly emerge from their degraded condition and share the blessings of civilization with Europe. The colonized must be grateful to the colonizers for being willing to assume that burden.

All this ideological cant may sound like a caricature today, but it was in fact the dominant legitimizing myth of European colonialism in the 19th and 20th century. Even radicals like Karl Marx thought that England was doing India a favor by leading her from the backward stage of feudalism to the higher stage of capitalism. Woodrow Wilson spoke of self-determination for the minorities of Eastern Europe, but for the supposedly backward peoples of Asia and Africa a system of "mandates" and "trusteeships" was established by the League of Nations first—then the United Nations. The entire spectrum of European ideologies, from right to left, saw colonialism, at its worst as economic exploitation, at its best as a civilizing mission. Colonialism was, or at least ought to have been, it was said, a vast exercise in parental guidance from the enlightened colonizers and obedient gratitude from the benighted natives.

Before paternalism was used to defend colonialism, it already had had a long history of use in the defense of slavery. Slaves too had been declared to be happy-go-lucky, incompetent, immature, irresponsible, grown-up children. Slavery was hailed as a benevolent institution for the uplifting of slaves under the benign guidance of their masters. Slaves too were expected to show gratitude for their enslavement. (A century later, the gates to the Nazi concentration camps proclaimed, *Arbeit macht frei,* "Freedom through labor.")

The prototype of this paternalistic idyl was, of course, the slave plantation, a little world unto itself, and an extended family of sorts, albeit an extraordinarily perverse one. Its patriarchal head was not only its unquestioned despot; he was also, not infrequently, the father or grandfather of some of his slaves. The extensive miscegenation that characterized all slave plantation regimes was perhaps the largest attempt in human history to combine on a commercial scale business and pleasure, exploitation and kin selection (van den Berghe, 1978b).

All these paternalistic ideologies based on an extension, however inappropriate, of principles of kin selection are more characteristic of agrarian societies than of industrial societies, but, as we have seen with Japan, they are not incompatible with even highly industrialized societies. In the West, at least in the core industrial countries of Europe and North America, paternalism is clearly no longer the dominant rationalization for exploitation. Instead it has been supplanted by invoking reciprocity as the basis of domination and parasitism. It goes by the name of democracy, socialism or liberalism, and has been, directly or indirectly, the ideological basis of every revolution since 1789. Even this new ideology of reciprocity, based on freedom and equality, did not entirely discard the idiom of kinship, however. The motto of the French Republic is *Liberté, Egalité, Fraternité.* The emphasis shifted from paternalism to fraternalism; the idiom of kin selection was revamped to project a more egalitarian image.

All the same, the ruling classes of industrial societies no longer seriously attempt to make the masses believe that they behave as benevolent parents to a big, happy family. Rather, they suggest that they govern through the consent of the governed—for the common good. They would have us believe that coercion is a regrettable necessity intended, not to fleece us, but to curb our selfish impulses. The theory of the modern "democratic" state, whether capitalist or socialist, is that the state is the benevolent arbiter that keeps us all honest in order to achieve the greatest possible good for the greatest possible number. The state exists, not to exploit us, but to control cheaters in a vast system of reciprocity held to be equally beneficial to everyone.

CONCLUSION

Let us recapitulate the central arguments of this book. We suggested at the outset that three main mechanisms accounted for human sociality: kin selection, reciprocity and coercion. Since our focus was on the family, we stressed kin selection as the most basic mechanism with the longest evolutionary history. We saw, however, that human systems of kinship and marriage are extremely elaborate, and involve not only kin selection, but also complex forms of reciprocity and coercion.

In this chapter, we suggested that the human family is so much the basic form of human social organization that many of its features have been extended to larger, nonkin groups. There too, we encountered the same three mechanisms of sociality, but we saw that kin selection has such *prima facie* legitimacy that it has been repeatedly invoked, even when it was, in fact, a fiction to justify the most exploitative forms of coercion. Increasingly, in the last two centuries, reciprocity rather than kin selection has become the main ideological underpinning of coercion.

A full understanding of human kinship and marriage, and, by extension, of human behavior in general can only be gained within a broad evolutionary perspective. Human behavior is the adaptive product of an extraordinarily complex interplay between a multitude of genotypes and a vast array of environmental factors. The issue, therefore, is not whether genes are more important than culture, for both are inextricably intertwined. Culture itself grew out of a process of biological evolution, but it gained sufficient autonomy from specific genotypes to become not only an array of behavioral phenotypes, but also a man-made part of the environment. Indeed, humans have now achieved the cultural capability of consciously controlling and modifying the genotype of their own and many other species. The feedbacks between heredity and environment, between nature and nurture, are more complex than ever. Therefore, it is becoming increasingly important to reincorporate the social sciences into the scientific theory that, for well over a century, has had no successful rival in explaining the modification of life forms on our planet: Darwinian evolutionism.

To be sure, culture is, in some respects, an emergent phenomenon for our species. It provides us with an additional method of adaptation that is Lamarckian in nature and therefore much faster than Darwinian natural selection. The emergent character of human culture does give the sciences of human behavior a special place, but it does not justify their separation from the natural sciences, anymore than the life sciences can be kept distinct from the physical sciences. Life, too, is an emergent principle in the organization of matter. Life is matter that achieved the capability of reproducing itself. Clearly, the subject matter of biology cannot be completely reduced to chemistry and physics; but, equally obviously, biophysics and biochemistry underlie a well-rounded understanding of life forms. Not only that, but, as biology advances, attempts to reduce the emergent phenomena of life to their underlying chemistry and physics have become increasingly successful.

This book has argued that the social sciences must now undergo the same process if they are to develop as scientific discipline. They are not purely and simply reducible to biology, but they must become an extension of the other sciences that specialize in lower levels of the organization of matter. Human behavior and culture can no longer be treated as closed systems understandable only in terms of themselves. They must be seen as one species' special way of adapting, and this perspective, in turn, implies a holistic and evolutionary view of the universe that incorporates the study of our behavior in a general theory of the organization of matter and more especially of living matter. Every emergent phenomenon brings forth a new level in the organization of matter and thus justifies a new spate of scientific specialties, but the higher level always includes all of the lower levels. This is what the mainstream of the social sciences largely chose to ignore for half a century. They must now either abandon their isolation from the rest of the scientific enterprise or, alternatively, abandon any claim to scientific status.

SUPPLEMENTARY READINGS

Though illustrative materials supporting the arguments of this chapter are abundant, and have been referenced in the text, the central ideas are largely my own and can be found in expanded form in van den Berghe (1978a) and in my introduction to van den Berghe (1978b). For partially parallel, partially divergent applications of sociobiology to humans, see Alexander (1971, 1979), the last chapters of the respective books by Dawkins (1976), Barash (1977) and Wilson (1975, 1978).

GLOSSARY

Affines   Persons related by marriage.

Agnates   Patrilineally related kinsmen, as distinguished from *cognates*.

Allele   One of several alternative forms of a gene located on a particular *locus* of a *chromosome*.

Alter   The other organism interacting with *ego*.

Altricial Birds   Birds whose fledglings have to be fed. As distinguished from *Precocial Birds*.

Altruism   In sociobiology, an act that increases the fitness of alter at some fitness cost to ego.

Arboreal Primate   A primate that spends most of its life in trees. As opposed to a *Terrestrial Primate*.

Avunculocal Residence   A rule whereby a male is expected to reside with his mother's brother, whose daughter he often marries.

Bifurcate Merging Kin Terminology   A system of kin terms in which some collateral relatives (e.g., uncles) are called by the same terms as lineal relatives (e.g., parents), and some are differentiated from lineal relatives. Often father's brothers and mother's sisters are called the same as parents, but not father's sisters, nor mother's brothers.

Bilateral Descent   A social rule of descent that ascribes equal or nearly equal significance to all ancestors.

Bilocal Residence   A rule that residence may be either *virilocal* or *uxorilocal*. Also sometimes called *Ambilocal* or *Utrolocal Residence*.

Biomass   The mass in kilograms of living matter in a given habitat.

Bridewealth   Sometimes also called *Brideprice.* A specified type and quantity of goods transferred from the kinsmen of the groom to the kinsmen of the bride to make marriage binding and to legitimate the offspring.

Chiasma   Chromosomal crossover during *meiosis.*

Chromosome   A strain of DNA material that carries genes.

Clan   A corporate kin group whose members, rightly or wrongly, claim common descent from a single, often mythical ancestor. *Patriclans* are based on *patrilineal descent; matriclans* on *matrilineal descent.* Clans are usually subdivided into *lineages.*

Coercion   The use of force or the threat of force to modify alter's behavior.

Cognates   Bilaterally related kinsmen.

Collateral Relatives   Relatives outside ego's direct line of descent, e.g., siblings, uncles, cousins.

Consanguineal Relatives   Persons related by common descent.

Conspecific   A member of ego's species.

Cross-Cousin   Ego's Mother's Brother's Child or Father's Sister's Child, as distinguished from *Parallel-Cousins.*

Culture   The social transmission of learned behavior by means of symbolic language, and the material artifacts resulting therefrom.

Diploid   A cell of organism with a double set of homologous chromosomes.

Dominant Allele   The allele of a gene which determines the phenotype of the heterozygote.

Double Descent   Also called "Double Unilineal Descent," exists in societies that have both *patrilineages* and *matrilineages,* usually with different functions.

Dowry   The passage of property from the kin group of the bride to the bride herself or to her husband on marriage. As distinguished from *Bridewealth.*

Ego   In kinship analysis, the hypothetical person of either sex from whose perspective a tie of kinship or marriage is traced. By extension, the organism from whose perspective a relationship is traced, as distinguished from *alter.*

Emi   The Nupe term for "house," referring to a localized patrilineage segment.

Endogamy   A rule that prescribes marriage within a socially defined group. Also a tendency to marry within a group, without an explicit rule to that effect, as distinguished from *exogamy.*

Epigamic Selection   The form of sexual selection in which one sex of a species seeks to gain reproductive access to the other by making itself attractive.

Eskimo Cousin Terminology   All cousins are referred to or called by the same term, which is different from the term used for siblings. (The United States has an Eskimo cousin terminology.)

Ethology   The study of animal behavior.

Eusociality   A condition among social insects whereby sociality is promoted by the presence of sterile castes (such as worker bees, ants and termites).

Exogamy   A rule that prescribes marriage outside a socially defined group, often a *lineage* or *clan*. Also a tendency to marry outside a group, without an explicit rule to that effect, as distinguished from *endogamy*.

Extended Family   A kin group consisting of other relatives in addition to parents and unmarried offspring.

Fitness   A measure of reproductive success.

Fraternal Polyandry   Marriage by a woman to a set of brothers.

Gamete   A reproductive cell, either sperm or egg.

Gene   The basic unit of DNA material that determines a hereditary trait.

Gene Pool   All the alleles present in a population.

Genotype   The genetic make-up of an organism, as distinguished from *phenotype*.

Group Marriage   The simultaneous mating of several men to several women.

Haploid   A cell or organism with a single set of chromosomes, as distinguished from *diploid*.

Hermaphrodite   An organism carrying both male and female sex organs.

Heterosis   A condition under which a *heterozygote* has greater fitness than either the *homozygote recessive* or the *homozygote dominant*.

Heterozygote   An individual possessing two different alleles of a given gene, as opposed to a *Homozygote*.

Homozygote   An individual possessing two identical alleles of a given gene, as opposed to a *Heterozygote*.

Hypergamy   A rule or preference for a woman to marry a man of higher status or rank than herself.

Ie   The Japanese patrilineal kin group.

Inbreeding   Breeding between biologically related individuals.

Incest Avoidance   The predisposition against mating with kin.

Incest Taboo   The social sanctions for *Incest Avoidance*.

Inclusive Fitness   Reproductive success in terms not only of ego's direct reproduction, but of the reproduction of all of ego's relatives, weighted by degree of relatedness.

Intrasexual Selection   The form of sexual selection whereby one sex of a species (usually the male) seeks to eliminate other members of that sex from reproductive access to the other sex.

Iroquois Cousin Terminology   A type of *Bifurcate Merging* kin terminology in which *Parallel-Cousins* are called by the same term as siblings, but differentiated from *Cross-Cousins*.

Jati   A Hindu endogamous caste group.

K Selection   Selection for small number of offspring with great investment in each, leading to relatively stable populations, as distinguished from *r Selection*.

Kibbutz   Utopian Jewish settlement in Israel in which all means of production are held in common, and in which most aspects of life, including child raising, are communal.

Kin Selection   The propensity to act beneficently toward related organisms. Nepotism. See also *Inclusive Fitness*.

Kindred   An ego-centered, bilateral kin group.

Lek   An area used by a species for communal courtship displays.

Levirate   Marriage by a man of his deceased brother's widow.

Lineage   A corporate kin group formed by a rule of unilineal descent. *Patrilineages* are groups that trace common descent to a known male ancestor. *Matrilineages* trace common descent through a female ancestor.

Lineal Relatives   Ego's direct ascendants or descendants.

Locus   In genetics, the particular site of a *gene* on a *chromosome*.

Marriage   Socially sanctioned mating in humans.

Matrifocal Family   A family in which an adult female assumes exclusive or nearly exclusive parental responsibility.

Matrilateral   On the mother's side. Not the same as *Matrilineal*, since "Matrilateral" refers to all relatives of the mother, not only to members of her *matrilineage*.

Matrilineal descent   A social rule of descent that emphasizes descent through females.

Matriclan   A clan tracing descent in the female line.

Matrilineage   A corporate kin group formed by a rule of *matrilineal descent*.

Matrilocal Residence   See *Uxorilocal Residence*.

Meiosis   The process through which the *diploid chromosome* number is reduced by half.

Mitosis   Reproduction by cell division.

Moiety   Half of a society composed of two and only two *clans* (from the French word *moitié* for "half ").

Monogamy   Stable mating between a single male and a single female.

Monozygotic Twins   Identical twins from a single fertilized egg.

Neolocal Residence   A rule whereby a couple, upon marriage, are expected to establish a residence separate from both the groom's and the bride's kinsmen.

Nuclear Family   A kin group consisting only of parents and unmarried offspring.

Ontogeny   The specific life history of a given organism, as distinguished from *phylogeny*.

Pair-bond   A stable mating relationship between an individual male and female.

Panmixia   A condition under which all members of one sex in a population have an equal probability of mating with any member of the other sex. Random mating.

Parallel-Cousin   Ego's Mother's Sister's Child or Father's Brother's Child, as distinguished from *Cross-Cousins*.

Parental Investment   Behavior of parents tending to increase fitness of offspring.

Parthenogenesis   Reproduction of individuals from unfertilized ova.

Patriclan   A clan tracing descent in the male line.

Patrilateral   On the father's side. Not the same as *Patrilineal,* since "Patrilateral" refers to all relatives on father's side, not only to members of father's *patrilineage.*

Patrilineage   A corporate kin group formed by a rule of *patrilineal descent.* Its members are called *agnates.*

Patrilineal Descent   A social rule of descent that emphasizes descent through males.

Patrilocal Residence   See *Virilocal Residence.*

Phenotype   The outward, observable appearance of an organism, as distinguished from *genotype.*

Phylogeny   The evolutionary history of a group of related organisms, as distinguished from *ontogeny.*

Polyandry   Stable mating between a single female and two or more males.

Polygamy   Stable mating between a single member of one sex and two or more members of the other sex. Can be either *Polygyny* or *Polyandry.*

Polygenic traits   Traits determined by more than one gene.

Polygyny   Stable mating between a single male and two or more females.

Population   In genetics, an in-breeding group distinct from other groups of the same species.

Precocial Birds   Birds that start feeding themselves soon after hatching.

Primates   An order of mammals which includes some 190 living species of prosimians, monkeys, apes and man.

Primogeniture   Inheritance by the oldest child, often the oldest male child.

Promiscuity   The absence of stable mating relationships between individual males and females. Indiscriminate mating.

Prostitution   Sexual promiscuity for gain.

r Selection   Selection for rapid population increase through large number of offspring with little investment in each, as distinguished from *K Selection.*

Recessive Allele   The allele of a *gene* which has no effect on the *phenotype* of the *heterozygote.*

Reciprocity   Doing alter a favor in expectation of return. Sometimes called *Reciprocal Altruism.*

Sexual Bimaturism   The difference in maturation time taken by the males versus the females of a species to become reproductive.

Sexual Dimorphism   The phenotypical differences between the males and the females of a species.

Sexual Selection   The competition between members of one sex of a species, usually the male, for reproductive access to the other sex, usually the female.

Sociobiology   The application of Darwinian evolutionary theory to animal behavior.

Sororal Polygyny   Marriage by a man to a set of sisters.

Sororate   Marriage by a man of his deceased wife's sister.

Spacing   The maintenance of physical distance between organisms of the same species.

Stem Family   A kin group consisting of parents, their unmarried offspring and one married son with his wife and children.

Terrestrial Primate   A primate that spends much of its life on the ground, as opposed to an *Arboreal Primate.*

Territoriality   The defense or marking of fixed space by an individual or group against occupation or use by other conspecifics.

Tradition   In ethology, a particular form of learned behavior, characteristic of a specific animal population, but not of the species as a whole.

Ultimogeniture   Inheritance by the youngest child, often the youngest male child.

Unilineal Descent   A social rule of descent that emphasizes a single line of descent, either *patrilineal* or *matrilineal.*

Uxorilocal Residence   A rule whereby a man, upon marriage, is expected to go and live with his wife and her relatives.

Virilocal Residence   A rule whereby a woman, upon marriage, is expected to go and live with her husband and his relatives.

Zygote   The *diploid* cell resulting from the fusion of two *haploid gametes.*

BIBLIOGRAPHY

Aberle, David F.
    1961a   "Matrilineal Descent in Cross-Cultural Perspective," in David Schneider and Kathleen Gough, eds., *Matrilineal Kinship*, Berkeley: University of California Press.
    1961b   "Navaho," in David M. Schneider and Kathleen Gough, eds., *Matrilineal Kinship*, Berkeley: University of California Press.

Aberle, David F., et al.
    1963   "The Incest Taboo and the Mating Patterns of Animals," *American Anthropologist* 65, 253–266.

Adams, Bert N.
    1968   *Kinship in an Urban Setting*, Chicago: Markham.

Adelman, Bob, and Susan Hall
    1972   *Gentleman of Leisure*, New York: New American Library.

Alexander, Richard D.
    1971   "The Search for an Evolutionary Philosophy of Man," *Proceedings of the Royal Society of Victoria* 84, 99–120.
    1974   "The Evolution of Social Behavior," *Annual Review of Ecology and Systematics* 5, 325–383.
    1975   "The Search for a General Theory of Behavior," *Behavioral Science* 20, 77–100.
    1977   "Review of Marshall D. Sahlins' *The Use and Abuse of Biology*," *American Anthropologist* 79(4), 917–920.

1979   "Natural Selection and the Analysis of Human Sociality," in C.E. Goulden, ed., *Changing Scenes in the Natural Sciences*, Philadelphia: Philadelphia Academy of Natural Sciences.

Ayala, Francisco J.
1978   "The Mechanisms of Evolution," *Scientific American* 239(3), 56–69.

Bachofen, Johann J.
1861   *Das Mutterrecht*, Stuttgart: Krais and Hoffmann.

Bandura, Albert
1969   *Principles of Behavior Modification*, New York: Holt, Rinehart and Winston.

Barash, David P.
1975   "Ecology of Parental Behavior in the Hoary Marmot (Marmota caligata)," *Journal of Mammalogy* 56, 612–615.
1977   *Sociobiology and Behavior*, New York: Elsevier.

Barkow, Jerome H.
1978a   "Culture and Sociobiology," *American Anthropologist* 80(1), 5–20.
1978b   "Social Norms, the Self and Sociobiology," *Current Anthropology* 19(1), 99–118.

Barnes, J.A.
1971   *Three Styles in the Study of Kinship*, Berkeley: University of California Press.

Bartell, G.D.
1971   *Group Sex*, New York: New American Library.

Beach, Frank A.
1976a   "Cross-Species Comparisons and the Human Heritage," in Frank A. Beach, ed., *Human Sexuality in Four Perspectives*, Baltimore: The Johns Hopkins University Press.

Beach, Frank A., ed.
1976b   *Human Sexuality in Four Perspectives*, Baltimore: The Johns Hopkins University Press.

Beardsley, R.K., J.W. Hall and R.E. Ward
1959   *Village Japan*, Chicago: The University of Chicago Press.

Beattie, J.H.M.
1964   "Kinship and Social Anthropology," *Man* 64, 101–103.

Befu, Harumi
1963   "Patrilineal Descent and Personal Kindred in Japan," *American Anthropologist* 65(6), 1328–1341.

Bell, Alan P., and M.S. Weinberg
1978   *Homosexualities*, New York: Simon and Shuster.

Bell, Norman W., and Ezra Vogel, eds.
1968   *A Modern Introduction to the Family*, Glencoe, IL: The Free Press.

Bellah, Robert N.
1952   *Apache Kinship Systems*, Cambridge: Harvard University Press.

Berndt, Ronald M.
    1962   *Excess and Restraint. Social Control Among a New Guinea Mountain People,* Chicago: The University of Chicago Press.

Bigelow, Robert
    1969   *The Dawn Warriors,* Boston: Little Brown.

Bodmer, W. F., and L. L. Cavalli-Sforza
    1976   *Genetics, Evolution and Man,* San Francisco: Freeman.

Bohannan, Paul
    1963   *Social Anthropology,* New York: Holt, Rinehart and Winston.

Bohannan, Paul, and John Middleton, eds.
    1968   *Marriage, Family and Residence,* New York: Doubleday.

Bowlby, John
    1969   *Attachment,* New York: Basic Books.

Broude, Gwen J., and Sarah J. Greene
    1976   "Cross-Cultural Codes on Twenty Sexual Attitudes and Practices," *Ethnology* 15(4), 409–429.

Burgess, Robert L., and Don Bushell, eds.
    1969   *Behavioral Sociology,* New York: Columbia University Press.

Campbell, B., ed.
    1972   *Sexual Selection and the Descent of Man, 1871–1971,* Chicago: Aldine.

Campbell, D. T.
    1975   "On the Conflicts Between Biological and Social Evolution and Between Psychology and Moral Tradition," *American Psychologist* 30, 1103–1126.

Carden, Maren L.
    1969   *Oneida: Utopian Community to Modern Corporation,* Baltimore: The Johns Hopkins University Press.

Carneiro, Robert L., and Daisy F. Hilse
    1966   "On Determining the Probable Rate of Population Growth During the Neolithic," *American Anthropologist* 68(1), 177–181.

Carter, Hugh, and Paul C. Glick
    1976   *Marriage and Divorce,* Cambridge: Harvard University Press.

Cavalli-Sforza, L. L., and W. F. Bodmer
    1971   *The Genetics of Human Populations,* San Francisco: Freeman.

Chagnon, Napoleon A.
    1966   *Yanomamö Warfare, Social Organization and Marriage Alliances,* Ann Arbor: University of Michigan Ph.D. Dissertation.
    1974   *Studying the Yanomamö,* New York: Holt, Rinehart and Winston.
    1977   *Yanomamö, The Fierce People,* New York: Holt, Rinehart and Winston.

Chagnon, Napoleon A., and William Irons, eds.
    1979   *Evolutionary Biology and Human Social Behavior,* North Scituate, MA: Duxbury Press.

Clignet, Rémi
    1970   *Many Wives, Many Powers: Authority and Power in Polygynous Families,* Evanston, IL: Northwestern University Press.

Clignet, Rémi, and Philip Foster
1966   *The Fortunate Few,* Evanston, IL: Northwestern University Press.

Clutton-Brock, T.H., and Paul H. Harvey, eds.
1978a   *Readings in Sociobiology,* Reading: Freeman.
1978b   "Mammals, Resources and Reproductive Strategies," *Nature* 273, 191–195.

Cohen, Yehudi
1978   "The Disappearance of the Incest Taboo," *Human Nature* 1(7), 27–78.

Colby, Benjamin N., and Pierre L. van den Berghe
1961   "Ethnic Relations in South-Eastern Mexico," *American Anthropologist* 63, 772–792.

Coleman, J.S., et al.
1966   *Equality of Educational Opportunity,* Washington, DC: U.S. Government Printing Office.

Constantine L., and J. Constantine
1973   *Group Marriage,* New York: Macmillan.

Coser, Rose L., ed.
1964   *The Family: Its Structure and Functions,* New York: St. Martin's Press.

Cowgill, George L.
1975   "On Causes and Consequences of Ancient and Modern Population Changes," *American Anthropologist* 77(3), 505–525.

Daly, Martin, and Margo Wilson
1978   *Sex, Evolution and Behavior,* North Scituate, MA: Duxbury Press.

D'Andrade, Roy G.
1966   "Sex Differences and Cultural Institutions," in Eleanor E. Maccoby, ed., *The Development of Sex Differences,* Stanford: Stanford University Press.

Darlington, C.D.
1960   "Cousin Marriage and the Evolution of the Breeding System in Man," *Heredity* 14, 297–332.

Darwin, Charles
1871   *The Descent of Man and Selection in Relation to Sex,* New York: Appleton.

Davenport, William H.
1976   "Sex in Cross-Cultural Perspective," in Frank A. Beach, ed., *Human Sexuality in Four Perspectives,* Baltimore: The Johns Hopkins University Press.

Davis, Kingsley, and W.L. Warner
1937   "Structural Analysis of Kinship," *American Anthropologist* 39, 291–313.

Dawkins, Richard
1976   *The Selfish Gene,* London: Oxford University Press.

Deaux, Kay
1976   *The Behavior of Women and Men,* Belmont, CA: Wadsworth.

Denniston, R. H.
1965   "Ambisexuality in Animals," in Judd Marmor, ed., *Sexual Inversion,*
New York: Basic Books.

De Vos, George, and Hiroshi Wagatsuma
1967   *Japan's Invisible Race,* Berkeley: University of California Press.

Dore, R. P.
1965   *City of Life in Japan,* Berkeley: University of California Press.

Dorjahn, Vernon
1954   *The Demographic Aspects of African Polygyny,* Evanston, IL: Northwestern University Ph.D. Dissertation.

Durkheim, Emile
1915   *The Elementary Form of Religious Life,* London: Allen and Unwin.

Dyson-Hudson, Rada, and Eric A. Smith
1978   "Human Territoriality, an Ecological Reassessment." *American Anthropologist* 80(1), 21–41.

Eaton, Randall L.
1978   "Why Some Felids Copulate So Much," *Carnivore* 1, 42–51.

Eibl-Eibesfeldt, Irenäus
1977   *Ethology: The Biology of Behavior,* New York: Holt, Rinehart and
Winston.

Eisenberg, J. F., and W. S. Dillon, eds.
1971   *Man and Beast, Comparative Social Behavior,* Washington, DC: Smith-
sonian Institution Press.

Ellis, Albert, and Albert Abarnabel, eds.
1973   *The Encyclopedia of Sexual Behavior,* New York: Jason Aronson.

Ember, Melvin, and Carol R. Ember
1971   "The Conditions Favoring Matrilocal Versus Patrilocal Residence,"
American Anthropologist 73(3), 571–594.

Embree, John F.
1939   *Suye Mura, A Japanese Village,* Chicago: The University of Chicago
Press.

Emlen, Stephen T., and Lewis W. Oring
1977   "Ecology, Sexual Selection and the Evolution of Mating Systems,"
Science, 197 (4300), 215–223.

Engels, Frederick
1884   *The Origin of the Family, Private Property and the State,* New York:
International Publishers (reprinted in 1942).

Evans-Pritchard, E. E.
1940   *The Nuer,* London: Oxford University Press.

Farber, Bernard
1973   *Family and Kinship in Modern Society,* Glenview, IL: Scott, Foresman.

Feldman, M. W., and R. C. Lewontin
1975   "The Heritability Hang-up," *Science* 190, 1163–1168.

Firth, Raymond
1936   *We the Tikopia,* London: Oxford University Press.

Fogel, Robert W., and Stanley L. Engerman
1974   *Time on the Cross,* Boston: Little, Brown.

Ford, Clellan S., and Frank A. Beach
1951   *Patterns of Sexual Behavior,* New York: Harper and Row.

Forde, Daryll
1955   "The Nupe," in *Peoples of the Niger-Benue Confluence,* Part X, Ethnographic Survey of Africa, London: International African Institute.

Fortes, Meyer
1949   *The Web of Kinship Among the Tallensi,* London: Oxford University Press.
1953   "The Structure of Unilineal Descent Groups," *American Anthropologist* 55, 17–41.
1959   "Descent, Filiation and Affinity," *Man* 59, 193–197, 206–212.
1969   *Kinship and the Social Order,* Chicago: Aldine.
1970   *Time and Social Structure,* London: Athlone.

Fortes, Meyer, and E. E. Evans-Pritchard, eds.
1940   African Political Systems, London: Oxford University Press.

Foster, George M.
1953   "Compadrazgo in Spain and in Spanish America," *Southwestern Journal of Anthropology* 9, 1–28.

Fox, Robin
1962   "Sibling Incest," *British Journal of Sociology* 13, 128–150.
1967   *Kinship and Marriage,* Harmondsworth: Penguin.
1972   "Alliance and Constraint," in B. Campbell, ed., *Sexual Selection and the Descent of Man, 1871–1971,* Chicago: Aldine.

Fox, Robin, ed.
1975   *Biosocial Anthropology,* New York: John Wiley and Sons.

Francis, E. K.
1976   *Interethnic Relations,* New York: Elsevier.

Frazer, James G.
1910   *Totemism and Exogamy,* London: Macmillan.

Frazier, E. Franklin
1948   *The Negro Family in the United States,* New York: Citadel Press.

Freud, Sigmund
1918   *Totem and Taboo,* New York: A.A. Brill.

Friedl, Ernestine
1975   *Women and Men: An Anthropologist's View,* New York: Holt, Rinehart and Winston.

Fukutake, Tadashi
1972   *Japanese Rural Society,* Ithaca, NY: Cornell University Press.
1974   *Japanese Society Today,* Tokyo: University of Tokyo Press.

Gagnon, John H.
1977   *Human Sexualities,* Glenview, IL: Scott, Foresman.

Gagnon, John H., and William Simon

1973   *Sexual Conduct, The Social Sources of Human Sexuality,* Chicago: Aldine-Atherton.

Gluckman, Max
1950   "Kinship and Marriage Among the Lozi of Northern Rhodesia and the Zulu of Natal," in A.R. Radcliffe-Brown and Daryll Forde, eds., *African Systems of Kinship and Marriage,* London: Oxford University Press.

Goffman, Erving
1976   "Gender Advertisements," *Studies in the Anthropology of Visual Communication* 3(2), 65–154.

Goode, Erich
1978   *Deviant Behavior,* Englewood Cliffs, NJ: Prentice-Hall.

Goode, William J.
1956   *After Divorce,* New York: The Free Press.
1963   *World Revolution and Family Patterns,* New York: The Free Press.
1964   *The Family,* Englewood Cliffs, NJ: Prentice-Hall.

Goody, Jack
1976   *Production and Reproduction,* London: Cambridge University Press.

Goody, Jack, and S.J. Tambiah
1973   *Bridewealth and Dowry,* Cambridge: Cambridge University Press.

Gordon, Michael
1978   *The American Family,* New York: Random House.

Gough, E. Kathleen
1959   "The Nayars and the Definition of Marriage," *Journal of the Royal Anthropological Institute* 89(1), 23–34.
1968   "Is the Family Universal?" in Norman W. Bell and Ezra F. Vogel, eds., *A Modern Introduction to the Family,* New York: The Free Press.

Greene, Penelope
1978   "Promiscuity, Paternity and Culture," *American Ethnologist* 5(1), 151–159.

Gregory, Michael S., et al., eds.
1978   *Sociobiology and Human Nature,* San Francisco: Jossey Bass.

Gutman, Herbert
1976   *The Black Family in Slavery and Freedom, 1750–1925,* New York: Pantheon.

Hall, E.T.
1969   *The Hidden Dimension,* Garden City, NY: Doubleday.
1973   *The Silent Language,* Garden City, NY: Doubleday.

Hamburg, David A., and Donald T. Lunde
1966   "Sex Hormones in the Development of Sex Differences in Human Behavior," in Eleanor Maccoby, ed. *The Development of Sex Differences,* Stanford: Stanford University Press.

Hamilton, William D.
1964   "The Genetical Evolution of Social Behaviour," *Journal of Theoretical Biology* 7, 1–52.

1967   "Extraordinary Sex Ratios," *Science* 156, 477–488.
1972   "Altruism and Related Phenomena," *Annual Review of Ecology and Systematics* 3, 193–232.

Hanley, Susan B., and Kozo Yamamura
1977   *Economic and Demographic Change in Preindustrial Japan, 1600–1868,* Princeton, NJ: Princeton University Press.

Harlow, Harry F., and Margaret K. Harlow
1965   "The Effect of Rearing Conditions on Behavior," in John Money, ed., *Sex Research: New Developments,* New York: Holt, Rinehart and Winston.

Harris, Marvin
1968   *The Rise of Anthropological Theory,* New York: Thomas Y. Crowell.
1974   *Cows, Pigs, Wars and Witches,* New York: Random House.
1975   *Culture, People and Nature,* New York: Thomas Y. Crowell.
1977   *Cannibals and Kings, The Origins of Culture,* New York: Random House.

Hartung, John
1976   "On Natural Selection and the Inheritance of Wealth," *Current Anthropology* 17(4), 607–622.

Hawley, Amos H.
1950   *Human Ecology,* New York: The Ronald Press.

Hayashida, Cullen Tadao
1976   *Identity, Race and the Blood Ideology of Japan,* Seattle: University of Washington Ph.D. Dissertation.

Hendrix, Lewellyn
1975   "Nuclear Family Universals," *Journal of Comparative Family Studies* 6, 125–130.

Henriques, Fernando
1968   *Prostitution and Society,* London: Macgibbon.

Hinde, Robert A.
1974   *Biological Bases of Human Social Behaviour,* New York: McGraw-Hill.

Hoffman, Martin
1976   "Homosexuality," in Frank A. Beach, ed., *Human Sexuality in Four Perspectives.* Baltimore: The Johns Hopkins University Press.

Holloway, Ralph L., ed.
1974   *Primate Aggression, Territoriality and Xenophobia,* New York: Academic Press.

Homans, George C., and David M. Schneider
1955   *Marriage, Authority and Final Causes,* New York: The Free Press.

Hrdy, Sarah B.
1977   "Infanticide as a Primate Reproductive Strategy," *American Scientist* 65(1), 40–49.

Jencks, Christopher, et al.
1972   *Inequality: A Reassessment of the Effect of Family and Schooling in America,* New York: Basic Books.

Jenni, D. A.
1974   "Evolution of Polyandry in Birds," *American Zoologist* 14, 129–144.

Jensen, Arthur R.
1969   "How Much Can We Boost IQ and Scholastic Achievement?" *Harvard Educational Review* 39, 1–123.

Kando, Thomas M.
1978   *Sexual Behavior and Family Life in Transition*, New York: Elsevier.

Kawai, M.
1965   "Newly Acquired Precultural Behavior of the Natural Troop of Japanese Monkeys on Koshima Islet," *Primates* 6, 1–30.

Kenyatta, Jomo
1964   *Facing Mount Kenya*, New York: Vintage Books.

Kephart, William M.
1976   *Extraordinary Groups*, New York: St. Martin Press.

Keyes, Charles F.
1976   "Towards a New Formulation of the Concept of Ethnic Group," *Ethnicity* 3(3), 202–213.

Kinsey, A.C., et al.
1948   *Sexual Behavior in the Human Male*, Philadelphia: Saunders.
1953   *Sexual Behavior in the Human Female*, Philadelphia: Saunders.

Kluckhohn, Clyde, and Dorothea C. Leighton
1946   *The Navaho*, Cambridge: Harvard University Press.

Kummer, Hans
1968   *Social Organization of Hamadryas Baboons*, Chicago: The University of Chicago Press.
1971   *Primate Societies*, Chicago: Aldine-Atherton.

Kuper, Hilda
1947   *An African Aristocracy*, London: Oxford University Press.

Lack, D.
1968   *Ecological Adaptations for Breeding in Birds*, London: Methuen.

Lancaster, C.S.
1976   "Women, Horticulture and Society in Sub-Saharan Africa," *American Anthropologist* 78(3), 539–564.

Lancaster, Jane B.
1975   *Primate Behavior and the Emergence of Human Culture*, New York: Holt, Rinehart and Winston.

Lasch, Christopher
1977   *Haven in a Heartless World, The Family Besieged*, New York: Basic Books.

Laughlin, Charles D., and Eugene G. d'Aquili
1974   *Biogenetic Structuralism*, New York: Columbia University Press.

Laws, Judith L., and Pepper Schwartz
1977   *Sexual Scripts, The Social Construction of Female Sexuality*, Hinsdale, IL: The Dryden Press.

Leach, Edmund R.
1961   *Rethinking Anthropology*, London: Athlone Press.

LeBoeuf, Burney J.
1974   "Male–Male Competition and Reproductive Success in Elephant Seals," *American Zoologist* 14, 163–176.

Lee, Gary R.
1977   *Family Structure and Interaction*, Philadelphia: Lippincott.

Lee, Richard B., and Irven De Vore, eds.
1968   *Man, the Hunter*, Chicago: Aldine.
1976   *Kalahari Hunter-Gatherers*, Cambridge: Harvard University Press.

Leibowitz, Lila
1978   *Females, Males, Families, A Biosocial Approach*, North Scituate, MA: Duxbury.

Leighton, Dorothea, and Clyde Kluckhohn
1947   *Children of the People*, Cambridge: Harvard University Press.

Lenneberg, E. H.
1967   *Biological Foundations of Language*, New York: John Wiley and Sons.

Lenski, Gerhard, and Jean Lenski
1978   *Human Societies*, New York: McGraw-Hill.

Lerner, I. Michael
1968   *Heredity, Evolution and Society*, San Francisco: Freeman.

Lévi-Strauss, Claude
1953   "Discussions" in Sol Tax, ed., *An Appraisal of Anthropology Today*, Chicago: The University of Chicago Press.
1963   *Structural Anthropology*, New York: Basic Books.
1969   *The Elementary Structures of Kinship*, Boston: Beacon Press (*first edition in French in 1949*).

Lewontin, R. C.
1974   *The Genetic Basis of Evolutionary Change*, New York: Columbia University Press

Lizot, Jacques
1976   *Le Cercle des Feux*, Paris: Editions du Seuil.
1977   "Population, Resources and Warfare Among the Yanomami," *Man* 12(3–4), 497–517.

Maccoby, Eleanor, ed.
1966   *The Development of Sex Differences*, Stanford: Stanford University Press.

Maclean, Paul D.
1965   "New Findings Relevant to the Evolution of Psychosexual Functions of the Brain," in John Money, ed., *Sex Research, New Developments*, New York: Holt, Rinehart and Winston.

Majumdar, D.N.
1960   *Himalayan Polyandry*, New York: Asia Publishing House.

Malinowski, Bronislaw
1929   *The Sexual Life of Savages*, London: Routledge.
1960   *A Scientific Theory of Culture*, New York: Oxford University Press.

Maquet, Jacques J.
1961   *The Premise of Inequality in Ruanda*, London: Oxford University Press.

Marmor, Judd
1965   *Sexual Inversion*, New York: Basic Books.

Marshall, Donald S., and Robert C. Suggs, eds.
1971   *Human Sexual Behavior*, New York: Basic Books.

Marshall, Lorna
1959   "Marriage Among the !Kung Bushmen," *Africa* 29, 335—364.
1965   "The !Kung Bushmen of the Kalahari Desert," in James L. Gibbs, ed., *Peoples of Africa*, New York: Holt, Rinehart and Winston.
1976   *The !Kung of Nyae Nyae*, Cambridge: Harvard University Press.

Martin, Del, and Phyllis Lyon
1972   *Lesbian Woman*, San Francisco: Glide Publication.

Martin, M. Kay, and Barbara Voorhies
1975   *Female of the Species*, New York: Columbia University Press.

Masters, William H., and Virginia E. Johnson
1966   *Human Sexual Response*, Boston: Little, Brown.

Mathur, A.S., and B.L. Gupta
1965   *Prostitutes and Prostitution*, Agra: Ram Prasad.

Maynard Smith, John
1964   "Group Selection and Kin Selection," *Nature* 201(4924), 1145–1147.
1966   *The Theory of Evolution*, Baltimore: Penguin.
1971   "What Use Is Sex?" *Journal of Theoretical Biology* 30, 319ff.
1978   "The Evolution of Behavior." *Scientific American* 239(3), 176–192.

Mayr, Ernst
1978   "Evolution," *Scientific American* 239(3), 47–55.

Mazur, Allan
1973   "A Cross-Species Comparison of Status in Small Established Groups," *American Sociological Review* 38, 513–530.

Mazur, Allan, and Leon S. Robertson
1972   *Biology and Social Behavior*, New York: The Free Press.

Mead, Margaret
1935   *Sex and Temperament*, New York: Morrow.
1949   *Male and Female*, New York: Morrow.

Meillassoux, Claude
1977   *Femmes, Greniers et Capitaux*, Paris: Maspero.

Millett, Kate
1970   *Sexual Politics*, New York: Doubleday.

Money, John, ed.
1965   *Sex Research; New Developments*, New York: Holt, Rinehart and Winston.

Montagu, M. F. Ashley
1969   *Sex, Man and Society*, New York: Putnam.

Montagu, M. F. Ashley, ed.
1962   *Culture and the Evolution of Man*, London: Oxford University Press.
1968   *Man and Aggression*, London: Oxford University Press.

Morgan, Lewis Henry
1877   *Ancient Society*, New York: Henry Holt.

Morris, Desmond
1969   *The Human Zoo*, London: Jonathan Cape.

Moynihan, Daniel P.
1965   *The Negro Family*, Washington, DC: U.S. Government Printing Office.

Muncy, Raymond Lee
1973   *Sex and Marriage in Utopian Communities: 19th Century America*, Bloomington: University of Indiana Press.

Murdock, George P.
1949   *Social Structure*, New York: Macmillan.
1957   "World Ethnographic Sample," *American Anthropologist* 59, 664–687.
1959   *Africa; Its Peoples and Their Culture History*, New York: McGraw-Hill.
1967   *Ethnographic Atlas*, Pittsburgh: University of Pittsburgh Press.

Murdock, George P., and D. R. White
1969   "Standard Cross-Cultural Sample," *Ethnology* 8, 329–369.

Nadel, S. F.
1940   "The Kede" in M. Fortes and E.E. Evans-Pritchard, eds., *African Political Systems*, London: Oxford University Press.
1942   *A Black Byzantium*, Oxford: Oxford University Press.
1951   *The Foundations of Social Anthropology*, London: Cohen and West.
1954   *Nupe Religion*, London: Routledge and Kegan Paul.

Nakane, C.
1966   *Kinship and Economic Organization in Rural Japan*, London: London School of Economics Monographs on Social Anthropology, No. 32.

Needham, Rodney
1962   *Structure and Sentiment*, Chicago: The University of Chicago Press.
1964   "Descent, Category and Alliance in Siriono Society," *Southwestern Journal of Anthropology*, 20, 229–240.

Needham, Rodney, ed.
1971   *Rethinking Kinship and Marriage*, London: Tavistock.

Nimkoff, M. F.
1965   *Comparative Family Systems,* Boston: Houghton Mifflin.

Norbeck, Edward
1954   *Takashima: A Japanese Fishing Community,* Salt Lake City: University of Utah Press.

Orians, Gordon H.
1969   "On the Evolution of Mating Systems in Birds and Mammals," *American Naturalist* 103, 589–603.

Otterbein, Keith F.
1965   "Caribbean Family Organization," *American Anthropologist* 67, 66–79.

Packer, C.
1977   "Reciprocal Altruism in Papio Anubis," *Nature* 265(Feb. 3), 441–443.

Parker, Seymour
1976   "The Precultural Basis of the Incest Taboo," *American Anthropologist* 73(2), 285–305.

Parsons, Talcott
1977   *The Evolution of Societies,* Englewood Cliffs, NJ: Prentice-Hall.

Parsons, Talcott, and Robert F. Bales
1955   *Family, Socialization and Interaction Process,* New York: The Free Press.

Pasternak, Burton
1976   *Introduction to Kinship and Social Organization,* Englewood Cliffs, NJ: Prentice-Hall.

Peter, Prince of Greece and Denmark
1963   *A Study of Polyandry,* The Hague: Mouton.

Peterson, Nicolas
1975   "Hunter-Gatherer Territoriality," *American Anthropologist* 77(1), 53–68.

Pfeiffer, John E.
1977   *The Emergence of Society,* New York: McGraw-Hill.

Population Reference Bureau
1977   *World Population Data Sheet,* Washington, DC.

Radcliffe-Brown, A. R.
1952   *Structure and Function in Primitive Society,* Glencoe, IL: The Free Press.

Radcliffe-Brown, A. R., and D. Forde, eds.
1950   *African Systems of Kinship and Marriage,* London: Oxford University Press.

Reichard, Gladys A.
1928   *Social Life of the Navaho Indians,* New York: Columbia University Press.

Reiss, Ira L.
1976   *Family Systems in America,* Hinsdale, IL: The Dryden Press.

Rosenberg, George S., and D. F. Anspach
1973   *Working Class Kinship,* Lexington, MA: Lexington Books.

Rossi, Alice S.
1977   "A Biosocial Perspective on Parenting," *Daedalus* 106, 1–31.
1978   "The Biosocial Side of Parenthood," *Human Nature* 1(6), 72–79.

Rowell, T. E.
1972   *Social Behaviour of Monkeys,* Harmondsworth: Penguin.

Ruitenbeek, Hendrik M., ed.
1973   *Homosexuality,* London: Souvenir Press.

Sahlins, Marshall D.
1965   "On the Sociology of Primitive Exchange," in M. Banton, ed., *The Relevance of Models for Social Anthropology,* New York: Praeger.
1976   *The Use and Abuse of Biology,* Ann Arbor: University of Michigan Press.

Sahlins, Marshall D., and Elman R. Service, eds.
1960   *Evolution and Culture,* Ann Arbor: University of Michigan Press.

Scanzoni, John
1972   *Sexual Bargaining; Power Politics in the American Marriage,* Englewood Cliffs, NJ: Prentice-Hall.

Schneider, David M.
1965   "Kinship and Biology," in A.S. Gale et al., eds., *Aspects of the Analysis of Family Structure,* Princeton: Princeton University Press.
1968   *American Kinship,* Englewood Cliffs, NJ: Prentice-Hall.

Schneider, David M., and K. Gough, eds.
1961   *Matrilineal Kinship,* Berkeley: University of California Press.

Schneider, David M., and Raymond T. Smith
1973   *Class Differences and Sex Roles in American Kinship and Family Structure,* Englewood Cliffs, NJ: Prentice-Hall.

Service, Elman
1962   *Primitive Social Organization,* New York: Random House.
1966   *The Hunters,* Englewood Cliffs, NJ: Prentice-Hall.
1971   *Cultural Evolutionism,* New York: Holt, Rinehart and Winston.

Shepher, Joseph
1971   "Mate Selection Among Second Generation Kibbutz Adolescents and Adults," *Archives of Sexual Behavior* 1(4), 293–307.
1978   "Reflections on the Origin of the Human Pair-Bond," *Journal of Social and Biological Structures* 1, 253–264.
1979   *Incest, The Biosocial View,* Cambridge: Harvard University Press.

Shepher, Joseph, et al.
1977   "Female Dominance and Sexual Inadequacy," Paper Read at American Anthropological Association Annual Meeting, Houston.

Silberbauer, G. B.
1965   *Bushman Survey Report*, Gaberone: Bechuanaland Government.

Silberbauer, G. B., and Adam Kuper
1966   "Kgalagari Masters and Bushman Serfs," *African Studies* 25(4), 171–179.

Skinner, B. F.
1971   *Beyond Freedom and Dignity*, New York: Knopf.

Smith, Michael G.
1960   *Government in Zazzau, 1800–1950*, London: Oxford University Press.

Smith, Robert J., and Richard K. Beardsley, eds.
1962   *Japanese Culture: Its Development and Characteristics*, Chicago: Aldine.

Souen K'i
1968   *Courtisanes Chinoises à la Fin des T'ang*, Paris: Presses Universitaires de France.

Spencer, Herbert
1874   *The Study of Sociology*, London: Appleton.

Spiess, Eliot B.
1977   *Genes in Populations*, New York: John Wiley and Sons.

Spiro, M. E.
1956   *Kibbutz: Venture in Utopia*, Cambridge: Harvard University Press.
1958   *Children of the Kibbutz*, Cambridge: Harvard University Press.

Stephens, William N.
1963   *The Family in Cross-Cultural Perspective*, New York: Holt, Rinehart and Winston.

Steward, Julian H.
1955   *Theory of Culture Change*, Urbana: University of Illinois Press.
1977   *Evolution and Ecology*, Urbana: University of Illinois Press.

Stine, Gerald James
1977   *Biosocial Genetics*, New York: Macmillan.

Taeuber, Irene B.
1958   *The Population of Japan*, Princeton, NJ: Princeton University Press.

Temple, O.
1922   *Notes on the Tribes, Provinces, Emirates, and States of the Northern Provinces of Nigeria*, Lagos: The C.M.S. Bookshop.

Thomas, Elizabeth Marshall
1959   *The Harmless People*, New York: Knopf.

Tiger, Lionel, and Robin Fox
1971   *The Imperial Animal*, New York: Holt, Rinehart and Winston.

Tiger, Lionel, and Joseph Shepher
1975   *Women in the Kibbutz*, New York: Harcourt, Brace, Jovanovich.

Trivers, Robert L.
1971   "The Evolution of Reciprocal Altruism," *Quarterly Review of Biology* 46(4), 35−57.
1972   "Parental Investment and Sexual Selection," in B. Campbell, ed., *Sexual Selection and the Descent of Man*, Chicago: Aldine, pp. 136−179.
1974   "Parent−Offspring Conflict," *American Zoologist* 14(1), 249−264.

Udry, J. Richard
1966   *The Social Context of Marriage*, Philadelphia: Lippincott.

UNESCO
1975   *Statistical Yearbook*, Paris: UNESCO Presses.

United Nations
1973   *Demographic Yearbook, 1972*, New York: United Nations Statistical Office.
1976   *Demographic Yearbook*, New York: United Nations Statistical Office.

U.S. Bureau of the Census
1961   *Historical Statistics of the United States*, Washington, DC: U.S. Government Printing Office.
1973   *Persons by Family Characteristics*, 1970 Population Census, PC(2)-4B, Washington, DC: U.S. Government Printing Office.
1974   *Statistical Abstract of the United States*, Washington, DC: U.S. Government Printing Office.
1977a   *Population Characteristics*, Series P-20, No. 306, Washington, DC: U.S. Government Printing Office.
1977b   *Household and Family Characteristics, March 1976*, Series P-20, No. 311, Washington, DC: U.S. Government Printing Office.

U.S. Department of Health, Education and Welfare
1977a   *Vital Statistics of the United States, 1973*, Vol. 1, *Natality*, Rockville, MD: U.S. Public Health Service.
1977b   *Vital Statistics of the United States, 1973*, Vol. 3, *Marriage and Divorce*, Rockville, MD: U.S. Public Health Service.
1977c   *Vital Statistics Report*, Vol. 26, No. 2, Rockville, MD: National Center for Health Statistics.

van den Berghe, Gwendoline, and Pierre L. van den Berghe
1966   "Compadrazgo and Class in Southeastern Mexico," *American Anthropologist* 68(5), 1236−1244.

van den Berghe, Pierre L.
1973a   *Age and Sex in Human Societies*, Belmont, CA: Wadsworth.
1973b   *Power and Privilege at an African University*, London: Routledge and Kegan Paul.
1974   "Bringing Beasts Back in," *American Sociological Review* 39(6), 777−788.
1977   "Territorial Behavior in a Natural Human Group," *Social Science Information* 16(3−4), 419−430.
1978a   *Man in Society*, New York: Elsevier.

1978b   *Race and Racism,* New York: John Wiley and Sons.

1978c   "Bridging the Paradigms, Biology and the Social Sciences," in Michael S. Gregory, Anita Silvers and Diane Such, eds., *Sociobiology and Human Nature,* San Francisco: Jossey-Bass.

van den Berghe, Pierre L., and David Barash

1977   "Inclusive Fitness and Human Family Structure," *American Anthropologist* 79(4), 809–823.

van Lawick-Goodall, Jane

1971   *In the Shadow of Man,* Boston: Houghton Mifflin.

Van Velsen, J.

1964   *The Politics of Kinship,* Manchester: Manchester University Press.

Vogel, Ezra

1971   *Japan's New Middle Class,* Berkeley: University of California Press.

Wallace, Bruce

1970   *Genetic Load,* Englewood Cliffs, NJ: Prentice-Hall.

Washburn, Sherwood L.

1978   "The Evolution of Man," *Scientific American* 239(3), 194–207.

Washburn, S.L., and I. De Vore

1961a   "Social Behavior of Baboons and Early Man," *Viking Fund Publications in Anthropology* 31, 91–105.

1961b   "The Social Life of Baboons," *Scientific American* 204, 62–71.

Weinberg, Kirson S.

1963   *Incest Behavior,* New York: Citadel Press.

Weinrich, J.D.

1977   "Human Sociobiology: Pairbonding and Resource Predictability," *Behavioral Ecology and Sociobiology* 2, 91–118.

Weiss, Robert S.

1975   *Marital Separation,* New York: Basic Books.

Weitz, Shirley

1977   *Sex Roles,* New York: Oxford University Press.

Wells, John W.

1970   *Tricks of the Trade,* New York: New American Library.

West-Eberhard, M.J.

1975   "The Evolution of Social Behavior by Kin Selection," *Quarterly Review of Biology* 50, 1–34.

Westermarck, Edward A.

1891   *The History of Human Marriage,* London: Macmillan.

White, Leslie

1958   "The Definition and Prohibition of Incest," *American Anthropologist* 50, 416–435.

1959   *The Evolution of Culture,* New York: McGraw-Hill.

Whiting, Beatrice B., and John W.M. Whiting

1975   *Children of Six Cultures,* Cambridge: Harvard University Press.

Williams, G.C.
  1966   *Adaptation and Natural Selection,* Princeton: Princeton University Press.
  1975   *Sex and Education,* Princeton: Princeton University Press.
Williams, Juanita H.
  1977   *Psychology of Women,* New York: Norton.
Wilson, Edward O.
  1971   *The Insect Societies,* Cambridge: Harvard University Press.
  1975   *Sociobiology: The New Synthesis,* Cambridge: Harvard University Press.
  1978   *On Human Nature,* Cambridge: Harvard University Press.
Winans, Edgar V.
  1962   *Shambala; The Constitution of a Traditional State,* Berkeley: University of California Press.
Winch, Robert F.
  1977   *Familial Organization,* New York: The Free Press.
Witherspoon, Gary
  1975   *Navajo Kinship and Marriage,* Chicago: The University of Chicago Press.
Wolf, Arthur P.
  1966   "Childhood Association, Sexual Attraction and the Incest Taboo," *American Anthropologist* 68(4), 883–898.
Wynne-Edwards, V.C.
  1962   *Animal Dispersion in Relation to Social Behaviour,* Edinburgh: Oliver and Boyd.
Young, Michael, and Peter Willmott
  1957   *Family and Kinship in East London,* Glencoe, IL: The Free Press.
Zuckerman, S.
  1932   *The Social Life of Monkeys and Apes,* London: Kegan Paul.

INDEX